Unearthing the Power of Place

Secrets of Sacred Space is an informative guide to understanding and creating sacred places of power for meditation, renewal, and connection with the earth.

Chuck Pettis comprehends the sacred and powerful design of ancient monuments like the pyramids and Stonehenge. He has learned how to communicate with devas and other spiritual beings to discover the spiritual essence of a site. He will teach you to discover how ley lines, water lines, and power centers define a sacred space. You'll learn age-honored methods: dowsing, cosmic geometry, geomancy, astronomical alignment, symbolism, earth spirituality, and archetypes.

Secrets of Sacred Space offers unprecedented resources and information on the art, science, and spirituality inherent in places of power, including:

- 85 illustrations demonstrating principles of sacred space design
- 61 photos of ancient and contemporary sacred sites
- an 8-page color insert
- 2 essential appendices: the Table of Astronomical Alignments and the Solar Calendar

Secrets of Sacred Space will help you decode the myst
and guide you in designing and creating a power place c

Chuck Pettis (Washington) has designed and built sacred places according to the tenets of art, science, and spirituality since 1970. He created the first modern energetically and astronomically aligned stone circle in the United States, the Ellis Hollow Stone Circle. He dowsed the Seattle Ley-Line Map (funded with a grant from the Seattle Arts Commission), which was featured on the television show *Sightings*. Pettis holds a B.A. in Psychology from Carnegie-Mellon University and an M.S. in Design from Southern Illinois University.

Secrets of
Sacred Space

Discover and Create Places of Power

Chuck Pettis

1999
Llewellyn Publications
St. Paul, Minnesota 55164-0383, U.S.A

FIRST EDITION
First Printing, 1999

Cover design:
Lisa Novak

Cover photo:
Stephen Miller ©1979

Editing, book design:
Kjersti Monson
Tom Lewis

Library of Congress Cataloging-in-Publication Data
Pettis, Chuck, 1948-
    Secrets of sacred space: discover and create places of power/
Chuck Pettis.—1st ed.
        p.   cm.
    Includes illustrations, bibliographical references and index.
    ISBN 1-56718-519-3
    1. Sacred space.   2. Architecture and religion.   3. Spiritual
    life—Miscellanea.   I. Title
    BL580.P48   1999
    291.3'5—dc21   99-41549

Llewellyn Worldwide does not participate in, endorse, or have any authority or responsibility concerning private business transactions between our authors and the public.

All mail addressed to the author is forwarded but the publisher cannot, unless specifically instructed by the author, give out an address or phone number.

Llewellyn Publications
A Division of Llewellyn Worldwide, Ltd.
P.O. Box 64383, Dept. K519-3
St. Paul, MN 55164-0383, U.S.A.
WWW.LLEWELLYN.COM

Printed in the United States of America

Dedicated to John and Kate Payne . . .

A true magus (wizard) is a person who studies the essential reality behind appearances, who understands the doctrine of correspondences in nature, has prepared for and received the traditional secrets of his craft, and works with and for the benefit of his native society.

— John Michell
The Old Stones at Land's End

Contents

Preface

In 1975, I visited the Rollright Stone Circle near Oxford, England. As I stepped into this beautiful circle of oddly-complexioned standing stones, my consciousness was altered. Meditation in the middle of the stone circle was deep and memorable. With recently acquired college degrees in psychology and design, and a fascination that such a space, obviously carefully designed, could immediately change one's state of consciousness, I felt a sense of predestination. On that day, I resolved to study the design techniques used to build ancient monuments and then design and build a stone circle myself to see if a new, contemporary sacred space could alter and uplift consciousness.

The Ellis Hollow Stone Circle, the first modern, energetically and astronomically aligned, stone circle in the United States, was completed in 1977. One early visitor to the site reported, "As I approached the upright stone, I suddenly felt that I had entered an area of high energy, an awareness of a special dimension that heightened my perceptions, as well as an intensified awareness of energy flows in my body. Walking around the stone at close range, I felt several surges of energy. I later found out that the areas where I had felt this surge seemed to correlate where ley lines ran through the area. As I walked away from the stone circle, I was aware of how balanced, whole, light, and happy I felt."

Our world needs more sacred spaces like this that can evoke the spiritual experience. *Secrets of Sacred Space* summarizes the design techniques and spiritual practices historically used to create places of power all over the world. This book will show you how to connect with the earth spirit in a deeper, more profound way. It will give you tools to help heal Mother Earth and bring you closer to enlightenment. Most importantly, this book is meant to be a service to all people who feel the need for their own place of retreat, safety, and spiritual renewal and would like a practical, step-by-step approach to find and create their own place of power, large or small.

— Chuck Pettis

chapter one

Monuments and Sacred Spaces

Sacred places of power move and enliven the soul—they take you to higher states of consciousness, inspire feelings of awe and wonder, and are places for retreat, self-renewal, and enlightenment. The making of the sacred space is as important, if not more important, than its use when complete. Indeed, building a sacred space—a cosmic monument—is a high form of meditation and the epitome of spiritual service.

Conspicuous ancient monuments like Stonehenge, Avebury, Carnac, and the Great Pyramid along with many thousands of smaller stone circles, earthworks, and holy places mark the earth's power centers all over the world. While ancient monuments are from another time and culture, the use of stone and earth to design uplifting and inspiring sacred spaces is just as relevant today as it was thousands of years ago.

Figure 1.1—*Full moon at* Avebury Stone Circle, *the world's largest stone circle.*

Photo © Tom Bullock

Increasing numbers of people are seeking out and visiting the most powerful and beautiful places on earth to retreat from the pressures of the modern world. Regular time off for retreat serves the spiritual needs of the soul and refuels us with life energy. On a day-to-day basis, parks, gardens, and special spaces around and within our homes are vital to our soul's well-being and serve as reminders of the relationship we have with nature and the cosmos.

Learning how to find, understand, and create places of power is similar to learning a language. There is a vocabulary, a grammar, and a pictographic handwriting called *geomancy* that ties earth and stone together into an artistic whole that speaks to the soul. The first step in learning to become a geomancer (or earth wizard) is to understand the varieties of ancient monuments and contemporary environmental artworks. After reading this book, you will know what messages and symbolism the ancient magi built into their monuments. Also, you will be able to pick the appropriate monument type to artistically express your own spiritual needs and feelings.

Photo ©1979 Stephen Miller

Figure 1.2—*Large standing stones at the western end of the Kermario Stone Rows in Carnac, France. In this set of stone alignments alone, 982 remaining stones are grouped in ten lines, 3,675 feet in length.*[1]

Earth Art

The artist within wants to find beauty all around us. *Sacred space* is defined as an artwork in a consecrated space; it is a place set apart as holy and devoted to spiritual use. A sacred space can be large (a monument) or small (simple arrangements of leaves or small stones). A small garden is an ideal place for a sacred space, using the earth as easel and plants as paint.

Sacred space is the universe in miniature. In Japanese gardens, a miniature version of a beautiful existing or idealized landscape is created in a concentrated space. Similarly, the large-scale megalithic monuments illustrated and discussed in this chapter can be miniaturized and simplified in any form. Keep in mind that the large monuments shown herein are really archetypes (more on this in chapter eleven), and powerful at any scale. What is important is not the size, but the intention or symbolism of the space and its effect upon you and your friends and family.

Earth art can be created with inherent spiritual and transcendental power. Ancient artists created optimal archetypal monument forms using earth and stone to maximize the energy of place and create portals to higher states of consciousness. These ancient monuments range from large isolated standing stones to colossal works of stone and earth that even today would be major construction projects. Related groups of them inscribe the earth over hundreds of square miles. Some are simple, without embellishment. Others are complex, elegant, and dramatic. The great investment of physical human effort required to build thousands of these monuments—not only in one or several geographic locations, but all over the world by virtually every ancient culture—gives universal significance to their existence.

Within us is the need to encapsulate our collective identity. Monuments—large works of enduring value or significance—fulfill that need. The word *monument* comes from the root word *monere*, meaning to remind or warn.[2] The fact that some of the monuments illustrated herein are over 5,000 years old is proof of their endurance. The key question is: what did the builders and designers wish to remind us about or, perhaps more intriguing, what did they wish to warn us about?

One characteristic seems to be common to our perception of all monuments: a mixed feeling of reverence, fear, and imposing wonder caused by the greatness of their construction, and something more than this sense that is beyond words. Call it awe, inspiration, wonder, or just respect. The feeling is there. It is this feeling that sacred space is all about.

Monuments are enigmas and riddles, distinguished by the synthesis of many design elements and simplicity of form. They are earth forms, layered illustrations, and large-scale terrestrial sculpture artistically and scientifically woven into the fabric of the earth. They are consciously created spaces that have been surveyed, measured, and constructed for special psychological, social, and spiritual rites of passage. This book will help visitors to ancient monuments unravel and answer centuries-old riddles and better understand what the ancients were trying to tell us. It also functions as a manual for designing large contemporary monuments and sacred spaces of all types.

Contemporary Land Projects

The mid-1960s saw increased involvement with the landscape by artists. They began to engage and play with the landscape rather than just depict it. The landscape became an artistic medium, serving as a vehicle for the mindful experience of space, location, and direction. The land took on elements of life, vitality, and spirit.

Some of these projects are temporary relocations of natural objects. Some are large permanent landscape changes as in Robert Smithson's *Spiral Jetty*, a 1,500-foot-long by 15-foot-wide stone jetty earthwork that makes two-and-a-half counterclockwise turns as it spirals into itself. Located on the northeastern shore of the Great Salt Lake in Utah, *Spiral Jetty* is now submerged and can only be seen from a plane.

My favorite environmental art piece in the Seattle area is Herbert Bayer's *Mill Creek Canyon Earthwork*, created in 1982 in Kent—a Seattle suburb.[3] More than

Photo ©1998 Chuck Pettis

Figure 1.3—Mill Creek Canyon Earthwork *in Kent, Washington by Herbert Bayer. The oval mound seen over the high berm is a perfect complement to the earthen ring in the center of the circular pool of water.*

just a work of art, Bayer's design is functional in its ability to contain and slow water flowing through the canyon during periods of heavy rain.

Contemporary land art, now generally termed *environmental art*, is thriving today and becoming more sculptural in form. *Sculpture* magazine regularly covers earth art. All earth art affirms a connection with the natural world and is a counterforce to urbanization. Furthermore, these land art forms challenge the traditional status of art as a transportable and collectable object. Now, let's briefly review each of the basic types of megalithic monuments and earthworks.

Megalithic Monuments

Megalithic (*mega*, great or mighty + *lithos*, stone) monuments, by definition, are constructed with large stones. The physical presence of large stones is impressive and commands respect. Stone is a symbol of cohesion, wholeness, and strength. Stone is the epitome of the physical; its omnipresence in the universe lends it great power because its vibration is so pervasive.

Megalithic monuments can take the form of standing stones, recumbent stones, stone circles, stone lines and avenues, stone figures, cairns, medicine wheels, dolmens, or pyramids. Most monuments and sacred spaces can also be prototyped with wooden posts. This is a relatively simple way to see how a sacred space design or layout will work before going to the trouble and greater expense of installing stones.

Standing Stones and Recumbent Stones

The standing stone is the most elementary megalithic monument, consisting of a single stone embedded vertically in the ground. The recumbent stone is simply a stone set on its side. Clearly, the vertical dimension is emphasized in standing stones while the horizontal dimension is emphasized in recumbent stones. Stones in these arrangements may be carved with symbols or decorated with images or objects using wood, metal, feathers, cloth hangings, and pennants.

Photo ©1975 Chuck Pettis

Figure 1.4—*The King Stone near the* Rollright *Stone Circle in Oxfordshire, England. The standing stone, a universal symbol of the masculine force, is the most elementary megalithic monument.*

Photo ©1979 Stephen Miller

Figure 1.5—*Standing stone near the* Moustoir Tumulus, *Carnac, France.*

Stone Circles

In many ways, the stone circle is the most elegant of the megalithic monuments. The stone circle or *cromlech* (*krom*, curve + *lech*, a stone) consists of standing or recumbent stones arranged in a circle, ellipse, or egg-shape. A stone circle is a consciously created space that has been surveyed, measured, and constructed for special psychological, artistic, and spiritual uses. The circle is the symbol of wholeness, oneness, and perfection. It symbolizes perfect harmony and all cyclic processes because it has neither beginning nor end.

Figure 1.6—Oddly complexioned stones make up the Rollright Stone Circle, *located near Oxford, England, a site that is widely acknowledged to be a place of power. Usually connected with the sun and moon, stone circles represent our cyclic, mystical relationship with the seasons.*

Photo ©1975 Chuck Pettis

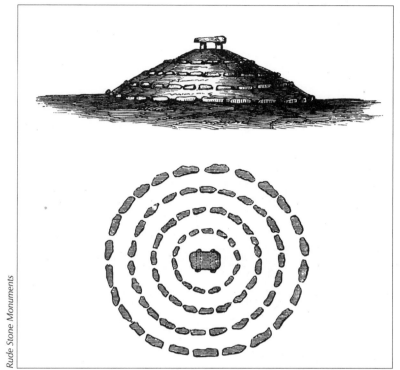

Figure 1.7—*A circle naturally sets a space apart for holy use. African stone circles.*

Stone Lines and Avenues

Stone lines are formed when two or more stones are consciously aligned to a special location or celestial event. A symbol of strength, the stone line is a vector— a pointing finger directing one's attention. Stone avenues (*ad*, to + *venire*, to come), formed by parallel rows of stones, are usually a way of approach or departure from a central monument. They are symbolic of transformation and the spiritual path. Many stone avenues and stone circles were preceded by and prototyped with wooden posts (as described previously) and totem poles—an excellent technique for sacred space artists to emulate.

Figure 1.8— Carnac, France stone lines.

Photo ©1979 Stephen Miller

Figure 1.9—The Avebury Stone Circle *originally had two "spirit path" stone avenues used to approach and leave the central stone circle.*

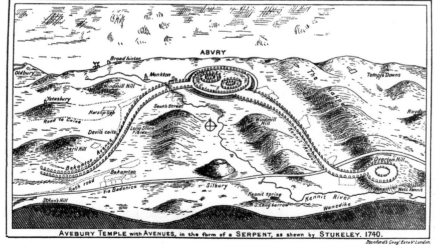

Archaic England

Figure 1.10—*Stone avenue on a western Massachusetts hilltop.*

Photo ©1975 Chuck Pettis

Stone Figures, Labyrinths, and Mazes

Stone figures (*figere*, to form a shape), as the name clearly suggests, are stones that have been arranged to represent the outline or shape of a figure, symbol, or likeness. The labyrinth symbolizes our own path of spiritual growth, climaxing at the central point of revelation and inner peace. Walking a labyrinth, with one path to the center and back (unicursal), is a profound meditative experience. A maze (*masen*, to confuse, puzzle), consists of many intricate pathways (multicursal) leading to a hidden central point. Exploring a multicursal maze with multiple pathways and dead ends is an adventure. Such a maze may make us feel confused and bewildered, symbolizing the times when we experience our own self-doubt and we ask *Who am I?* or *What should I do in this situation?* Both labyrinths and mazes are spiritual tools that bring out our intuitive, pattern-seeking, symbolic self (rather than engaging our thinking mind).

Cairns

There are two types of cairns: simple stone piles, historically used as tombs or coffins, and highly sophisticated megalithic observatories built with alternating layers of organic (turves)[4] and inorganic material (small stones). In the latter, carefully constructed passages oriented to sun risings and settings (chapter ten explains how this can be done) lead into a central chamber decorated with sun and moon symbols. One of the best examples of this type of cairn are the Loughcrew cairns, located about fifty miles northwest of Dublin, Ireland. Originally over fifty chambered mounds covered four hills that provide a 360-degree view of the beautiful Irish countryside. Over 5,000 years old, this grouping of sophisticated artworks are aligned to not only the solstices and equinoxes, but to the holidays Candlemas, May Day, Lammas, and Martinmas as well.

Figure 1.11—*West Virginia cairn.*

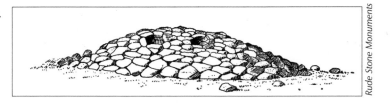

Rude Stone Monuments

Figure 1.12—*Cairn T at Loughcrew (Ireland), oriented to the autumn equinox sunrise, is one of the best-kept megalithic secrets on the planet.*

Photo ©1997 Chuck Pettis

Medicine Wheels

Primarily found in northwestern America and southwestern Canada, medicine wheels are stone circles that have the additional features of a marked center and a radiating pattern of stone "spokes." Often aligned to solstice risings and settings and other astronomical events, medicine wheels symbolize healing and the union of self with the Great Spirit.

Dolmens

Dolmens (*dol*, table + *men*, stone) are stone structures enclosed with a cap stone. Typically, a large flat stone is supported by three or more stones in such a way as to enclose a space or chamber beneath it.

There are six major types of dolmens: triangular, round, rectangular, corridor, boulder, and lean-to dolmens. *Triangular dolmens* are the simplest, comprised of three standing stones that support a capstone. *Round dolmens* consist of vertical stones set in a circle with a stone slab set over all of them. *Rectangular dolmens* have four standing stones, forming a square or rectangular space under the capstone. *Corridor dolmens* are extended rectangular dolmens with two rows of standing stones over which multiple stone slabs have been positioned to create a

Photo ©1977 Chuck Pettis

Figure 1.13—*Locally called the "pilgrim's picnic table," the Hassensack Dolmen (Rhode Island) is actually the source of the area's name; "hassensack" is a Native American word for stone table.*

Figure 1.14—The key distinguishing factor of the dolmen is the cover, or capstone. For that reason, stone trilithons are included in this category. The use of the trilithon is perhaps best known at Stonehenge, where roughly shaped capstones are held in place securely by two vertical standing stones using a clever pinning arrangement.

Photo ©1975 Chuck Pettis

Figure 1.15—A turban stone consists of a standing stone with a second "cap" or "turban" stone on top. A trilithon consists of a pair of stones set close together supporting a third stone laid across the top.

Rude Stone Monuments

corridor chamber. *Boulder dolmens* are dolmens built with boulders and have no distinct geometric shape. The *lean-to dolmen* consists of a single stone slab leaning against a recumbent stone, resembling a stone "lean-to."

The key distinguishing feature of the dolmen is the cover, or capstone. For that reason, stone trilithons are included in this category. A trilithon consists of a pair of stones set close together supporting a third stone laid across the top.

Pyramids

Pyramids are carefully constructed four-sided stone structures, usually massive with four triangular sides converging at a point. The majority of pyramids are found in Egypt and Mexico.

The Great Pyramid: Its Divine Message

Figure 1.16—*The most sophisticated megalithic structure, the base side of the* Great Pyramid *is 755.78 feet (about two-and-half football fields) long.*

The pyramid is an elemental symbol of the path from material to spiritual. The four-sided square base is a basic earth symbol of matter and the physical kingdom. From this base, the four sides rise toward an apex, forming four triangles. The triangle is the intermediary between the purely physical base and the purely spiritual apex point. In all natural structures, it is the triangle that holds all matter together. The apex of the pyramid is the spiritual goal, the point of union.

The word *pyramid* can be dissected etymologically into *pyr* (fire) and *mid* (middle): "fire in the middle." Fire burns gross elements into less dense gases and exhausts—a transformation from matter to gas occurs. This process is symbolized by the presence of a chamber in most pyramids near the center of the structure. This chamber is the focal point of the pyramid, both physically and spiritually. A person in the middle of the pyramid is "in the fire" or in a transformation mode.

Earthworks

Earthworks are monuments constructed by piling earth into banks and mounds. They can range in size from a small ring of earth six inches high to mounds as large as hills. Earthworks come in a number of different forms: mounds, henges, cursuses, long barrows, passage tombs and chambers, earth figures, turf labyrinths and mazes, and earth pyramids.

Mounds, Henges, and Cursuses

Mounds (or *tumuli*, as they are sometimes called) are the simplest of earthworks and the easiest to construct. Earth is heaped in a pile, which naturally assumes a hill-shape. Because its form is reminiscent of the bulging convexity associated with pregnancy and the woman's breast, the mound symbolizes fertility and the Great Mother.

Small mounds were a key part of the 1980 exhibition *Art in Nature* by Deborah Jones (New York). Her artwork consisted of two concentric circles around a central fire pit. The outer circle contained ten masks hanging from nine triangular sumac supports while the inner circle consisted of nine bark bowls, each resting on an earthen mound representing a birth image. Each of the nine bowls was of a different design. Close to the opening of Ritual Bowl No. 2 (figure 1.21) are jagged forms suggesting a toothed vagina configuration. Historically and mythically, bowl forms have been identified with the female. Vessels have always been symbols of change, from simple cooking conversion to alchemical transformation.

The henge is a ring of piled earth enclosing a circular sanctuary. The circular bank of the earth henge is another beautiful expression of the vessel symbol. The circle is the perfect distinction, container, or vessel. The symbolism of protection is also present in henges, since a vessel holds *out* as well as holds *in*. In mandala symbolism, the outer ring is always protective, acting as a defensive barrier for the self against threat of harm.

Photo ©1998 Chuck Pettis

Figure 1.17—An earth goddess symbol, Silbury Hill *is the largest human-made earthwork in Europe, measuring 520 feet in diameter by 130 feet in height.*

Photo ©1975 Chuck Pettis

Figure 1.18— Visible for many miles around, Glastonbury Tor *in southern England is a place of mythological legend and enchantment.*

Figure 1.19—*The mound builders of the American Midwest made many mounds in huge geometric shapes. Even though the sides of the square in this Circleville, Ohio earthwork (now destroyed) measured almost 900 feet and the diameter of the circle was over 1000 feet, this earthwork was considerably smaller than other Midwestern earthworks.*

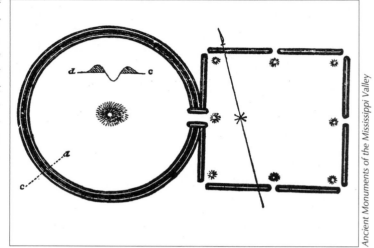

Ancient Monuments of the Mississippi Valley

Figure 1.20—*There used to be thousands of mounds, feminine symbols for fertility, in the United States. The* Grave Creek Mound, *located in Moundsville, West Virginia, is the largest conical mound in the country, measuring over 300 feet in diameter by 70 feet in height.*

Ancient Monuments of the Mississippi Valley

A henge can also create a level artificial horizon, blocking out distracting features around the monument. From the outside, a henge can control the approaching viewer's sight of the monument, directing them to a defined entrance for the all-important first impression, which can dramatize and strongly enhance the power of the site.

Perfect for processional ceremonies, a cursus is a long narrow passageway enclosed by two inner mounded banks and two outer ditches. Stonehenge had a straight cursus avenue at one time, with paired standing stones on top of the banks that started at an outer henge and extended to the northeast, framing the Summer Solstice sunrise when viewed from the center of the site.

Photo ©1980. Artist–Deborah Jones. Photographer–Carol Betsch.

Figure 1.21—Ritual Bowl No. 2, *1980 (no longer extant) is 8 inches high by 15 inches wide by 9 inches deep. Materials include a tree knot, an elmwood frame, pressed wood, and pierced bark. This vessel artwork atop a gravel mound is part of a sacred space designed and built by Deborah Jones in Ithaca, New York.*

Figure 1.22—The Plantations Earthwork, designed by Cheryl Nickel and Chuck Pettis for The Cornell Plantations in Ithaca, New York (never built). This henge has a diameter equal to one second of the earth's circumference (a little over 101 feet). It surrounds a circle of large standing stones that point to true north and south and to the point of sunrise and sunset on the spring and autumn equinoxes.

Photo ©1979 Chuck Pettis

Figure 1.23—The 382-foot-diameter "sacred festival circle" of Wisconsin is also known as "the sacrificial pentagon" because according to legend, the oldest male was sacrificed as an offering to the sun and moon in the spring and autumn.

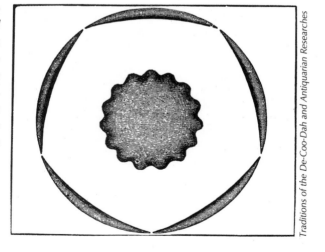

Traditions of the De-Coo-Dah and Antiquarian Researches

Ancient Monuments of the Mississippi Valley

Figure 1.24—*Circular henge surrounding a mound in Greenup County, Kentucky.*

Photo ©1975 Chuck Pettis

Figure 1.25—*The original ditch just inside the large henge of the Avebury Stone Circle was actually over 32 feet deeper than seen today—so deep that a telephone pole would not reach the "bottom." In its original form, the ditch had smooth and vertically cut chalk sides.*

Long Barrows, Passage Tombs, and Chambers

Long barrows are banks of earth characterized by one dimension being significantly longer than the other (like extended mounds). Barrows and mounds are often found with an underground room or chamber at one end, constructed with stone walls and stone slab ceilings. Chambered mounds are also referred to as passage tombs.

Earth Figures and Turf Mazes

Earth figures use piles of earth and turf to form various shapes and figures. Turf mazes are formed by removing the top part of the ground to create a channel. Either the raised turf or the channel (i.e., trench) can become the path.

Figure 1.26—*The West Kennet Long Barrow, located near Silbury Hill and Avebury in southern England, is an excellent example of a chambered barrow. 330 feet long, its eastern end has a multichambered area which is entered from behind an impressive facade of large standing stones.*

Photo ©1975 Chuck Pettis

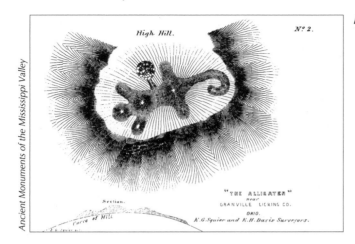

Ancient Monuments of the Mississippi Valley

Figure 1.27—The Alligator *earth mound.*

Photo © 1974 James Pierce

Figure 1.28—Dug from 1972 to 1974, The Turf Maze *by James Pierce is the first of its kind in the New World. The one-third mile maze forms an equilateral triangle.*

Earth Pyramids

Earth pyramids are square or rectangular mounds of earth with flat slanted sides and a flat top area. The largest pyramid in the United States is part of the Cahokia Mound group, located east of St. Louis (once called Mound City). Termed Monk's Mound since a monastery was built on it (which is no longer there), the pyramid is believed to have been the ceremonial center for this important community. The site covers sixteen acres, more space than even the Great Pyramid. Surrounding it for miles were originally hundreds of mounds of all types and descriptions.

Figure 1.29—Monk's Mound *is the largest pyramid in the United States.*

Prehistoric America

Twelfth Annual Report (Smithsonian), 1890-91

The Geomancer's Mission Today

A geomancer (*geo*, earth + *manteia*, divination) is any person who appreciates and is sensitive to the power at ancient monuments and sacred places. With higher awareness comes added responsibility. The geomancer's mission with regard to sacred space is two-fold:

- Strengthen the spiritual presence at ancient monuments.
- Design and build contemporary sacred spaces.

Strengthen the Spiritual Presence at Ancient Monuments

Millions of people visit ancient monuments all over the world to experience the sense of awe, wonder, and fascination that resides at these places of power. I have visited ancient monuments for over twenty years and it has become very apparent that too much is being taken from these sites and not enough is being put back in.

Power centers take on the strong emotions of people who visit and experience them. Ancient cultures invested a lot of spiritual feeling in their sacred places, and not enough is being done to maintain this sensibility. If there are no positive spiritual thoughts and feelings being put into a sacred site, then the level of that site's power gradually diminishes.

Here's what you can do to reverse this decline in the power of ancient places.

- Treat ancient monuments as sacred, consecrated places.
- Don't leave garbage. If there is garbage, pick it up.
- Meditate at the site.
- Bless the site (see chapter two).

Build Contemporary Sacred Spaces

Visiting an ancient monument is one thing. Actually building one is another thing altogether. Indeed, the making of a sacred space is special in and of itself; the archaeological study of Stonehenge shows nearly continuous building and change over the course of 2,000 years! When built over ley-line power centers by spiritually aware people, contemporary sacred spaces immediately have the same level of power experienced at most ancient monuments. With meditation, ceremony, and other spiritual practices, new sacred spaces can have *more* power than ancient monuments. New sacred spaces are important for many reasons:

- They facilitate personal and group spiritual experiences.
- They heal the earth and contribute to world peace.
- They can alter, uplift, and expand our consciousness.
- They facilitate enlightenment.
- They give us symbols of home, the ancestral past, and the promise of a more spiritual and positive future.

Anyone who creates a sacred space is an artist. Artists have a tendency to mirror our social needs before they become overtly obvious, like leading indicators of the collective psyche. The art of creating sacred space is a powerful yet subtle tool for meaningful social change.

To make your own sacred space, speak not in words or argument, but in symbols and peace. Take an idea here, an image or analogy there, and combine these with your feelings of love and spirituality. Plan a sacred space using the many resources in the following chapters and appendices and build it, or plan a simple arrangement and build it now: on a shelf or in your garden, arrange small stones or special objects into a circle.

Monuments: Cosmic Communicators

Monuments are receptacles of universal knowledge. To visitors, they should be seen as cosmic puzzles. Their builders put a lot of energy into communicating something they felt was important enough to build with enduring materials and construction. To artists, monuments are the ultimate artistic medium, affirming the beliefs we hold sacred and symbolizing them structurally for others to discover in the future.

Underlying all sacred space is the need for places where we can go to be close to our inner self. These sacred places offer magical opportunities to help us maintain contact with the spiritual world.

Secrets of Sacred Space Revealed in This Chapter

+ Ancient monuments all over the world mark places with the power to alter consciousness.

+ The most effective building materials for creating places of power are earth and stone.

+ Each type of monument has a cosmic message for us that is communicated through the language of symbolism.

+ Creating sacred space is a powerful yet subtle tool for meaningful social change.

+ Sacred spaces facilitate spiritual feelings and experiences.

Suggested Projects and Exercises

+ Visit ancient monuments and contemporary sacred spaces located near where you live, or visit them on your next vacation or trip. Nothing can take the place of actually being in the field of a charged sacred space.

+ Build small-scale replicas of ancient monuments in a part of your yard.

Notes

1   Stephen Miller's web site (www.mkzdk.org) is one of the most incredible sites on the internet. To see more beautiful Carnac photos by Stephen, go to www.bretagne.com/doc/mega/.

2   Etymology of key words appears throughout this book. My primary reference for etymological data was *Origins: A Short Etymological Dictionary of Modern English* (New York: The Macmillan Company, 1959) by Eric Partridge. I also used *Webster's New World Dictionary of the American Language* (Cleveland and New York: The World Publishing Company, 1966).

3   The Mill Creek Canyon Earthwork is located at Titus and Canyon Streets in Kent, Washington.

4   Plural for "turf," referring to the surface layer of earth with grass, roots, and dirt.

The Sacred Experience

The main reasons to visit and build sacred power centers are to have profound and mystical experiences, grow spiritually, and enjoy great meditations leading to higher states of consciousness. The peak moments of my own spiritual growth are intimately connected with sacred space. More than a contact high, power centers facilitate and inspire deep and meaningful spiritual experiences. Because power centers store strong emotions in their electromagnetic field, they are filled with the variety of sacred feelings and human emotions. This chapter is a mini-cookbook of the spiritual practices (prayer, meditation, invocation, and blessing) that are effective for tapping into and enhancing the power of sacred places.

A sacred experience is special and intrinsically personal. The word *sacred* means something set apart as being holy and inviolable. The sacred represents something to be regarded with respect and reverence—something not to be profaned or violated. Attempts to move or destroy ancient monuments are chronicled as being met with severe and unearthly retribution. Folklore tells of stones being dragged away only to be found returned to their original place the next day. Attempts to move stones or dismantle a monument are met with mysterious circumstances and events.

A sacred experience is the antithesis of the material world. Only *you* can feel it, experience it, and be it. You can't buy it. No one can do it for you or even tell you what it feels like. I can tell you that a spiritual experience makes me at one with the universe, but these words mean nothing to you until you have experienced the feeling yourself. It's like trying to describe what something tastes like. Fortunately, there is a solution. You can get the recipe for a food dish, make it for yourself, and taste and experience it. The same is true for a sacred experience.

Spirituality is on its own time schedule. My mother once expressed it beautifully: "I never know if I'm coming or going, except when it's time." When it *is* your time, the right way will appear for you. However, you can begin living virtuously and in a spiritual manner today. You can choose not to get angry, lie, gossip, covet, steal, kill, or hate. You can choose to express your love and have compassion for those who are in pain or suffering. You can give to those who are in need. You can speak pleasantly. These activities are important because when we die, the only things we take with us are the results of our virtuous and nonvirtuous actions and deeds.

The Spiritual Path

Dharma is a Sanskrit word referring to characteristics that make a thing unique. For example, the dharma of bees is to make honey and the dharma of fire is to burn. Dharma is an innate quality like a flower always turning to face the sun. Our dharma as human beings is to always look for something greater than ourselves. It is this inner force which has created the many forms of spiritual practice. Ultimately, dharma is the teaching that guides us to toward enlightenment—the direct understanding of the true nature of reality.

If you are looking for a spiritual path, proceed carefully. There are organizations that exploit people under the guise of helping them spiritually. Therefore, check out spiritual and religious organizations, as well as their leaders, very carefully. Do your homework. Be patient.

Spiritual Practices

In order to be able to reliably perform the intuitional practices explained in this book, it is essential that you have a solid foundation in spiritual practice and a feeling of connectedness with God (or *the Supreme Consciousness*, my preferred term for the highest spiritual being). Here are descriptions of the basic forms of spiritual practice.

Prayer

Prayer is a request, question, or conversation directed to a spiritual being. Use prayer to ask for help and guidance along the spiritual path. Ask for more devotion, compassion, and love in your attitude and actions. With a proper attitude, sincere prayers are usually answered, although not necessarily in the exact way we expect.

Pray only for what is really necessary and needed. Pray with the idea that, in any event, God's will should be done. This feeling of *surrender* is probably the most important aspect of prayer. Who are we to "know" the right way for our need to be met? Indeed, some Native American tribes consider it presumptuous to ask the Great Spirit for particular items—the all-knowing deity is already aware of what we need. True prayer is the method for us to implement divine will in our world. It is our highest visualization of the future.

Meditation

Meditation is a deep and continued contemplation or reflection on a sacred matter. In prayer, we *talk* to God. In meditation, we *listen* to God. To meditate, the mind concentrates on one specific idea for an extended period of time. Rather than projecting the idea outward like in prayer, the mind assumes a receptive state.

Meditation is like turning off the mind. We all have a little voice inside that is continuously providing a running commentary on our life. It doesn't want to stop talking. But with regular and continued meditation over a period of time, the voice can become more and more quiet. As you gain the ability to quiet the mind, many things are "seen" by the mind's eye and "heard" by the mind's ear that couldn't be heard before. This is the process of self-realization—the layers of dust on our soul gradually drop off as we get to know ourselves a little better. Success in knowing our inner self has many rewards: reduction in frustrated desire for material objects, less anxiety, more self-security, and improved self-esteem.

How to Meditate. To meditate, sit in a comfortable, relaxed position, cross-legged on the floor or in a chair. Relax your body. Keep your back straight. Take several deep, slow breaths. Let your muscles and tensions loosen up. Then, concentrate your awareness on your breath. Try not to get involved in the stream of thoughts and feelings just beneath the surface of your consciousness. Simply *observe* your thoughts. Let your mind's conversation gradually become quieted and brought to stillness. Try to make your body and mind as still as a calm mountain lake.

Increase your ability to concentrate and empty your mind by focusing your sight on a single object, squinting your eyes and, for a short period, not thinking. Say to yourself, *For one minute only, I will not think. I will quiet and empty my mind of all thoughts.* Hiking is a time when it is easy for me to empty my mind and enjoy mental silence. When I stop for a break, I squint and concentrate on a mountain, a knot in a tree, or a stone in a stream. This is very relaxing. I find that I can remember these short moments quite clearly long after the hike is done.

Raise your consciousness by contemplating a spiritual being (like Buddha or Jesus), a spiritual image (yantra, cross), a spiritual quality (love, compassion), or a spiritual sound (mantra).

Mantra Meditation. Mantra meditation is done by repeating a mantra (*man*, mind + *tra*, liberation) which is a special sound, usually a Sanskrit word or words with a sacred meaning. Mantra meditation keeps the mind active on a spiritual idea rather than random, everyday thoughts. Try the mantra "Baba Nam Kevalam" which means "Everything is an expression of the Supreme." When breathing in, say *"Baba Nam"* mentally to yourself and as you breathe out, say *"Kevalam."* Repeat the mantra in rhythm with your breath. As with all spiritual practices, finish by offering your actions to the Supreme Consciousness and for the benefit of all beings.

You might also try the Buddhist mantra "Om Mani Padme Hum," which means "Om . . . the jewel in the lotus . . . Hum," the jewel being love and compassion and the lotus being the wisdom of ultimate reality."[1] *Padme* is pronounced with a silent *d*, as in "pay-me," and with a long *a*. *Hum* is pronounced as "hung."[2]

Invocation

Invocation (*in*, on + *vocare*, to call) is similar to prayer, but rather than asking for something, you are calling on the highest spiritual beings for help, protection, inspiration, or blessing. A synthesis of prayer and meditation, invocation is very potent. Like prayer, it is a heartfelt appeal for help or intervention and, like meditation, it is an opening of the mind to receive the proper guidance. So, invocation combines the use of feeling (prayer), the mind (meditation), and will (affirmation). The well-known "Great Invocation"[3] is often used after a group meditation:

> *From the point of Light within the Mind of God*
> *Let light stream forth into the minds of men.*
> *Let Light descend on Earth.*

> *From the point of Love within the Heart of God*
> *Let love stream forth into the hearts of men.*
> *May Christ return to Earth.*

> *From the center where the Will of God is known*
> *Let purpose guide the little wills of men—*
> *The purpose which the Masters know and serve.*

> *From the center which we call the race of men*
> *Let the Plan of Love and Light work out*
> *And may it seat the door where evil dwells.*

> *Let Light and Love and Power restore the Plan on Earth.*

Blessing

A deliberate and conscious service to others, blessing is a spiritual technique that uses the power of concentration and thought projection[4] to help others, as well as oneself. Blessing can be as simple as saying or thinking, *May our family, home, pets, and plants be blessed.* Or the blessing technique can be applied to all normal activities like eating ("May all beings gain the food of meditation") or walking ("May all beings move quickly along the spiritual path"). To bless:

- Find a time when you won't be hurried or distracted. Get into a meditative state. Offer the act of your blessing to the Supreme Consciousness, God. Attune yourself to the Supreme Consciousness.

- Pick the idea or feeling (perhaps love, strength, or healing) you want to project and concentrate your heart and mind on it.

- Concentrate on the person or place you would like to bless and visualize a beam of divine white light (*chi*) projecting your idea or feeling from your heart to the recipient. For example, think of your mother and all the sacrifice, love, and care she has given you since you were a child. Imagine the love all mothers have felt for their children throughout history. Take that feeling of love and direct it with appreciation to your mother.

- Give thanks for the opportunity to be of service.

Make blessing a part of your life by projecting love and energy to those you come into contact with throughout the day. Because there is an infinite amount of love and life energy, you don't have to worry that you will lose energy by doing this. Actually, the more you project love, the more love you experience.

You can bless: animals, plants, food, money, material objects, obstacles, loved ones who have passed on, your ancestors, friends, family, all those you come into contact with, people in places of responsibility all over the world, and humanity as a whole. You are limited only by your imagination. Through the act of blessing, we affirm that we are a part of one divine manifestation, free ourselves of worries and fears, and make the world a better place.

Spiritual masters can project love and spirituality through specific hand gestures called *mudras*. When I attended the first Spirit of Place conference organized by Jim Swan—author of several books, including *Nature as Teacher and Healer* (New York: Villard–Random House, 1992)—Professor Lin Yun, the feng shui master, gave a mudra blessing that I experienced as a wave of white light and love.

Self-surrender

Right thought and action is essential to any spiritual practice. Every religion has a moral code. For Christians, it is the Ten Commandments. For many Eastern religions, it is *Yama* and *Niyama*, specific observances and abstinences such as non-injury, benevolent truthfulness, abstinence from stealing, having a cosmic outlook, frugality, contentment, cleanliness, service to humanity, spiritual study, and self-surrender.

The best technique for living a sacred life and for creating sacred places is self-surrender to Supreme Consciousness. Supreme Consciousness is God, Brahma, Buddha, and the Allness of existence—matter and consciousness. There is no greater being. Self-surrender is accepting what is best for you and living life as a flow. I try to live my life by seeing everything that happens to me as being in accordance with the divine plan.

There is a charisma and radiance that emanates from people who have surrendered to the Supreme and have come to "know" and express themselves deeply in some way. The presence of a saint is a blessing for anyone who comes into contact with her. A hero projects strength and courage. A true believer inspires faith and confidence.

Life is like being on a river. Our job is to stay in the middle of the river where life's current flows fastest, to avoid the distracting eddies, and follow the flow of meaningful coincidences. A good canoeist knows that there are ways to paddle the canoe in harmony with the water so only a minimum effort is required to keep moving forward safely and smoothly. This is how to live life.

The same approach works very nicely when designing and creating sacred places of power. The subtle questions of which stones should be used, in what place, at what time, are best made with the following attitude: "I want to create a beautiful sacred place. Supreme Consciousness and earth spirits, please let events guide me to make the best decisions."

The Laws of Manifestation

Our state of mind has a lot to do with how things happen to us. As we think, so we become. In his out-of-print book, *The Laws of Manifestation,* David Spangler talks about how every legitimate desire we have creates a magnetic vortex that attracts fulfillment of the need. I have observed that when people have a strong and clear vision of what they want, the universe seems to facilitate the manifestation of that desire. Of course, there is also karma, the unfulfilled reactions to all those virtuous and nonvirtuous actions from our many many past lives. Whether originating as a result of karma or the desire for a future good, I try to see everything that happens to me as significant, with the potential to make me more whole and closer to enlightenment.

Observe water moving. If flowing water runs into an obstruction, it just keeps following the line of least resistance. I feel the same thing should happen in daily life, especially when dealing with sacred space. So, when working with sacred space, only do what feels *right* (based on principle, not transitory emotion). Do what seems to happen naturally without a lot of wasted friction. Take resistance as a sign that you should reevaluate, change direction, or stop and rest for a while. Treat obstacles as blessings.

Spiritual practice is a vital part of developing a sacred space. When designing and creating a sacred space, meditate regularly to keep in tune with your higher self and your intuition. Even as you are reading this book, if an idea catches you, take just a moment, close your eyes, and meditate on it. Use your sacred space regularly as your special place and refuge to be alone and meditate.

Life is Short

From the small animals and fish in the ocean to insects, birds, rodents, wildlife, livestock, and pets, there are billions and billions of animals alive on the earth right now. In proportion to these animals, the number of humans is incredibly small. How small? Imagine that there is a long-lived tortoise in the ocean that only comes up to the surface every hundred years. On the surface of the ocean is one circular life preserver. Eventually, the tortoise will put its head through that one life preserver. The probability of being born a human is even more rare than that.[5] Because it is so rare to be born as a human, we need to make the most of our life.

Every life form dies, and we are no exception. Every day is a countdown to the day we die—and when we leave our bodies, we won't be able to take along our money, our car, our home, or any of our material possessions. The *only* thing we take with us is our self and the karma we have earned from our virtuous and nonvirtuous actions.

Death can come at any time, as I learned when I took a course in mountain climbing ten years ago. We were climbing Mount Baldy, north of Mount Rainier in the state of Washington. The leader grabbed for a rock as he was climbing up and the rock broke loose. He yelled, "Rock!" As I was trained to do, I immediately got down and pulled myself behind the rock I was climbing. The falling rock passed within a few feet of me and as I watched, seemingly in slow motion, the rock hit a fellow climber in the head. He tragically died that day on the mountain. I realized that the rock could have hit me—I could have died on the mountain that day. I resolved to live each day as if it were my last.

Death can come at any time; our time on earth is short. We cannot afford to procrastinate and put off the virtuous and spiritual activities that contribute to our spiritual growth, enlightenment, and self-realization. If you have the desire to build a sacred space, do it today. Don't put it off until tomorrow. If you have too many demands on your time, evaluate your priorities—try to put materialistic or "unwholesome" activities off until tomorrow.

Service to Humanity

The creation of sacred space is an artistic act. The goal of a sacred space, by definition, is to uplift the viewer and raise their consciousness. Art, itself, is a form of worship. The fourteenth-century artist Cennino Cennini advised artists to pray and adorn themselves with sacred robes symbolizing love and reverence. If you purify yourself and meditate before creating a work of an art, that piece will naturally tend to take on the form of one's noble dreams and aspirations. The creation of sacred spaces, consciously located over power centers, is an ideal way for artists of all levels to express their own spirituality in their homes and backyards

Here are some objectives for the creators of sacred space to consider:

+ Promote the ideals of service and spirituality.

+ Help society develop and evolve intellectually and spiritually.

+ Avoid and crusade against narrow-mindedness, bigotry, sectarianism, all –*isms*, and excessive commercialization of art.

+ Encourage new artists to base their art on higher values.

+ Be positive.

Figure 2.1—*Sacred landscape created by landscape designer Dan Boroff in collaboration with Chuck and Claudia Pettis.*

Photo ©1998 Chuck Pettis

Secrets of Sacred Space Revealed in This Chapter

- The main reasons to visit and build sacred power centers are spiritual growth, profound and mystical experiences, and great meditations leading to higher states of consciousness.

- Only *you* can feel and experience higher states of consciousness. You can't buy it. No one can do it for you.

- Spiritual practice is a vital part of developing a sacred space. When designing and creating a sacred space, meditate regularly to keep in tune with your higher self and your intuition.

- Art is a form of worship. If you purify yourself and meditate before creating a work of an art, that piece will instinctively tend to take on the form of one's noble dreams and aspirations.

Suggested Projects and Exercises

- Try each spiritual practice (prayer, meditation, invocation, and blessing) at a time when it feels right to you. Try to make spiritual practice a more integral part of your life.

- Go and hear lectures and introductory talks on various spiritual groups. Don't set out with the goal of joining one. Use the experience to gain understanding of what different people believe in and how they practice. When I lived in Ithaca, New York, I was a member of the Foundation of Light, a spiritual organization that regularly sponsors "Meetings for Spiritual Understanding." Representatives from local religious and spiritual organizations give a presentation of their beliefs and lead a meditation or prayer. These kinds of meetings are very successful in creating understanding, tolerance, and respect for everyone's beliefs.

◆ Pick a blessing technique that you enjoy and try doing it regularly for a week. For example, when you enter a store, mentally ask that everyone in the store be blessed. Fill the store with love.

◆ Go to a place that is special for you, like a beautiful glen, overlook, park, or ancient site. Meditate there. Bless the spot.

Notes

1   Thurman, Robert A. F. (translator), *The Tibetan Book of the Dead: Liberation Through Understanding In The Between* (New York: Bantam Books, 1994), 267.

2   The CD *Tibetan Incantations* from Music Club (available on Amazon.com) has the best recording of "Om Mani Padme Hum" I've heard.

3   This Invocation has been used for over 25 years by countless spiritual groups the world over.

4   For an excellent, detailed presentation of blessing, read *The Science and Service of Blessing* (Kent, England: Sundial House, 1968) by Robert Assagioli.

5   Lhundrub, Ngorchen Konchog, *The Beautiful Ornament of the Three Visions* (Ithaca, NY: Snow Lion Publications, 1991), 58. Also, Deshung Rinpoche's *The Three Levels of Spiritual Perception* (Boston: Wisdom Publications, 1995), 146-147.

Finding Places of Power

Potent ancient monuments around the world have one thing in common: the presence of earth energies that have the power to alter and uplift human consciousness. Dowsing is the intuitional practice or technique for locating these earth energies. This chapter explains the types of dowsing tools and how to use them to find underground water lines, ley lines, and power centers.

Sensing the Invisible

Our senses can pick up only a limited range of vibrations. For example, we can see color, but not X-rays. We can hear sounds, but only if they are loud enough and only if they are within our hearing range. Many of these invisible spectrums can be detected and "seen" by the extension of our senses via various technologies llke films, amplifiers, scopes, or transducers. Until technologies are developed to reliably detect the presence of earth energies, we must rely on the sensitivity of our bodies and minds.

The human body is the best "receiver" on earth. We can detect many things that machines and technologies cannot, especially in the areas of emotion and consciousness. Two subtle energy systems on the frontiers of human perception—the electromagnetic fields of underground water streams and ley lines—are beginning to be recognized, studied, and used today. These earth energies are important because ancient monuments such as stone circles, as well as cathedrals and all kinds of historic sacred spaces, are invariably situated on centers of earth energies.

Before I get too much further into this subject, a few introductory comments are appropriate. There is a difference between what I explain in this book and modern scientific knowledge of the subject of groundwater and geology. The idea that there is another significant source for water (i.e., magmatic or juvenile water) other than rainwater is not generally accepted by the scientific community.

My own personal experiences with water-well dowsing have all been successful. In several cases, I found water wells that contradict the water table theory. One of these was for some friends who had already paid a well driller for a 300-foot dry hole. I found an underground water stream only ten feet away from this hole; it was thirty-two feet deep and had a sixteen-gallons-per-minute flow.[1]

I believe that some of the "radical" ideas presented herein will eventually be seen as true, just as the theory of continental drift overcame initial scientific scorn. I beg the scientific reader to be open-minded about this presentation on earth energies.

Dowsing

Dowsing (*deuten*, to declare and *douse*, to plunge) refers to the technique for finding water and ley lines, among other things, by using a dowsing instrument (such as a dowsing rod). The use of the dowsing rod—a Y-shaped forked stick or rod—is as old as humankind. The dowsing rod is still used commercially by many well-drillers and contractors who have to dig around underground pipes and lines. A good dowser can find good, pure water ninety-five percent of the time.

Dowsing is the act of searching by projecting an intent to sense the thing desired and receiving confirming (or nonconfirming) feedback through the body, usually by the movements of a dowsing instrument. Dowsing is a form of *clairvoyance,* the ability to see at any given moment what is happening elsewhere. Our senses are more powerful than we think. Because our physical and psychological capabilities are designed to help us fulfill our desires, they realize their full potential only to the extent that we wish to utilize them.

Divining is a close synonym of dowsing and gets to the root of what dowsing is all about. Divining comes from the word *divinus* meaning of, or by, or for a god (or gods), or inspired by them. Hence, divining is a spiritual practice—the success of which rests on a stable and spiritual state of mind.

Dowsing is simply a natural tool. It enables you to amplify what you are already perceiving but have not bothered to pay attention to before. Dowsing makes it easier for us to focus on the abstract world of feeling, intuition, and the sacred. A very important technique for anyone working with sacred or haunted spaces, dowsing can be used to:

- Locate underground water lines and springs. The direction of flow, depth, and quantity of flow (gallons-per-minute) can also be ascertained.
- Locate ley lines and their direction of flow.
- Find power centers—places where the earth's field alters human consciousness.
- Determine if a water line or ley line is having a negative effect on the health of the people living or working above the line.
- Communicate with and receive spiritual guidance (this involves spiritual beings such as devas and angels, and will be covered in chapter four).
- Map underground earth energies in order to design and build sacred spaces.

Water Lines

According to my experience (and the experience of many other dowsers), there is a network of running water beneath the earth's surface. This primary water system originates deep inside the earth as steam that, as it is forced upward under pressure, condenses into pure water. As illustrated in figure 3.1, the water travels upward in a vertical shaft called a "pipe" until its flow is stopped by an obstruction. This point is called a *dome of water* because the water is, in effect, domed up. If fissures or cracks in the earth are connected to the pipe, the pressure of the water pushes the water into the cracks becoming underground streams, or water lines.

Figure 3.1—
Section and plan of underground water spring and water lines.

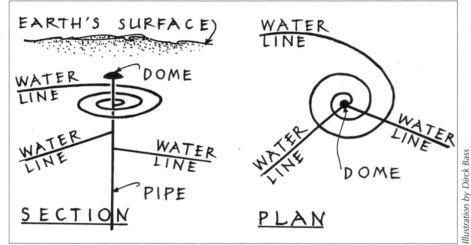

Illustration by Dirck Bass

There is a difference between *ground water* and the primary water system described above. Primary water is not affected by drought. Ground water *is*, because it is part of the above-ground hydrological cycle involving evaporation, cloud formation, rain, rivers, oceans, and the underground water table.

When I first learned dowsing, I practiced on existing water wells. After a time, I learned what a water line *feels* like, and I started dowsing for new wells. My technique (learning the sensation associated with existing wells before trying to dowse new ones) was strongly affirmed: everyone who drilled at exactly the place I indicated found water. In one case, the well-driller thought it would be convenient to drill five feet from my mark. The result was a dry hole. Since underground water streams are usually only a foot or two wide, you simply miss the stream unless you drill directly over it.

Primary water is found at most ancient monuments and temples. The close relationship of water lines and springs with ancient monuments was first established by Louis Merle and Charles Diot, French archaeologists who published papers on the subject in 1933 and 1935. In 1935, Captain Robert Boothby, R.N., claimed in an article that prehistoric sites were crossed by underground streams. In 1939, Reginald Allender Smith, Keeper of British and Roman Antiquities Department of the British Museum, wrote a paper for the British Society of Dowsers in which he said, "The constant presence of underground water at the exact centers of these circles and earthworks is a significant feature easily verified by others."[2]

What Do Water Lines Feel Like? Within each person is a quality, or original instinct, which is attracted by and responds to the influence and the power of holy, sacred places. Virtually everyone who has participated in my "Dowsing Earth Energies and Creating Sacred Space" workshop has been able to feel and dowse for a water line.

As water flows through underground streams, it creates a subtle electromagnetic field, several feet wide, that rises vertically above the water line, even through multiple floors and stories. This vertical planar field of electromagnetic energy affects people physically, mentally, and spiritually.

Most people need artificial assistance in the form of a pendulum, forked stick (dowsing rod), or some other dowsing instrument to find water. When a dowser using a dowsing rod passes over a water line, the arm muscles tense slightly, causing an almost imperceptible reflex movement in the hands. The stick or rod then dips down, indicating the presence of water. Here are some comments from dowsing students describing what standing over a water line feels like to them:

"Slow and warm and fuzzy."
"Heavy in my arms."
"Faint undulating energy."
"Pulsing, flowing."
"Surprise. Electric. Pleasing."

"A flowing directional pull, like ripples."
"Gravity, a pulling downward."
"Cold, powerful."
"Chocolate syrup."
"Calming energy."
"Too quiet, too serene, yet refreshing."

It's one thing to experience the effect of a water line by standing over it for a short time. It's another thing to work or sleep over a water line. Spending a lot of time over a water line will tend to slow you down and make you feel lazy or apathetic. People who work at desks over water lines often have problems finding enough energy to get work done or even started. Also, water lines can have serious negative effects when the water line is physically or psychically polluted. Such negative water lines not only create a place of passivity, but can be detrimental to one's physical and mental health. I consider negative water lines to be one of the world's major causes of disease. The negative effects of water lines and how to be aware of them are explained further in chapter five.

Ley Lines

Ley lines are the other earth energy found at most ancient monuments and sacred places. The honor of the rediscovery of the ley-line system belongs to Alfred Watkins,[3] who on one summer afternoon in the 1920s "saw a web of lines linking the holy places and sites of antiquity."[4] Watkins' basic postulate was that ancient monument sites align with one another in straight lines. Many ancient sites found on British ordinance maps can actually be connected to form an incredible coincidence of interconnecting lines. The question that arises is what came first? The alignment of prehistoric sites or the lines linking the sites? With an Ordinance Survey map in England, it's not hard to find ley lines—that is, three or more ancient monuments in alignment. For us, the creators of contemporary sacred space, what is important is the presence of a ley line and its associated sensations. In this context, ley lines are often termed *energy leys* to distinguish them from the definition of ley lines based on aligned prehistoric sites.

Ley, as a word, is related to *leoht* (light illumination) and the Middle English word *lea* (a pasture or meadow that is open to the sun). *Ley* is also related to *lay* and *lee*. This etymological sequence describes a sort of cosmic roadway system upon which people traveled in pre-Renaissance times: cleared hilltop notches (ley); cleared forest pathways (lay); and cleared fields (lee). Imagine standing on a hilltop at dusk and seeing an aura of lighted ley lines passing through earthworks and stone circles, the darkened groves of trees glowing with soft light.

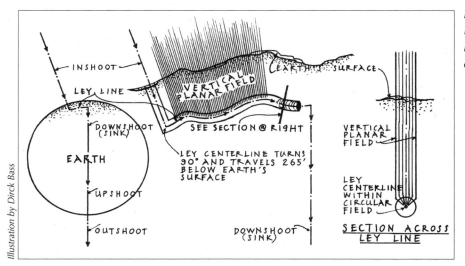

Figure 3.2—
Illustration of ley-line flow through earth.

Ley lines are cosmic forces originating outside of the earth. Just like all phenomena, ley lines and ley-line power centers can emerge or cease existing. I have seen cases of both events. According to dowsing research done in the 1970s by T. Edward Ross (who served as the President of the American Society of Dowsers) and John Payne (my teacher, now deceased), ley lines penetrate and then leave the earth vertically, at nodes. The penetrating nodes are called power centers. As illustrated in Figure 3.2, when entering, ley lines continue inward to a point 265 feet below the surface of the earth. At this point, they make a ninety-degree right-angle turn and travel in a perfectly straight line (when seen from a plan, or "birds-eye" view) and in an undulating motion (when seen from a section, or side view), always maintaining a depth of 265 feet relative to the surface of the earth. The width of the line on the ground is approximately six to eight feet. The ley line exits the earth by again turning ninety degrees, passing straight through the center of the earth, and going out the other side.

Everyone always asks, "Why 265 feet?" My answer is simply that when we dowse for the ley line that's what we find. Honestly, I don't know exactly why. I *do* know that when I'm over a ley line, it alters my consciousness.

What Do Ley Lines Feel Like? Like water lines, a vertical field extends up from the ley line, even through buildings. The nature of this field is energetic or *yang*. A person who sits or lies over a ley line for an extended time will tend to be hyperactive. This can work to one's advantage in healing or in situations where extra energy is useful. However, if someone is already very energetic, the ley line may cause an unhealthy situation—and if the ley line is negative, the negative aspects of extra energy will manifest in tension, anxiety, and neurosis. Dowsing students have described what standing over a ley line feels like to them as follows:

"Energizing."
"Light...a glowing line that goes with the direction of flow."
"Began to feel like I was weaving."
"Faint smooth energy."
"Lightness. A pulling upward."
"Pulsing, flowing, deep lively sensation just below my solar plexus."
"Warm and solid."
"Crisp, clear."

Power Centers

At every point where ley lines enter the earth (inshoots) and at approximately seventy percent of the nodes where ley lines leave the earth (outshoots), there is an underground water spring.[5] The ley-line inshoot or outshoot and accompanying water spring are the universal prerequisites for power centers. It is not just the water spring or the ley line, but the *union* of the two that determines the site selection of monuments and sacred spaces.

The power of ancient monuments lies in the interaction of the telluric earth field of water lines with the cosmic solar field of ley lines. Their combination creates a synergetic, holistic field, which is greater than either of the two energies alone. This fusion of the fundamental components of the universe, yin and yang, is the source of all matter, energy, and consciousness.

Photo ©1989 Chuck Pettis

Figure 3.3—*There are many power centers on mountain tops, such as this one on Mount Dickerman in the Cascade Mountains of Washington state (view toward Glacier Peak).*

A power center radiates a universal energy that affects consciousness and can also be influenced and changed by consciousness. In fact, just as silt becomes sedimentary rock over time, strong human emotions experienced at a power center create layers of consciousness over time that future visitors can feel and experience. I had such an experience during my visit to the Calendar II underground chamber located in central Vermont (see Figure 3.4). The story follows.

In the late 1970s, I belonged to a group called the New England Antiquities Research Association (NEARA), which studies and helps locate and preserve the historic and prehistoric past of New England. From them, I learned of the location of many prehistoric sites and visited them.

One summer day, I drove to the top of a mountain in central Vermont. At the top, I parked and started walking around. I tend to get a certain feeling at power centers and I was picking up on this feeling that day when I found a standing stone and recumbent stone with Iberian ogam inscriptions (believed to have been written by European Celts 3,000 years ago).[6] At the center of this cosmic place is a beautifully preserved underground chamber. It's called *Calendar II* because of its orientation to the midwinter sunrise. If you sit inside the chamber and look out the entranceway on the morning of the Winter Solstice, December 21, the sun will rise in the center of the entrance. This is one of many such sites found all over New England.

Figure 3.4— *"Calendar II" is an underground chamber located on a central Vermont mountaintop and oriented to the Winter Solstice sunrise.*

Photo ©1977 Chuck Pettis

This chamber, like most such chambers, is located over an underground water spring and a ley-line power center. As I entered the chamber, I felt a palatable presence in the air—an increase in energy density, an intensity of experience. It came to me that this chamber was specially designed to evoke these kinds of feelings.

Monuments harbor the potential for universal creative power that can be directed for the progress of humanity. In India, such spots are places for liberation and enlightenment. These sacred places have a very spiritual vibration, facilitating deep meditation and contemplation.

There are other kinds of earth energies that affect us, including those found in *kivas*—Native American circular underground ritual chambers that are located in the southwestern United States. When visiting Bandelier National Monument in New Mexico, I stood in the area where a kiva, now ruined, had been. I could feel power and a yin telluric forcefield. The kiva was a sort of magnetic center into which energies were drawn from the surrounding countryside, then drawn upward into a concentrated vortex.

This feeling of power sensed by our consciousness and body is the key thing to seek at any sacred place—it is the *effect* of the field on our consciousness that really counts, not the name, technicalities, or details. When you visit ancient monuments or sacred places of any kind, be aware of and *experience* your level of consciousness. Feel how you change in mood, note what kinds of thoughts you have, and pay attention to what "comes to mind." Ancient monuments are a blessing because they elegantly mark power centers. In many parts of the world, all you have to do is find a megalithic monument, mound, or ceremonial place and you've found an important power center.

What if you want to find a power center and there isn't a monument or ancient place near you? What if you are interested in analyzing power centers to find out how they work or how the patterns of earth energy are manifested? Well, unfortunately there are no commercial earth energy meters (yet) on the market. Currently, there are two ways to find power centers. One is just to be able to feel them, naturally. I have one friend who can just walk to a power center and say, "Here it is." People like this are quite rare. The more common way to find power centers and earth energies is through the technique of dowsing.

Underground Energy Patterns Marked By Megalithic Sites

During my research into ancient monuments, I carefully dowsed and mapped the earth energies flowing through a number of power centers. In doing so, I found that the stones and earth *above* the ground often mark earth energies *underneath* the ground. For example, the interior passage and side chambers of the West Kennet Long Barrow in southern England mark ley lines, and the interior walls map underground water lines.

Figure 3.5—
Standing stone, stone chamber, and dolmen at Mystery Hill.

Illustration by Dirck Bass

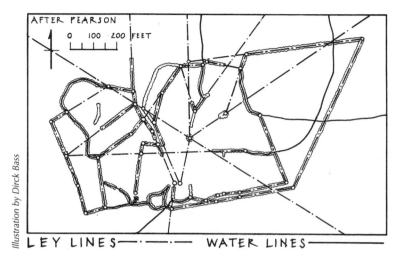

Figure 3.6—*Overall survey of Mystery Hill site showing stone walls marking ley lines and water lines (after Pearson).*

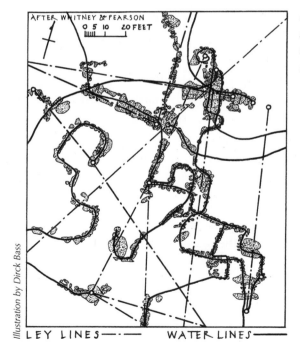

Figure 3.7—*Central area of Mystery Hill showing stone constructions marking ley lines and water lines (after Whitney & Pearson).*

While the British Isles are well known for their megalithic sites, many people do not know that several hundred megalithic monuments are located in New England. Of these, Mystery Hill, located in southern New Hampshire, is the largest and most complex (as well as the most controversial). Standing stones, underground chambers, dolmens, as well as long stone walls and wells are all found on this twenty-five-acre site. Mystery Hill stands out among megalithic monuments because its entire structure is an actual map of the ley lines and water lines located directly beneath the monument.

Getting Started with Dowsing

There are many theories of why dowsing works; each dowser has his or her own theory and mode of operation. Here's the way I do it, based on my research and field practice. You can try it my way or modify the method to suit you. Remember, it's not *how* you do it that counts, it's the *results* that count.

Levels of Dowsing

Physical Dowsing. There are three basic levels of dowsing: physical, mental, and spiritual. Start with physical dowsing. With practice, the body can be trained to physically respond to an electromagnetic field or emanation. When the dowser's body senses the field, muscular responses make the dowsing rod flip down or the pendulum spin. At this level, the body is like a radar receiver and the dowsing device is like a blip on the screen.

Mental Dowsing. Mental dowsing is a step higher than physical dowsing. At this level, we can map-dowse, which means to dowse a location while physically removed from the site (usually with the aid of a map or photo).

Spiritual Dowsing. Spiritual dowsing is the highest level of dowsing. At this level, you actually become one with the object, idea, or consciousness you are exploring. You merge with the underlying and unifying consciousness pervading all existence—the Supreme Consciousness, God.

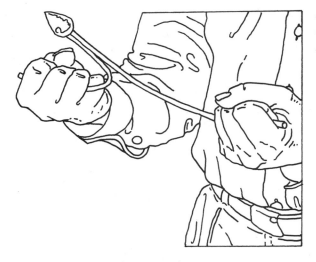

Figure 3.8—*The trick to using a dowsing rod is learning how to hold it.*[7]

This dowsing section is based on my own experience dowsing places of power. There are many books that deal with the broader field of dowsing that you can read to explore dowsing further (see bibliography). The best way to learn to dowse, though, is with the guidance of an experienced dowser.

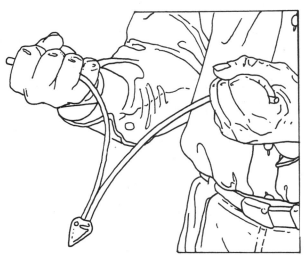

Figure 3.9—*When over a water or ley line, the dowsing rod flips down (or up).*

Types of Dowsing Tools

To get started with dowsing, you must first make, buy, or borrow a dowsing rod, pair of L-rods, or a pendulum.

Dowsing Rod. The dowsing rod is probably the most widely used dowsing tool. You can make a dowsing rod by cutting a Y-shaped stick from a tree or bending a plastic tube and fastening the bent end. As shown in Figure 3.8, the two open ends of the dowsing rod are held with one end in each hand. Then, a kind of outward and upward movement is made by the hands to make the end of the

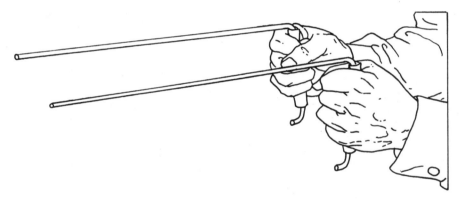

Figure 3.10—
Hold L-rods out in front of you so they are almost level.

rod very "twitchy," ready to flip up or down with the smallest muscular reaction in the arm. When one passes over a water or ley line, the rod is activated by the arm muscles and moves up or down, indicating the presence of a line.

The dowsing rod is good for general field work. It gives a good, positive signal with its quick, flipping action and is not affected by wind or walking.

L-rod. An L-rod is a piece of metal rod bent into a right angle. L-rods are held in both hands with the long ends positioned to point straight ahead. Both hands are held about chest high, so that the short ends are held vertically and the long ends point forward, parallel to the ground. To get the L-rods into the "ready" position, tip the hands so the long ends point down toward the ground in front of you. Then, gradually lift the ends up until just before they begin to swing out or in.

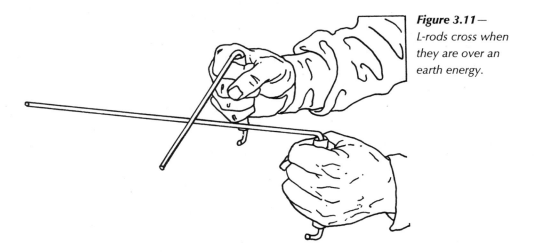

Figure 3.11—
L-rods cross when they are over an earth energy.

Held in this dynamically balanced position, they swing easily when a dowsing response is received.

L-rods can respond in several different ways. When both rods swing out or in (crossed), they indicate an earth energy such as a water stream or ley line. Or both

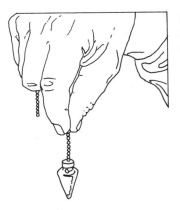

Figure 3.12—*Hold the pendulum with the thumb and forefinger so it hangs naturally.*

rods can move to the same direction, pointing in the direction of line flow. Flow can also be found by using just one rod and having it point in the direction of flow.

You can make your own L-rods by cutting two coat hangers with wire clippers and bending them to form a right angle. Use copper rods to make high-quality L-rods. For more sensitivity, slip a plastic tube over the short ends. Then, you can grip the tubes firmly and the rods can still move freely and smoothly. Without

***Figure 3.13**—*
The pendulum swings in a circle when over an earth energy.

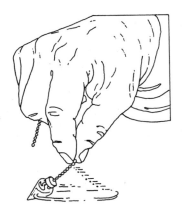

plastic tubes, the friction of the rod against your hand can make the dowsing reaction less sensitive. You could pass over a line and not even pick it up because the rod could not swing quick enough. This can also happen when your arms get tired and let the ends of the rods dip too low to rotate.

Pendulum. A pendulum is simply a weighted object hanging from a string or bead chain. The chain is held between the thumb and forefinger, which should be pointing down so the fingers look like a long beaked bird. The pendulum can be held at rest, but more often it is held so that it swings back and forth, which allows a quicker dowsing response than just holding it at rest. The typical pendulum response is to swing clockwise or counterclockwise in a circular motion when you pass over a water or ley line. The clockwise and counterclockwise motions can also be coded to imply opposites like positive or negative, yes or no, yang or yin.

You can make pendulums in a variety of ways. One of the easiest is to get a nut (the bolt kind of nut) and tie a thread or light string to it. You can also use a stone, crystal, button or another small object. You'll get a better response if the object is circular and balanced. Otherwise, the pendulum swing may be slightly off.

The portability of the pendulum makes it a good general-purpose dowsing tool. I carry one in my pocket. It can be used for all types of dowsing. It's best for map dowsing and close detail work.

Coding the Movements of Your Dowsing Instrument

Our bodies are wonderful receivers, capable of picking up many signals. The dowsing instrument doesn't move all by itself; it simply reinforces the body's natural dowsing response, making it more visible and reliable. When you adjust your radio, a red light indicates when the station is tuned in. When dowsing, the dowsing rod or pendulum is your "red light," alerting you that you have found what you were searching for.

Each dowsing tool has a different *code,* or dowsing reaction. For the dowsing rod, the code is easy. You want the rod to dip down (or up if you wish) when you pass over what you are looking for. With L-rods, you can code the rods to spread out or cross inward to indicate a water or ley line. With the pendulum, you can establish that any circular spin will indicate a line.

The pendulum is the most versatile dowsing instrument and is adaptable for uses other than looking for water or ley lines. For example, you can find the polarity of a water line (positive or negative) or set up a yes/no communication system (a code between you and your body) for yourself. A clockwise spin is usually yes or yang (positive). A counterclockwise spin is usually no or yin (negative). The yes/no correlation with the direction of spin varies from person to person. Therefore, establishing your spin direction for yes and no is the first thing dowsers should learn.

Establishing Your Yes/No Code. Start with the pendulum. Sit on a chair, upright, with your feet spaced about a foot and a half apart. Do not let the feet or legs cross. Hold the pendulum between your legs and let it swing back and forth. The back-and-forth swing is like the neutral gear in your car—the engine is running, but the car isn't moving. Next, make the pendulum move in a clockwise circle. Then make it move in a counterclockwise circle. Play with it for awhile to get a feel for how the pendulum feels when it's moving in different directions.

To find what *yes* (yang) is for you, hold the pendulum about two feet above your right knee. Slowly lower the pendulum toward your knee. When the pendulum enters your aura—the electromagnetic field of your body—it will begin to spin. Because the right side of most people's body is yang in nature, the direction the pendulum spins is your code for *yes*. Bring the pendulum back between your legs and let it return to the neutral back and forth swing. Then, follow the same process over your left knee to find your code for *no* (yin). If it's not working, make sure your legs aren't crossed, meditate for a few minutes, take a deep breath, and concentrate on the task. In a few cases, I've found people who aren't positive and negative on the right and left sides of their body, but rather are positive and negative on the top (head) and bottom (legs).

Check your yes/no code out with places or questions you know the answer to and confirm that your code is consistent with the results you actually get. The goal is to find a yes/no code that works reliably for you.

Get Used to the Feel of Your Dowsing Instrument

Hold the dowsing rod as previously illustrated and walk around with it as if you were actually dowsing. Then imagine that you find something and make the rod flip down. Move away and let the rod return to its original balanced position. If you have L-rods, practice making the rods spread apart, cross inward, or swing together to one side. If you have a pendulum, practice making it spin. Practice is important because the main problem beginning dowsers have is getting the feel of the dowsing instrument. Remember, the dowsing instrument is not moving magically on its own. *You* are making it move. Like learning to play a musical instrument, it takes a while to get used to how each dowsing instrument works and reacts. So, play with your dowsing rod for a little while just to get the feel of it. After you're comfortable with your dowsing rod, L-rods, or pendulum, you're ready to dowse water lines.

Dowsing Earth Energies

There are five basic steps for dowsing earth energies:

- Calm your mind and attain a state of mindfulness.
- Concentrate your mind on the desired object.
- Survey the area by walking around the site.
- Mark power centers, water lines, and ley lines.
- Have your results checked.[8]

Our body, mind, and inner self (soul) together form the most sophisticated machine on the earth. Each of our "machines" is capable of extraordinary feats of endurance and performance. Our eyes, ears, nose, skin, and tongue help us see, hear, smell, feel, and taste what is going on all around us. Besides these five senses, there is a sixth sense which all of us have and can use to tune in to just about anything we desire.

Biofeedback has shown that we can train ourselves to monitor and regulate our own bodily processes, which are usually automatically handled by our body with only minimal awareness by us. For example, biofeedback programs have been used to teach people to reduce stress, relax, treat headaches, help partially paralyzed stroke victims activate muscles, and reduce the anxiety of dental patients. Similarly, we can train our mind and body to pick up subtle earth energies and indicate their presence through a series of muscle and nerve interactions, resulting in an a visible response by the dowsing instrument.

Tuning in to whatever you are looking for is as easy as *thinking* about what you are looking for. If you are looking for water lines, imagine water flowing underneath the ground in a crack or fissure. If you are looking for ley lines, it's a little more subtle, since there isn't a physical substance to detect there. It's an *energy* you are seeking, yang in nature.

Your state of mind is all-important in dowsing. If you meditate, you can get in the dowsing state of mind automatically. Put your mind in a receptive and open state. If you don't meditate, use your powers of concentration to focus your attention on what you are looking for.

The key to understanding dowsing is that whatever you *think* is necessary for successful dowsing to occur is exactly what *is* necessary (for you). For example, some people can only dowse with one kind of forked stick. In this endeavor, you are limited only by what you believe.

Whatever you tune in to is what you are going to find, so be careful and very specific about what you want. Several times when I've dowsed for water wells, the client has pointed out a place another dowser had indicated. When I then checked the spot out, I wouldn't get a dowsing reaction until I tuned into *all* kinds of underground water (including polluted water). When I dowse for a water well, I generally concentrate on finding pure, potable drinking water, excluding all ground water and water with salt, sulfur, or iron. If you focus on just any water at all, you will get the bad as well as the good.

Finding ley lines is much more difficult that finding water lines. Even experienced dowsers have made mistakes when searching for ley lines. Don't dowse for ley lines until you can practice on a known ley line and experience what ley energy feels like. Remember, the reason to dowse at all is to find places of power that change and uplift our consciousness. If possible, learn to dowse from an experienced dowser over known water and ley lines. Have your results checked by someone whose expertise is proven.

Survey the Area or Site

To dowse a piece of land on-site, tune your mind in to what you are looking for and begin walking. You can check the entire area by walking the perimeter and either marking lines for later connection or following each one as you get to it.

After your initial survey is completed, mark the power centers, springs, and important lines with a small stone pile or a wooden stake. This will provide an easy-to-find reference point for future work.

To find power centers, begin by dowsing for ley lines. As you follow the ley line, it will eventually end. When this happens, the dowsing indication (the bent dowsing rod, for example) stops. You can then check for the presence of a ley line entering the earth by holding your left hand above the spot and use a pendulum with your right hand to check for the inshoot. Then, check for an underground water spring. When you have an inshoot and a blind spring, you have located a ley-line power center.

Have your results checked. None of us is infallible, especially when dealing with subtle earth energies, which are dependent on our ability to concentrate. It is very easy to get off on a wrong track when dowsing, especially when working with ley lines. Here's a way to double-check your ley-line dowsing. Tune in to and dowse for the center of the ley line (the *center line*). Mark the center line on the ground with a wooden pole. Do this at three different points. Because ley lines are perfectly straight, the three poles should all line up. If they don't, something is off. Either you haven't got a ley line or you haven't been careful enough about your dowsing.

Map Dowsing

When I first learned to dowse, some friends had just bought forty acres of land. I used their property to try out my dowsing skills. First, I walked the perimeter of the land looking for water lines. When I found a water line, I would follow it and mark its course on a map of the area. One line could take me up and down and through fields, brambles, and ditches. When I finished dowsing and mapping water lines, I did ley lines in the same way. It was great exercise, but it took a long time.

Actual on-site dowsing is, without doubt, the best way to dowse a site. However, in some cases it is not possible or convenient to visit the actual site in person. In other cases, the area to be dowsed may cover many acres requiring an inordinate amount of time to dowse by a "walking" survey. One handy and time-saving technique that solves both of these problems is map dowsing.

Map dowsing is excellent for checking out an area to see if anything is there, to see if the place is worth a trip, and to save time at the site itself. By map-dowsing a site beforehand, you have an excellent idea of where to start. You can confirm each of your findings directly on the site with "physical" dowsing.

How to Dowse with a Map. With map dowsing, you "let your fingers do the walking." Start with a map of the selected area. Then, after tuning in to the area with the help of the Landscape Angel (see "How to Contact and Communicate with Devas" in chapter four), use a pointer held in one hand—I use a pen—and a pendulum in your other hand. Attune to what you are looking for (water lines, ley lines). Start at a corner of the map and move your pen or pencil slowly around the perimeter of the area. When the pen passes over a water or ley line or whatever you are looking for, the pendulum indicates that presence by moving in a circle.

Once you find a water line or ley, hold the pendulum over the point on the perimeter where you found the line and have the pendulum swing back and forth in the direction that the line is flowing at that point, with the back swing ending at the perimeter and the forward swing showing the direction the line is taking. Use your pen to mark the direction the line is taking. Then move the pendulum over a little. Now the back swing starts at your pen mark and the pendulum's forward swing marks the next segment of the line's flow. In this way, you use the pendulum to follow and mark the location of the line on the map. Using this method, I can follow a line quickly, noting its course with a pen as I go. If I reach a water spring or ley-line power center, my system is to have the pendulum spin in a circle over the spot and go back to neutral if I pass the spot.

Finding Polarities

One last important point. Almost all stones found at ancient monuments are polarized. When building sacred spaces with stone, you should use polarized stones. Polarized stones have a positive and a negative end. They seem to hold a "charge" better than other stones—it's something like the difference between a battery that's live and one that's dead.

To find if a stone is polarized, use one hand as your "receiver" and your other hand to hold your pendulum. Run your receiver hand slowly over the stone's surface. If the stone is polarized, you will find that there is a point on the stone that is positive and another point, usually on the opposite side of the stone, that is negative. To create the best energy network, place each stone with the positive (yang) point facing straight up and the negative (yin) side down in the ground. Also, only use stones that the landscape angel and stone deva give permission to use. I'll describe how you can use meditation to determine "permission" in chapter four.

To amplify the power of the earth energies, put one or more quartz crystals under the stones. Meditate and ask for guidance from the landscape angel to determine if quartz crystals should be put under any or all of the stones and, if so, what number and orientation in each hole.

Work and Study with Other Dowsers

Dowsing represents a whole new frontier in humankind's perception of the world. We can do just about anything we set our minds to. With so much potential for knowledge at hand and, at the same time, so much potential for confusion, it is especially important to work and study with other dowsers and sympathetic people. So, seek out dowsers, talk, share experiences, and have a good time!

Cosmic Capacitors

Through dowsing, we can locate places that possess special electromagnetic fields and are receptacles of power and earth spirit. These places include ancient monuments, ley-line power centers, trees, stones, mountains, caves, water springs, wells, and rivers. We, as human beings, also have a field and are receptacles of power and spirit.

Thought forms can be transferred from the human field to the earth field and back again. A thought form is the visualization of a form, feeling, perception, or state of consciousness. Usually the thought-form transference takes place when a thought is highly charged emotionally or spiritually. Both positive and negative feelings can be transferred—the earth field does not discriminate between positive and negative thoughts. Through this process, thought forms are built up within the earth field until a person comes along who is receptive to one or more of the "stored" visualizations.

This phenomenon of thought transference is analogous to the operation of a capacitor. A capacitor is an electrical device, consisting of two or more conductor plates separated from one another by a dielectric (nonconducting material) and used for receiving and storing an electrical charge. This charge is induced by exposing the capacitor to the influence of a field of force. The charge builds up gradually, but is released all at once. Imagine standing stones as conductor plates with the earth acting as a dielectric. In this model, human consciousness and thoughts act as the field of force.

When we "implant" a thought form into the capacitor (monument), potential energy is produced; the monument becomes home to a charge of stationary consciousness that can be transferred *back* to human consciousness if the receiver (a person) is functioning at about the same frequency as the thought form—in other words, if the receiver possesses a sympathetic vibration.

The phenomena of thought and emotion transference from a space to a person has two consequences. First, there are accumulated layers of emotionally charged thought forms in many ancient monuments and sacred places that can uplift our spirit and boost our awareness and evolution toward self-realization. At the same time, some spaces may have negative thought-forms associated with them. You can *feel* potential danger—so if a space does not feel right, avoid it. Second, with all this in mind, each of us has a responsibility to future visitors of a sacred space to be very mindful of our thoughts when inside a sacred space. Our thoughts should be kept as pure and spiritual as possible.

Secrets of Sacred Space
Revealed in This Chapter

◆ Potent ancient monuments around the world have one thing in common: the presence of earth energies that have the power to alter and uplift human consciousness.

◆ Dowsing is the intuitional practice or technique for locating earth energies.

◆ The human body is the best receiver on earth.

◆ Underground flowing water and ley lines create subtle electromagnetic fields, several feet wide, that rise vertically above the water line—even through multiple floors and stories. These vertical planar fields of electromagnetic energy affect people physically, mentally, and spiritually.

◆ Spending a lot of time over a water line will tend to slow you down and make you feel lazy or apathetic.

◆ Water lines can have serious negative effects when they are polluted physically or psychically.

◆ A person who sits or lies over a ley line for an extended period of time will tend to be hyperactive.

◆ At every point where ley lines enter the earth (inshoots) and at approximately seventy percent of the nodes where ley lines leave the earth (outshoots), there is an underground water spring. The ley-line inshoot or outshoot and accompanying water springs are the universal prerequisites for the site selection of monuments and sacred spaces.

◆ A power center radiates a universal energy that affects consciousness and can also be influenced and changed by consciousness.

◆ Stones and earth *above* the ground mark earth energies *beneath* the ground.

◆ Polarized stones (stones with a positive and negative end) should be used in sacred spaces.

◆ Be aware of your feelings and thoughts when you are in sacred spaces.

Suggested Projects and Exercises

♦ Read some books on dowsing (see Tom Graves and Sig Lonegren in the bibliography). Everybody has their own approach and personal prejudices (myself included), so by getting a variety of viewpoints, you'll get a more balanced understanding of dowsing and earth energies.

♦ Join the American Society of Dowsers (P.O. Box 24, Danville, Vermont 05828; e-mail: ASD@Dowsers.org) or the dowsing society where you live.

♦ Buy or build some dowsing tools and give it a try! You can do it!

Notes

1 Since I am no longer in the water-well dowsing business, contact the American Society of Dowsers (see website address in bibliography), or the dowsing society in your country for a referral if you need a well dowsed.

2 Information in this paragraph was found in *The Pattern of the Past* (New York: Abeland–Schuman, Ltd., 1973) by Guy Underwood.

3 Watkins, Alfred. *The Old Straight Track: Its Mounds, Beacons, Moats, Sites, and Mark Stones* (London: Abacus/Sphere Books, 1976 reprint).

4 Michell, John. *The View Over Atlantis* (London: Garnstone Press, 1975).

5 Watkins, op. cit.

6 Dowsing research findings by Terry Ross and John Payne.

7 Dowsing illustrations by Carrie Westfall.

8 Trento, Salvatore Michael, *The Search for Lost America* (Chicago: Contemporary Books, Inc., 1978), 58–59.

chapter four

Earth Spirit Communication

The earth is a living organism, the body of a higher individual who has a will and wants to be well, who is at times less healthy or more healthy, physically and mentally. People should treat their own bodies with respect. It's the same thing with the earth. Too many people don't know that when they harm the earth they harm themselves, nor do they realize that when they harm themselves they harm the earth.[1]

—Rolling Thunder, American Indian medicine man

At ley-line power centers, spiritual feelings are more easily experienced. The veil separating the manifest and the unmanifest worlds is thin at these special places and much is possible in the way of personal development and spiritual experiences, both on an individual and a group level.

Healing the earth at sacred places and power centers is one of the most important services that can be done for humanity and the planet. In Chinese medicine, acupuncture techniques use needles placed at special points on the body called *meridians* to facilitate the flow of chi (life energy) through the body. Power centers are to the Earth Spirit as meridians are to acupuncture. By finding the earth's energy centers, embedding stones at those places, and carefully creating beautiful sentient spaces, we help heal the earth and improve the well-being of the earth spirit.

Just as people get diseases like cancer in specific parts of their body, the earth spirit is sick in areas where physical negativity (like hazardous waste dumps) and psychological negativity (like concentration camps) exist. By neutralizing the negativity at these places, we can heal the Earth Spirit, making our planet stronger and more balanced. The result is less war and conflict.

The Spiritual Hierarchy

Some readers will be very comfortable with the following presentation about spiritual beings and others may be skeptical. Therefore, I beg the skeptical reader to be open-minded about this presentation on the spiritual hierarchy. I am not proselytizing on behalf of the spiritual hierarchy—I believe that each person should follow whatever religion or path that they feel right for them. I do ask that you consider increasing the time and energy you devote to your own spiritual growth.

Depending on your religion or spiritual beliefs, the spiritual hierarchy is referred to by many names: heaven, enlightened ones, the elder brethren, a "sister" evolution, the angelic kingdom, and so on. I'm not a religious scholar, so I'm sure there are other examples that I haven't represented here. Each religion sees and describes their own spiritual beings and ideology a little differently, but the idea of the "spiritual being" seems to be common to all religions. All spiritual beings, regardless of religion, want to help us with our spiritual development. Because we are building sacred space for our own and others' well-being and spiritual growth, it makes sense to learn about the spiritual beings of your own faith or religion and ask for their help when creating our own sacred places.

The important thing to get from this chapter is that you can (and should) integrate your own religious beliefs into your sacred space. Let me continue now with a brief summary of some of the established ideology and beliefs about the spiritual hierarchy.

In addition to the Earth Spirit, there is a whole universe of gods, devas, deities, angels and other spiritual beings. In Tibetan Buddhism, there are Buddhas, deities, and Bodhisattvas. In Christianity, there are angels, God, and Jesus. In mythology, there are gods and goddesses. In folktales, there are elves and nature spirits. The entirety of this spiritual world of beings is termed the spiritual hierarchy. The beings and forces of the spiritual hierarchy act in harmony with the Supreme Consciousness, God, to create the order, form, and consciousness of the cosmos.

Everything is a manifestation of Supreme Consciousness; everything is alive to some extent. To find and bring out the spirit in place, to create a sacred space, it is necessary to see the divinity in everything. Every stone, plant, and animal has an animating force—a divine essence that is responsible for its structure, health, and beauty.

The Earth Spirit, the embodiment of the earth as a living, divine being, is a part of a vast evolution of spiritual beings who act in harmony with our own earthly evolution. Communicating and getting guidance from these spiritual beings is vital to working with earth energies and places of power. The guidance and blessing of the Earth Spirit and other divine beings of the spiritual hierarchy helps us do the right thing at the right places at the right times.

The spiritual hierarchy includes many levels of divine beings, all varying in degrees of consciousness and responsibility depending on the role they play. At the top is Supreme Consciousness. Have you ever seen a *tangka*, a Buddhist painting depicting a hierarchy of meditating Buddha images? That is a literal representation of the spiritual hierarchy. When I meditate in a sacred space, I often visualize an ascending hierarchy of meditating Buddhas above the space. In 1997, I had the opportunity to spend a week in Thailand (a country where you see images and sculptures of Buddha everywhere). If you are ever in Bangkok, take the opportunity to visit and meditate in the Temple of the Emerald Buddha. In this incredible sacred space is a showcase of the spiritual hierarchy, which is impressive visually and in meditation.

Other than the Supreme Consciousness, most important to our work with sacred places are spiritual beings called *devas*, or angels. Devas (from Sanskrit, shining one) are nonphysical beings of subtle energy and consciousness. *Angel* is a Greek word meaning messenger or one sent to minister spirits. If you could "see" the true form of devas and angels, they would appear as whirling spheres or figures of light, color, sound, and even smell.

Devas are beings of love and light who stand ready to help us in our spiritual growth. They live in a world of feeling, thought, and spiritual will. They communicate via symbolism, color impressions, and thought forms. Devas are nature's engineers, the creative intelligence and form-builders behind the entire universe. What makes a rose look like a rose? What makes nature so marvelous? Devas. As omnipresent, superphysical agents of the Supreme Consciousness, devas join everything together into one unified and orderly creation. Devas are universal. They exist for everyone, everywhere. Although the form of their expression and apprehension varies by person, their essence is pure.

Under devas are nature spirits, who do the actual "work." Nature spirits include the gnomes of the earth, the elves and fairies of the woods, fields, and streams, and the salamanders of the fire element. Nature spirits are the builders of form, following the archetypal plans of the devas and wielding energies provided by the devas for this purpose.

In this chapter, we will focus primarily of the role of devas, since they are the Earth Spirits we most frequently encounter.

Devas

In our solar system, the highest deva oversees the entire workings of the planets and all chemical, physical, magnetic, gravitational laws which make our solar system the way it is—this deva is known as the Solar Lord. Other important devas include the Earth Spirit, the Landscape Angel, the Moon Deva, and the devas of each plant, animal, and mineral.

Devas help us work in harmony with the cosmic intention; they are divine messengers who can help us make sure that our work with the earth and power centers is done properly, with maximum benefit and least harm. The proper utilization of power centers is not only important for us personally, but is also important for the devas who are magnetically attracted to them.

There is a power center in my hometown (Seattle, Washington) that is a special deva place. Located in Interlaken Park, this place is surrounded by green with a scenic overlook. On sacred space field trips we approach this place quietly, put our symbolic offerings of flower, stone, and crystal on the power center, and hold hands in a circle. In such a place, love flows freely. Faces relax. Eyes squint with peaceful smiles. The fairies, nature spirits, and devas dance around and intertwine with our energies. Hugs come naturally.

Ignorance of the spiritual hierarchy as well as their gathering places weakens the well-being of *both* humans and devas. In the past, these places were revered and cared for by generation after generation. Today, it is doubly important for us to attune ourselves to the needs of the earth because we have not only lost the tradition of creating and caring for power centers and monuments, but are drawing out vast amounts of the earth's natural resources while our population continues to grow rapidly.

Ancient monuments need protection from vandalism, destruction, and damage. In addition, all the earth's power centers should be sought out, marked, and protected from inappropriate development. These places should be treated as parks and left unspoiled.

Discovering a Deva

While visiting a deva-assisted garden near Findhorn, my friends and teachers, Kate and John Payne, became conscious as they passed certain bushes of an outpouring of scents, slightly different from place to place. "When we first smelled it, we didn't think of the devas," says Kate. "We said, oh there's a skunk here. I wonder if they know it? So we went into lunch and we said, 'Did you know that you had a skunk out in the garden?' And they laughed and said, 'That's the devas. Now you know what it smells like . . . a skunk.'" John added, "And they don't *have* skunks over there."

One of the first modern documented instances of cooperation with the nature spirits and devas was at Findhorn in the 1960s. The account can be found at the Findhorn web site at www.findhorn.org or in a book authored by the Findhorn community, *The Findhorn Garden* (San Francisco: HarperCollins, 1976). With devic assistance, Peter and Eileen Caddy, along with Dorothy MacLean, grew remarkable flowers and the famous forty-pound cabbage in the sandy shore of the North Sea of Scotland.

"It was quite a remarkable garden they had there, a locally traditional perennial English garden," recounts Kate Payne, a visitor to Findhorn at that time. "We found this almost unbelievable incandescence of the flowers that were at least half again as big as the ones at this very good garden at the local inn."

Findhorn was the beginning of a groundswell of interest in and cooperation with devas. While many people are actively (but quietly) working with devas in their gardens, Findhorn is the biggest advertisement for the cause of mutual cooperation between the various evolutions (earthly and spiritual).

Eileen Caddy is the author of numerous books, including *The Spirit of Findhorn* (New York: Harper-Row, 1977), and Dorothy MacLean is the author of *To Hear the Angels Sing* (Hudson: Lindisfarne Books, 1994), among other books.

Be Careful

When I was first thinking of building monuments in the mid-1970s, I had dinner in London with Tom Graves, a well-known dowser. Tom's initial reaction was strong: "Be careful." He said there are powers beyond our understanding at stone circles and other ancient monuments that can be dangerous. He's right: there are powers beyond our understanding at work at ancient sacred places. The question is how to *deal* with unknown powers.

My answer has been to make every step in the creation of sacred space a spiritual practice and to endeavor to act in harmony with the will of the Supreme. If you do everything possible to act in harmony with the Tao (the spiritual path), if you see everything as a manifestation of Supreme Consciousness, if you meditate regularly, if you follow the traditional spiritual observances (like truthfulness) and abstinences (like non-injury), and if you mentally visualize that your actions are done in service to the Supreme, then you will be protected from harm and guided toward the right way.

That's the way I look at it, and it works for me. Without a strong spiritual foundation and meticulous care at every step, Tom Graves' warning of danger is right on.

How do you see everything as a manifestation of the Supreme? The first thing is to have a strong grounding in meditation and spiritual practice. A connection has to be developed between you and your higher self, your link to the Supreme. Look for the divine in everything.

When I build a stone circle, I attune myself to those members of the spiritual hierarchy who play a part in the design and use of my sacred space. I want my design to be positive, effective, and nonharmful. So, when a decision has to be made, I attune with the deva who is responsible for the plant, animal, or stone in question and act on the guidance provided.

You Can Communicate with Devas

Communication with devas is possible by anyone open to their presence. We must simply be willing to make the effort necessary to develop our latent abilities to tune in to and listen to our higher self.

It is pure joy to invite many devas to fill a room. To my eyes, the room begins to vibrate. I see shimmering halos, and auras appear over people's heads. I become conscious of my heart center. It feels like great power and consciousness is concentrated in the space. At the end of such an evening, there's a very special feeling in the room because everyone has sensed for themselves the presence, closeness, and love of spiritual beings of love and light. What a blessing! The look on people's faces is extraordinary.

The old spiritual truth "Know yourself and you will know God" is the way to tap into the vast devic evolution. Human beings are gods in the making. We are powerhouses with unplumbed potential. We can use our minds to tune into anything, anyplace, and any deva or spiritual being. The main problem with establishing a relationship with one's higher self and devas is thinking *I can't do it.*

When you think of a particular deva, she is there with you, whether you are outdoors or in your home.

When visiting a sacred space, how and what you are thinking is very important. If you think of the space as dull and lifeless, it will be. But, if you think that you are actually helping to heal a great spiritual being, the Earth Spirit, by loving one of its power centers, then your visit takes on new meaning, excitement, and a sense of responsibility.

How to Contact and Communicate with Devas. Contacting and communicating with devas is a holy act and one deserving of respect. It is best to learn deva communication from a person experienced in this realm. Unfortunately, at the current time, there are few teachers and few books with practical instructions. With that in mind, I believe it may be beneficial to outline my spiritual practice for communicating with devas:

- Offer the action to the Supreme Consciousness.

Ask, "May this action be offered to Supreme Consciousness." You want your contact and communication with devas be a service to the Supreme Consciousness, God. Spiritual practices and responsibility go hand in hand. The law of karma states that for every action that you make (physical, mental, or spiritual), you receive a reaction. Good actions bring back good events in your life, while bad actions bring back bad events. Like a cosmic bank account, you get back what you invest.

To help your soul's spiritual growth, see everything as a manifestation of the Supreme Consciousness and offer the results of your actions to the Supreme. In this way, you are surrendering the action to the will of the Supreme. The more often you do this, the lighter your karmic load of potential reactions, bad or good, becomes. This is the path to enlightenment—to a direct understanding of the true nature of reality and to the blissful merger of self with the Supreme Consciousness.

- Meditate on the Supreme Consciousness, God.

The combination of all consciousness, both in the earthly evolution and the spiritual hierarchy is the Supreme Consciousness. Bring the thought of Supreme Consciousness into your mind. Imagine that you *are* the Supreme Consciousness.

Deva contact is essentially a meditation in which one concentrates on the deva with whom communication is desired. Since devas are on a different spiritual level than we are, we must first attune to our inner (divine) self in order to reach the required vibration level. Use meditation as a vehicle to go into your higher self and to become one with your wholeness.

After attuning to the Supreme Consciousness, I also visualize and invoke the blessings and help of the landscape angel, Chenrezi and Kuan Yin (the Bodhisattvas of compassion), and my spiritual teachers.

The most important guidelines here are to follow your inner soul guidance, be sensitive to your conscience, and discriminate between right and wrong.

• Say a prayer of purification, cleansing, and protection.

You can use one of these prayers of protection or make up one of your own. I start by saying:

> *May I, and all the people near me who might be affected by this activity, be protected from any harm or consequences of this action.*

Alternatively, you might like to use the following, which is based on a traditional Christian prayer of protection:

> *In the Name, through the Power, and by the Word of the Supreme Consciousness/the living Christ/the Buddhas, build a wall of Light and Protection around myself, my loved ones, my home, my affairs, and any mode of transportation I may use. I give thanks for this protection. Amen.*

Next, I focus my concentration. As I breathe in, I silently say a mantra and I focus all of my concentration on a brilliant point of light—pure God-consciousness. Then, as I breathe out, silently saying my mantra, I expand that point of light outward, forming a sphere of spiritual light such that everything within that sphere is the Supreme Consciousness. I continue this breathing process until a dome of light surrounds and protects the space where I am working.

As you work through this process, you may want to visualize deities of protection all around you.

Please be aware that if it doesn't feel right for you, for any reason, to contact a deva in a specific situation or even to contact devas in general, *don't do it.*

- Ask (using a pendulum): "Can I make deva contact?"

This is the first of two "checkpoint" questions. Are you qualified and are you able to contact devas at this time? If the indication is *no*, respect this answer; it is for your own good and protection. This is no time or place to prove anything.

- Ask (using a pendulum): "May I make deva contact?"

Is it appropriate and right for you to contact devas, at this time? If the indication is *no*, do not proceed.

- Close your eyes. Think of and visualize the deva you wish to contact.
  When you think of devas, they are with you.

Imagine what the deva would look like if you could see it as a being. For example, to contact a flower deva, think of the different colors, shapes, images, smells, and feelings that you associate with that flower. Your focused concentration is like a spiritual lighthouse to the deva you are seeking.

I have been asked the question, "How do you know who you're communicating with?" One of the reasons to systematically follow this process is to be very safe about who you are communicating with. This is not some trivial psychic game. This is a serious spiritual practice. If you are a meditator and have diligently followed the above steps, you should be communicating with the deva you seek. You can confirm this with your pendulum. For example, you may ask your highest self (through the pendulum), "Is this the pine tree deva?"

A deva can communicate and be sensed in a number of ways: as a spiritual presence, as a mental image, or even as a smell. In almost all cases, the communication is telepathic and is manifested as messages, thoughts, feelings, or images.

In all cases, keep your thoughts as pure and spiritual as possible in order to perfectly reflect the light of the angelic being.

You can flow with the mental images your receive in the deva's presence. Or you can take a more active role, by concentrating on specific questions and tuning into the answers that come into your mind. Feel free to make quick notes occasionally so you can refer to them later.

This is a fluid world of archetypes and consciousness. By the power of your concentration, you have reached a level of oneness that transcends the separateness of our bodies. You are now in the last frontier, the frontier of consciousness, an inner universe much vaster than our physical universe. It is a very personal place because you are all alone—a unit of consciousness in a deep sea of cosmic consciousness. Go slowly and carefully. Be responsible. Take care.

• Treat the deva with respect, love, and cordiality.

Devas are divine beings. They respond according to your vibration. Love is the keynote to which the entire spiritual hierarchy responds most strongly. When you feel the presence of the deva near to you, send out waves of love and kindness to it. Imagine the deva is as dear to you as your child, spouse, or parent, and show your love and respect for it through your thoughts and heart feelings.

Those of us who are making some of the first deva contacts in modern times should see deva communication as a special responsibility. We should act as ambassadors for all those who will follow and act as though we are guests in a special place, always on our best behavior. By honoring the divinity of the deva, we are recognizing divinity in the physical flower or another manifest thing. We are seeing the world as beautiful, divine, and wonderful.

• End by giving thanks.

It is good practice in all spiritual practices to end each meditation with a mental sign of thanks or offering. I mentally offer a colored flower to the Supreme Consciousness as a symbol of surrender to the will of God. Offer the merits of your actions as a service and benefit for all sentient beings.

In Summary. This process is a very powerful spiritual practice. I recommend adapting it, as summarized below, and using it whenever you dowse as well.

- Offer the action to the Supreme Consciousness.
- Meditate on God, the Supreme Consciousness, the landscape angel (to connect you spiritually with the site), and your spiritual teachers.
- Say a prayer of cleansing, purification, and protection.
- Ask, "Can I do this?"
- Ask, "May I do this?"
- Visualize the deva you wish to contact and listen/communicate with an attitude of loving kindness.
- End by giving thanks and an offering.

What It Feels Like to Communicate with Devas

Here are some experiences that my students have had with devas:

"A feeling of *connection* . . ."
"Devas of old forest groves are those that I feel an affinity with."
"Saw deva as streaming golden light."
"When I am around trees, I notice them. I had expectations. As I
lose them, I find deva experience."
"Uplifting communication with tree deva."

Some Helpful Hints

Deva communication is an inner experience, so it is different for each one of us. Because it is experiential, it is difficult to precisely explain how to communicate with devas and what actually happens. It is not a vicarious experience. Devic contact is a very holy act. Don't ever lose sight of this. You may find it helpful to use one deva, who you can contact easily, as an intermediary to contact other devas. For example, I tune into the Landscape Angel to ask general questions or get guidance on how to proceed in a particular area.

Deva communication involves establishing a resonance or parallel vibration with the deva we wish to contact. It's like a tuning fork. If we strike a tuning fork with a specific pitch, other tuning forks with the same pitch will begin to vibrate or resonate spontaneously. Similarly, our reception is only as good as our ability to attune to the exact vibration or higher quality we wish to contact.

When we attune to a deva, our soul begins vibrating at the same level as the deva. By invoking devas, we are calling on those qualities within ourselves. Through interaction with these divine beings, we enlarge our understanding of ourselves and our inner divinity. Use this spiritual technique wisely, for service to all.

Working with the Earth Spirit and Devas at Sacred Places

When a power center is found, the first thing to do is determine if the Landscape Angel and the devas want this space to be monumented. For example, I found one place with a very powerful vibration to it—so strong that my vision was affected (things got sort of misty). I meditated on the spot, tuned into the Landscape Angel, and understood that this place was primarily a sacred spot for the devas and nature spirits and if anything at all was to be done there, it should be very simple and minimal.

When a power center is found, meditate and tune into the Landscape Angel before any design work or building is done. Over time, ask for suggestions and guidance on what general type of monument should be erected, what the symbolism should be, and other details. When materials, particularly stones, are being selected for use in the monument, ask each one (each item or stone) if it *should* be a part of the monument. Every decision has a consequence, so ongoing cooperation with the Landscape Angel and devas is essential.

The spiritual hierarchy is facilitating the design and construction of new sacred spaces. They can assist us with our spiritual development in many ways, including thoughtful support in increasing the presence of earth energies essential to sacred space. During a walk up the path to the West Kennet Long Barrow, I was told by the Landscape Angel (in essence), "When you need ley lines, they will come." During the year that the Mutiny Bay Stone Circle was being built, two new ley lines emerged.

Secrets of Sacred Space Revealed in This Chapter

- At ley-line power centers, much is possible in the way of personal development and spiritual experiences on both an individual and group level.

- Power centers are to the Earth Spirit as meridians are to acupuncture. By finding the earth's energy centers, embedding stones at those places, neutralizing negative water lines and ley lines, and carefully creating a beautiful, sentient space, we help heal the earth and improve the well-being of the Earth Spirit.

- There are powers beyond our understanding at stone circles and other ancient monuments that can be dangerous. Therefore, make every step in the creation of sacred space a spiritual practice and endeavor to act in harmony with the will of the Supreme Consciousness.

- To help your soul's spiritual growth, see everything as a manifestation of the Supreme Consciousness and offer the results of your actions to the Supreme.

- There is a vast evolution of spiritual beings—the spiritual hierarchy—who act in harmony with our own "earthly" evolution. Communicating and getting guidance from these spiritual beings is vital to working with earth energies and places of power.

- Communication with devas—beings of love and light who stand ready to help us in our spiritual growth—is possible by anyone who is open to their presence. One must simply be willing to make the effort necessary to develop latent abilities to tune in to and listen to their higher, inner self.

- When a power center is found, the first thing to do is determine if the Landscape Angel and the devas want this space to be developed.

- When a decision has to be made regarding a sacred space, attune to the Landscape Angel or the appropriate deva and act on their guidance.

Suggested Projects and Exercises

- The Findhorn community in north Scotland has been a key force in publicizing the message of the devas. Through their amazing work with gardening, they have given visible evidence of the effect devic guidance can have. There are a number of books you can read about their work in this area, such as *The Findhorn Garden: Pioneering a New Vision of Man and Nature in Cooperation* (San Francisco: HarperCollins, 1976). The books by Geoffrey Hoddson, such as *Kingdom of the Gods* (Wheaton, IL: Theosophical Publishing House, 1952) and *Rolling Thunder* (New York: Dell Publishing, 1974) by Doug Boyd, explain other aspects and ways of thinking of the spiritual hierarchy. Read books on angels and devas to get different points of view on devas and the Earth Spirit.

- Try to contact the deva of a flower, tree, plant, or animal. Tune in to the deva according to the instructions in this chapter. Don't forget to follow each step, including protection.

- Try tuning into devas of your town, community, city, or country—or a mountain, valley, or location you feel particularly good about.

- Everything is part of one Supreme Consciousness. Everything has an ensouling intelligence, including soul qualities like courage, humility, and love. Try tuning in to your soul qualities and think about how you express one or more of them in your daily life.

- If you have a friend or family member who is ill, try tuning in to the healing angel and praying for healing help.

Notes

1   This is a quote from Doug Boyd's
     book, *Rolling Thunder* (New
     York: Dell Publishing, 1974), 51.

Entities, Ghosts, and Haunted Places

The world is not all love and light. There are many places with feelings of negativity, fear, and anxiety caused by the presence of negative (noxious) water lines and ley lines as well as the negative presence of human and nonhuman entities (ghosts). These places can and should be cleared of negativity because they are a major cause of ill health.

The hardest task of the geomancer is to pass over discarnate humans, deal with nonhuman entities, and neutralize negative earth energies. While not a subject to be taught in a book, visitors and creators of power centers and sacred places should at least be aware of this aspect of earth divination.

Many dowsers and doctors (especially in Europe) believe that earth energies—particularly negative or polluted underground water streams—are a major cause of disease. For a number of years, I have worked with a naturopathic doctor to help heal his patients' geopathic problems. Geopathic problems are caused by the detrimental physical, mental, and emotional effects of negative and polluted earth energies. Moreover, human entities (ghosts) and nonhuman entities (evil spirits) are sometimes present in homes or at ancient monuments, causing additional ill effects.

Entities, conscious forms without bodies, can be either human or nonhuman. They can range from being harmless to bothersome to destructive.

Human entities are those humans who have died and left their physical human body but did not cross over—they're "stuck" here without physical form. They can see, but not be seen. They can hear, but not be heard. I see human entities as being like the "hungry ghosts" of Tibetan Buddhism. Hungry ghosts are afflicted by hunger, thirst, heat, and cold due to their miserliness and avarice in past lives. I use the term *nonhuman entities* to describe demons and evil spirits. They are of the spiritual "dark" side, opposing deities, devas, and angels (of the "light" side).

Anyone involved in finding power centers and creating sacred space needs to be aware of the dangerous and "dark" side of the metaphysical realm. Negative water lines, negative ley lines, human entities, nonhuman entities, negative emotions, and black magic *do* exist. They are all potentially dangerous and are nothing to play with.

This chapter explains further what entities are, outlines the dangers of working with earth energies, suggests how to avoid problems and potentially dangerous situations, and describes the various types of geopathic problems. I've also included a few case histories about neutralizing negative earth energies and removing entities ("ghostbusting," or exorcism). If the topics in this chapter make you uncomfortable, go for a walk, meditate, or just skip to the next chapter.

Entities (Ghosts)

In the spring of 1993, I visited the Seattle Art Museum's special exhibit of Native American art and artifacts. Early in the exhibit, I was standing in front of a bear claw necklace. A feeling of great sadness overwhelmed me and I started crying. I felt several Native Americans around me in nonphysical form. That same experience occurred several more times as I walked through the exhibit. Eventually, over twenty human entities were all around me. They were all very sad about the display of their possessions and about being "stuck" in the museum. I sat down, meditated, and passed them all over to the other side.

As stranded consciousness, human entities are in a world of great suffering. For some reason, I have been taught how to pass these human entities over to the other side, where they can continue their karmic journey. When I am asked to help (through a request for a geopathic survey), I do it as a spiritual practice and as a service. I have been advised by one of my spiritual teachers *not* to detail the practice for publication. However, I can assure readers that it is done with great care and compassion in a mindset of nonattachment and selflessness.

Entities tend to take up residence around water lines or springs. They seem to be attracted to the field that the moving water gives off. If the water line happens to be negative, then their personality tends to become similarly slanted. If the entity is a nonhuman, this—combined with the effects of the negative stream—can be dangerous. The subject of entities is relevant for these important reasons:

- People who visit ancient power centers may be susceptible to their influence. It is better to be forewarned and forearmed than surprised by an invisible and possibly powerful antagonist.

- My experience has shown that entities are prevalent and are having a significant influence on people's lives, usually a negative one.

As I said, it is not within the scope of this book to go into how to "clean" a house or other place of negative energies and entities. If you think you may have a geopathic problem, consult your naturopath, spiritual teacher, or church.

Human and Nonhuman Entities

The process of dying is very important. We will all die someday; it is the culmination of our life. I recommend that readers think about death and what they will do when they die—most will conclude that there is indeed a life after life. The following explanation of the dying process is the result of my study and thinking on the subject. There has been some inspiring research into this process by a number of doctors who have studied near-death experiences. If you're interested in detailed accounts of this kind of research, I can recommend Raymond Moody's book, *Life After Life: The Investigation of a Phenomenon-Survival of Bodily Death* (New York: Bantam Books, 1988) and *Closer to the Light: Learning from the Near-Death Experiences of Children* (New York: Villard Books, 1990) by Melvin Morse, M.D. For more insights into death, I highly recommend *The Tibetan Book of Living and Dying* (San Francisco: HarperSanFrancisco, 1993) by Sogyal Rinpoche.

Regardless of whether you agree with my view as outlined below or not, what is important is that you come to your own understanding of the dying process, consistent with your own spiritual and religious beliefs, so that you are well prepared when your time to die comes.

The Dying Process. When a person dies, their spirit or soul leaves the physical body. For most people, dying is the process of changing from one plane of existence to another. As the physical body stops operating, their soul, or spirit, leaves the body. At this point, you can look back and see your body, the room, and any people around your body. You can hear, but you can't be heard. You can see, but you can't be seen. You then pass through a dark tunnel, like a cave, amid the sounds of rushing wind. You emerge from the tunnel in a place where you may be met by people who passed on before you as well as by a spiritual being of brilliant light and pure love. You may see many types of beings, both spiritual and frightening. Because you are not burdened by a physical body anymore, you are much more sensitive. This increased sensitivity is one reason it is so important to practice meditation, regularly and with vigor. With the ability to control your mind and not become attached to thought forms, your transition to the afterlife will be easier, safer, and less frightening.

What *actually* happens after death is a subject of great debate and one that cannot be completely resolved. Regardless of our views on the subject, one thing is certain: we will die. When we *do* die, we will not be able to take along our money, our job, our children, or our possessions. The only things we take are the virtuous and nonvirtuous actions from this life and our state of mind at the moment of death. The more I study this subject, the more determined I become to improve the quality of my actions and thoughts so that whatever happens when I die, I will have maximized my opportunities for spiritual growth in this lifetime.

Human Entities. Sometimes, a person cannot make the cross-over transition. Theories of why include the ideas that they were too disoriented with the after-life experience, were too attached to something in this life, they "got lost," or they didn't know how to pass over and hence stayed near to where they died or lived their life. In this sad situation, the human entity ends up lost between our world and the next. The Tibetans call this place the Bardo. Our culture calls these beings ghosts.

I am not an expert in Tibetan Buddhism, nor can I claim to be enlightened. All the same, I have found in my experience that a small number of human entities do not quickly pass through the Bardo and become reborn. These human entities may become attached to a familiar place such as the house they lived in or even the place where they died. It seems that souls are more likely to remain in the area where they died if they had a quick or violent death in an accident or battle. Often, entities will become attached to a water line or spring, drawing energy or a feeling of attachment from it. Once attached, the entity may become almost dormant, as though in hibernation. Conversely, they may be somewhat active and have subtle yet perceptibly negative effects on the people and space around them. Entities can also attach themselves to humans, literally sucking energy from their host.

Nonhuman Entities. I've already generally defined *nonhuman entities*, but to recap: this is a term used to describe a wide variety of nonphysical beings including, but not limited to, demons, poltergeists, evil spirits, and other hell-beings. These entities are the dark side of the spiritual hierarchy. Nonhuman entities are characterized by their darkness, propensity for evil, and the danger they pose to the people in the places they inhabit. These are the demons that priests are called upon to exorcise. It is best to avoid thinking about them or trying to understand them.

Geopathic Case History

One night, my friend Ellis Robinson asked me to map-dowse some property that friends of hers had just purchased in Port Townsend, Washington. The property was on a hill and not near any city water lines, so a well had to be drilled. I agreed to check for underground water streams on their ten acres.

I wanted to do the dowsing before we had dinner, since I work better when my mind and body are clear. Sitting around the table were Ellis, my wife, and Ellis' friends, Ursula and her husband. Here is Ursula's description of what happened that evening.

> It seems common knowledge to me that there are people who are sensitive to lots of things in this world, both seen and unseen. When our close friend, Ellis, suggested we ask Chuck to dowse our newly-bought property for water, I thought it a good idea.

> Sitting casually at the dinner table, Chuck quietly focused on the map of our land and, in time, began drawing lines indicating water. From there he asked if we'd like him to check for ley lines and for the presence of any entities mistakenly still there. I watched and I thought about what he'd asked.

> It was from his question that I began learning that evening about the concept of entities attaching themselves to unsuspecting folks— unsuspecting folks like me. I was intrigued to hear that within this philosophy one's health could be negatively affected by these misplaced attachments. For four years I had been dealing with one health challenge after another. My situation had become frustrating and at times I bordered on feeling hopeless. I rarely admitted to anyone how depressed I was becoming about my diminishing health. Having tried many routes, including alternative medicines, it was only natural that I asked Chuck if he thought he might be able to help me.

> From this point on, everything shifted for me that evening. I was able to tune in with Chuck and a very special synergy took place for me. Immediately I saw "blue crystalline lights" around Chuck's head. I began to see [lights like] these while I was pregnant with my son some

twenty years ago. They have often appeared to me when people shared their truths with me, and always resonate happiness. I'm not aware of having any control as to when I see them. It is more that they make their presence known on their own terms, which is fine with me. It tickled me that my blue lights would come. It indicated trust to me.

Time seemed to take on a different dimension. As he talked, I found myself in a dream I had just before my first husband's death. In it, I was walking in the woods and coming upon the spring, the headwater, the source of a deep water. As a movie, it reeled footage as Chuck was focusing his energy and doing his techniques.

As we continued to quietly talk, I was asked about objects that I had around me. I remember telling about the uncomfortable sense I had regarding our home. I felt that something was "out." Somehow, we got to the delight I had in going to garage sales, and that I'd purchased unusual things, such as one hundred pre-Columbian artifacts. Chuck zeroed in on this like a laser. He ascertained that there were four entities who'd attached to me and were affecting me negatively.

In a matter of minutes, he had them pass over, clearing me from their clutches. I experienced an immediate lifting and sense of being lightened. It was remarkable and significant. My energy was renewed, my pain disappeared, and my depression lifted. Once again, I am my optimistic, energetic self! I feel renewed to do all the things I've wanted to do and engaged with a full and happy life.

Negative Water Lines

Negative water lines or *black streams* are the most deadly of earth energies. A negative water line is a polluted underground water stream that is detrimental to good health. All water lines have an effect on health, but black streams are much more potent. Their effects on health can be mental as well as physical. This is because water is a conductor for emotions, magnifying small feelings out of proportion to their cause.

Polluted water streams are becoming increasingly prevalent. Spending an extended amount of time in a place which is directly over a polluted water line can contribute to cancer, arthritis, and other diseases. Any place where one spends a significant amount of time should be checked for water lines. Beds, desks, and workplaces are examples of areas where we may remain long enough for a negative water line to have an effect on us. The more negative lines that are present, the greater the effect.

Earth Energy and Entity Checklist

* Is there someone in your family who seems hyper, cranky, or moody for no apparent reason?

* Is there a place in your home or office that just doesn't *feel* right? That feels scary, or even evil?

* Are you moving into a new space that doesn't feel totally clear?

* Do you feel like energy is being drained from you?

* Do you ever feel someone or something is watching you—even though there's no one around?

* Do you feel unproductive or lacking in energy?

* Is there someone in your family with a disease or mental problems?

If you answered "yes" to any of these questions, it would be wise to check your home and place of work for water lines, ley lines, and entities. This process is called a *geopathic survey*. If you have water lines that run under your bed, seriously consider moving your bed. The same goes for your desk, the place where you work, and other areas you occupy for lengthy periods of time. If you have had problems like poor sleeping, wakeful children, anxiety, illness, or mental illness, a simple change in the location of your family's beds can change the atmosphere in your home overnight. A geopathic survey:

* Neutralizes negative earth energies that may cause ill health.

* Eliminates the influences of ghosts that may be draining your energy.

♦ Locates ideal sites for sacred spaces, gardens, and environmental artworks.

♦ Gives peace of mind.

♦ Facilitates environmental and planetary healing.

A comprehensive geopathic survey cleans your home or space of the detrimental effects of negative earth energies and entities. All underground water lines, ley lines, and ley-line power centers are identified. Negative lines are neutralized. The survey also checks for the presence of human entities (ghosts) and nonhuman entities (malevolent beings). If found, human entities are passed over and nonhuman entities are sent to where they belong according to the will of Supreme Consciousness. A geopathic survey is best done in cooperation with your naturopathic physician.[1]

As common sense dictates, you shouldn't rely on these tactics alone if you're facing a serious illness. People with medical problems should see a physician.

Neutralizing the Effect of Water Lines

A normal water line always has a yin field associated with it, which is a strongly passive influence. For example, I worked with a client who was having problems getting work done in her home office because there was a water line that passed under her desk. We solved the problem by the correct placement of a "cure"—in this case, a coat hanger that was cut and straightened into a rod and taped in proper alignment (parallel to and directly over the water line) to the floor under the desk. The rod must be positioned appropriately based on its polarity, which I use a pendulum to determine. This is a spiritual practice that requires the *essential* steps of protection and training. It must be learned from a teacher and practitioner and is well beyond the capacity of this book's instruction, which is why I do not include explicit directions for this or any other potentially dangerous spiritual practices.

It is important to know that new water lines can come in at any time and existing water lines can change to a negative polarity if a water line becomes polluted.

When a water stream becomes polluted and takes on negative polarity, the electromagnetic field that rises from the underground water line is changed. In nature, things like this happen. It's good to be sensitive to any changes in how a place feels to you and regularly check for new lines or changes in line polarity. The effects of water lines can be neutralized by a knowledgeable practitioner of geopathic survey.

My family used to live by a creek, and a new stream came in every couple of years or so. One stream (which was negative) came in under my son's bed. He couldn't sleep well and woke up crying at night. At this time, I was just learning about the effect of water lines on people. Kate and John Payne found the problem and neutralized the stream. The crying stopped.

Entities and Devas at Ancient Monuments

Many ancient monuments that I visit have discarnate human entities, often including the ancient ones who were involved in building the monument, or those who lived or were even buried there. The West Kennet Long Barrow was a ceremonial burial chamber for over 1,000 years. When I first meditated at the chamber, it was like meditating with the spirits of dead people who had been buried in this special place. I could feel them all around me; I could sense the feeling of death. This was a heavy meditation. Afterward, I was so spaced out I started driving on the right side of the road (the *wrong* side of the road in England). I can still remember the look on the approaching driver's face as he saw me driving toward him (luckily, we escaped).

Twenty years later, I meditated again in the West Kennet Long Barrow chamber. Again, I felt the same discarnate humans—but this time, I sensed they were ready to pass over. I helped them all cross over to the other side.

Now, when I visit ancient monuments, I can usually immediately sense the presence of discarnate human entities. In some way, they can also sense me as someone who can pass them over. When I visited Newgrange, an hour or two north of Dublin, Ireland, over 200 human entities gathered over my head at the entrance and followed our group into the very impressive and moving interior chamber. The corbelled ceiling of the chamber became the tunnel for all the human entities to pass over that day.

Ancient monuments with power are excellent places for you to meditate and communicate with devas. The strong electromagnetic field of a consecrated power center facilitates clear deva/human communication.

Avoid Places That Don't Feel Right

There are powerful invisible forces at work around centers of earth energies. These forces are often positive and uplifting. However, they can also be dangerous and harmful to your health. There are many discarnate humans and occasional nonhuman entities present at ancient monuments and places with ancient objects such as museums. Therefore, when you visit an ancient monument, a museum, or someone's home, be sensitive to the space and how it affects you. If the space doesn't feel right, avoid it. Don't collect souvenirs from ancient monuments (stones, artifacts) to bring home with you; you may inadvertently bring home unwanted "guests." Protect yourself (for instance, say a prayer of protection) before entering an ancient monument or a museum to prevent an entity from attaching itself to you and becoming a drain on your energy.

I once visited the home of a couple who spend their vacations visiting ancient monuments all over the world. As I walked into their home, I immediately began feeling the presence of many entities. They explained that when they visited a sacred space, they often brought back a souvenir. Unfortunately, these souvenirs were accompanied by over fifty human and nonhuman entities—a fact they immediately became aware of once I brought it to their attention. After I explained the situation and was allowed to clear their home of entities, the woman commented that the clearing was the simplest spiritual ceremony she had ever seen.

This story has two morals. First, it is not a good idea to bring back stones or artifacts from ancient power centers. These artifacts are convenient carriers of entities. Second, it is important to heighten your awareness when visiting ancient sites. If you sense any negativity or unease, do not enter the space.

Secrets of Sacred Space Revealed in This Chapter

♦ Negative or polluted underground water streams are a major cause of disease. Human entities (ghosts) and nonhuman entities (evil spirits) are sometimes present in homes and at ancient monuments, causing additional ill effects. These ill effects can usually be neutralized through a geopathic survey.

♦ Anyone involved in finding power centers and creating sacred spaces needs to be aware of the dangerous and "dark" side of the metaphysical realm. Negative water lines, negative ley lines, human entities, nonhuman entities, negative emotions, and black magic *do* exist. They are all potentially dangerous and are nothing to play with.

♦ Entities tend to take up residence around water lines or springs.

♦ Negative water lines and ley lines can be neutralized in a number of ways. However, these techniques need to be performed by an experienced practitioner.

♦ When you visit an ancient monument or even someone's home, be aware of how the space affects you. If the it doesn't feel right, avoid it. Don't collect "souvenirs" from ancient monuments to bring home with you; you may inadvertently bring home unwanted guests.

Notes

1   While I believe there is a connection between geopathic conditions and health, I have no medical or scientific proof and therefore can make no claims about the results of geopathic surveys. I am not a doctor, nor am I qualified to give medical advice or treatment. Therefore, if you have a medical problem, please see your physician.

The Ellis Hollow Stone Circle

I had returned to Ithaca, New York to attend my twenty-fifth high school reunion. Arriving early for a visit with my friend and teacher, Kate Payne, I went by the Ellis Hollow Stone Circle that I built with Mike Sweeney and the Foundation of Light's Cosmic Monument Study Group in 1977.[1] While I hadn't been back to the stone circle in ten years, it is a place I have always felt connected to. I can close my eyes and be there in spirit anytime. It is a place that has power for me.

A Visit to Ellis Hollow Stone Circle

The circle is composed of a ring of boulders and standing stones that enclose and encircle a seven-foot standing stone and a large recumbent sitting stone. Before entering, I stop and bow and then sit down on the recumbent stone to meditate. Legs crossed, hands clasped, and eyes closed, I quickly enter another world. There's a buzz sound, rapid eye movements, goose bumps. I surrender. The ancient ones are here. The Landscape Angel manifests above me and lowers herself down so I am inside of her glittering light. My little self begins to feel merged with the Supreme Consciousness.

The wind begins to blow. I hear the leaves moving in the wind. The level of chi rises. I can feel the nature spirits running and dancing around and between the stones. There is twinkling light. The wind picks up and clouds move in rapidly. The energy of the wind and gathering clouds fills the space between my cells. I am seven miles high. The power, the sense of oneness with nature, is incredible. More wind. More clouds. Thunder. Big drops of rain begin to fall, making wet spots on the stones and my clothes. Then, I walk to the car, slowly, feeling very happy.

Design Approach

With the philosophical and spiritual basics of sacred space design established in earlier chapters, it is time to see how it all fits together in actual practice. The Ellis Hollow Stone Circle will serve as an example. Subsequent chapters and the appendix will delve into the specifics of the more scientific and mathematic principles introduced here

In the first stage of design, the area around the Foundation of Light was dowsed. A ley-line power center, along with two springs (side-by-side) were located, and the site was identified as being an ideal spot for a sacred space.

Figure 6.1 — The Ellis Hollow Stone Circle.

Photo© 1997 Lydia Pettis

Our basic philosophical approach in designing and building the Ellis Hollow Stone Circle was to flow with what was happening. If we ran into resistance or problems with a particular approach or idea, we took it as a sign not to pursue that course of action. We only created what came naturally—what *worked*. The entire project was done in cooperation with the Landscape Angel and the many devas associated with the space. The deva of each stone was asked if it was meant to be a part of the stone circle. During construction, before each stone was placed in the ground, a Herkimer quartz crystal was placed underneath the stone and properly oriented using dowsing, according to the guidance of the Landscape Angel.

Geometry

The Ellis Hollow Stone Circle is actually an *ellipse*. An ellipse is a geometric figure that resembles an elongated circle with two *foci* or "centers." In the stone circle, the two foci are marked by an eight-foot-high standing stone and a flat recumbent stone which are located over a ley-line power center and water spring. The two center stones are surrounded by eight boulders, which form the circumference of the ellipse. The boulders mark where the ley lines pass through the stone circle.

The two axes of the ellipse are oriented to true north/south and east/west. The major axis is twenty-five feet in length and the minor axis is twenty-four feet. An inlaid observer's stone and the tall standing stone point to the horizon where the sun rises on the Summer Solstice, an annual ceremonial event.

Symbolism

The stone circle was designed to be a symbol of wholeness, harmony, and spiritual union, balancing yin and yang design elements to create a sentient environment for intuitional practice. The distance between the standing stone and the recumbent stone is seven "earth" feet. This unit of measure was chosen because one hundred "earth" feet are equal to one second or $1/1,296,000$ of the earth's circumference. In this way the human dimension (the foot) is linked to cosmic dimension (the circumference of the earth). The number *seven* symbolizes wholeness and spiritual perfection. In addition, the ellipse is based on a

Pythagorean triangle ($3^1/_2$ by 12 by $12^1/_2$) that makes the ellipse's circumference equal to seventy-seven earth feet.[2]

Polarized Rings of Energy

Three days after we set the eight-foot standing stone in the ground, a few circular polari zed rings of energy developed, extending approximately ten feet out from the stone. It was as if we dropped a stone in a pond, causing circular ripples to fan out over the water. In a week, bands developed out about two hundred feet. The bands finally stabilized at a distance of *seven miles* from the site! These bands now occur about every four to six feet and are easily detected by dowsing.

The Ongoing Evolution of the Ellis Hollow Stone Circle

My son, Bre, and I returned to Ithaca, New York for the twentieth anniversary of the Ellis Hollow Stone Circle on June 19, 1997. The first thing we did was go to

Figure 6.2—*Diagram of the Ellis Hollow Stone Circle.*

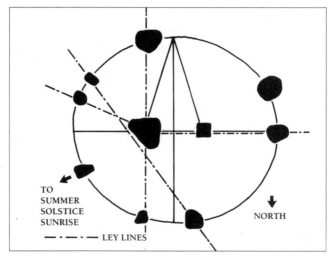

the stone circle and meditate. Afterward, we both felt that the stone circle needed more stones. After a beautiful sunrise on the Summer Solstice, I held a workshop at the Foundation of Light. An extraordinary group of people participated. By the end of the workshop on the day of the Summer Solstice, seven new stones had been properly selected, the first stone was in the ground, and a plan was in place to install the remaining six stones. My sister, Lydia Pettis, managed the completion of the Ellis Hollow Stone Circle expansion. Her description of the day that the remaining stones were placed in the circle is so inspiring that I will let her tell the story in her own words:

Figure 6.3—*Summer Solstice sunrise at the Ellis Hollow Stone Circle.*

Photo ©1978 Chuck Pettis

The Global Picture

Six new stones were planted in the Ellis Hollow Stone Circle on September 6, 1997, the day of Princess Diana's funeral and the day after the passing of Mother Teresa. The soft rain that began in Ithaca soon after Diana's memorial service made it appear that the world itself was weeping for the loss of these two great women. We came together at the circle mourning their loss, but choosing to celebrate the spirit and power of two very different embodiments of the Divine Mother.

These deaths were especially poignant because soon after the stones were selected at Summer Solstice, we identified a "Mother stone." Further, our initial date to install the stones was postponed due to a scheduling problem with the quarry. The postponement caused disappointment, but also a recognition that when—working with spiritual energies, "our" plan is not necessarily "the" plan.

We could not have imagined the events that triggered a worldwide opening of the heart and an outpouring of emotion unlike anything ever experienced. Nor could we have anticipated what may have been one of the most significant planetary events of all time: the joining together, during Princess Diana's memorial service, of tens (perhaps hundreds) of millions of people around the world saying the Lord's Prayer aloud. One world, one voice, one prayer in an outpouring of love for the Divine Feminine. The world shifted in that moment. That these events coincided with the placement of six simple stones in the Ellis Hollow Stone Circle is humbling and awe-inspiring.

But these are the energies, powers, and world events that were present in Ellis Hollow on September 6. We joined together to imbue the circle with the love, compassion, warmth, and grace of both Mother Teresa and Princess Diana. We brought our open and vulnerable hearts to the circle that day, and reached out to become a part of something very much larger than ourselves: the worldwide realization of the power of a loving touch, kind and gentle words, a warm laugh, and a welcoming glance. This embracing love, this commitment to giving and living from the heart is now, and forever will be, a part of the Ellis Hollow Stone Circle.

The Local Picture

Lydia's narrative continues:

A poem[3] read at the Solstice celebration this summer recalled the children and families present when the circle was created. There were no children at the celebration of the Summer Solstice this year; a "Child stone" was specifically selected to symbolically invite the children to return. Later, a "Mother stone" was identified, and these two now form the main entry into the circle. The new stones are all standing stones, and have been added to the ellipse between the existing boulders. The male energy of the new stones blends with the female energy of the existing boulders to create a powerful sense of balance and harmony.

Buried beneath each stone is a crystal. A friend blessed us with a gift of Herkimer crystals that he had mined, and the morning ceremony of September 6 included dowsing which crystal should be placed with each stone. A ritual dance was performed as each crystal left the sunlight to return to the dark richness of the earth. Two crystals were placed under the Mother stone. In the afternoon, the forklift arrived from the quarry to move the stones into place (unfortunately our levitation skills leave a little to be desired in this lifetime). A lot of sweat equity went into digging the holes for the stones, and maneuvering the stones, each weighing about half a ton, into place. We thank the God(dess) for heavy equipment and upper body strength!

In our closing meditation after the stones were placed, we were each profoundly moved by the feeling of the space we had just joined in creating and expanding. Warmth, safety, and a higher vibration are some of the first impressions. We will be placing a blank book in the stone circle, asking visitors to record their impressions of the new space.

When I visited the circle a few days later, and was looking at it from my "normal" perspective (which, for me, means viewing the perfections and imperfections—and worrying especially about the imperfections!) I gradually grew to realize that every stone was just as it should be, and that the deeper message, for me, was simply this: There is a place for everybody here.

Experience the Ellis Hollow Stone Circle

The Ellis Hollow Stone Circle is located at the Foundation of Light on the northwest corner of the intersection of Ellis Hollow Road and Turkey Hill Road in Ithaca, New York. There are no rules or prescribed rituals to be followed. Simply come into the circle. You may sit, stand, touch, lean against, and hug the stones, be quiet, talk to yourself, listen and watch. Empty your mind, or explore. This is your space as well as our space. Enjoy it, and let us know how it feels! There is now also a large labyrinth adjacent to the stone circle.

Secrets of Sacred Space
Revealed in This Chapter

◆ Before placing each stone in a sacred space, put a quartz crystal beneath it that is oriented according to the guidance of the Landscape Angel.

◆ Sacred spaces are meant to grow and transform according to the inspiration of the builders and of their custodians and guardians.

Poem for Summer Solstice

The old people are here now.
They come here at this time.
We build under the sky and
Under another's direction
The old one. The sun. Children run
Like hobos, we hear every sign,
Hear the sound of children on the run.
The night chill touches the vibrance of
Our bones. We are never alone.
Rise and sing. Fire in the air.
Hold my hand. There is an ancient
Man here now. There is a hum.
The vibrance is in the woods.
The tune rises in a wide circle
Marks and signs appear on the trees
Like gifts, thank God. Sun and sons
And hum of the children. The old
Man runs on the legs of that child
By the water fountain.
Now, it is time to walk through the
Colors. First red to signify we are
Not safe. Then white to signify we
Cannot see. Then blue to signify
We have forgotten how to move.
Then violet to signify we are already
Holy. And last, green. We plunge
Like kingfishers into the pool of
Summer. Like kingfishers, we fall to the
Edge of water and air.

The ancient one watches us fall,
Laughing. He hugs the stone, opens
The water with his beak, whistles
Us back into the air.
                    —Tom Hanna

Notes

1   The Foundation of Light was established in 1974 to promote spiritual understanding and practice as found in all the great world religions, and to promote service to humanity through meditation, creative expression, good will, and good works. For more information, write to the Foundation of Light at 399 Turkey Hill Road, Ithaca, NY 14850.

2   For more information on the mathematics involved in getting as many dimensions as possible in whole numbers, refer to A. Thom's *Megalithic Sites in Britain*, pp. 27–33.

3   This poem is reprinted here on page 105: "Poem for Summer Solstice," ©1980, 1998, Tom Hanna, 210 Eddy St., Ithaca, NY 14850 (tph3@cornell.edu).

chapter seven

The Seattle Ley-Line Project

In 1985, my friend Mike Sweeney and I started talking about building another stone circle or power center like the Ellis Hollow Stone Circle. Mike is a recognized sculptor and furniture builder in Seattle, Washington. Our opportunity came in 1987 when Mike came upon an opportunity to win a $5,000 grant from the Seattle Arts Commission encouraging collaborating artists to "explore their visions for the City of Seattle—to consider the fantastic as well as the realizable."

Together with a landscape architect and an architect, we formed The Geo Group and submitted a proposal to the Seattle Arts Commission to undertake the Seattle Ley-Line Project. The purpose of the project was to locate and map the major ley lines and ley-line power centers within the City of Seattle and plan a series of environmental artworks to mark and enhance Seattle's ley-line energies. The Seattle Arts Commission accepted our proposal and commissioned us to provide an artistic interpretation and spiritual vision of what Seattle, as a city, could become.

The Geo Group is a nonprofit organization dedicated to planetary healing and world peace. Our mission is to work (with the vision of the earth as a living being) to locate, heal, and create sacred spaces on power centers in order to improve the flow of earth energies for the well-being of the earth, as well as the expansion of peoples' and society's consciousness. You can learn more about The Geo Group by visiting our home page (www.geo.org).

The Seattle Ley-Line artwork is being exhibited as part of Seattle City Light's Percent for Art "Portable Works Collection." The Art Commission's artwork consists of a large cabinet with a metal veneer in the shape of the squared circle. In the center of the case is a large map of the Seattle ley lines and on either side of the map is a description of the project and proposed artworks to be built on the power centers in the city.

The artwork and map are on rotating display among city-owned buildings in Seattle. To find the artwork's current location, contact the Seattle Arts Commission.[1]

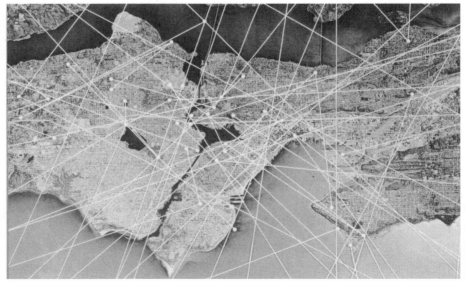

Figure 7.1 —
The Seattle Ley-
Line Map.
(Seattle photo
courtesy of
Cosmic Images,
Bellevue,
Washington.)

©1988 The Geo Group.

Description of Artworks

We identified and mapped the major ley lines and power centers located within Seattle using dowsing techniques. The Seattle Ley-Line Project made Seattle the first major city on earth to balance and tune its ley-line system in accordance with the will of the earth spirit. The map is an accurate artistic representation of all the ley lines and power centers we identified. We have deliberately kept this map representational to protect the privacy of property owners since most of the ley-lines power centers are on private property.

The Geo Group's vision is to mark and then enhance Seattle's ley line power centers with the following series of environmental artworks. Our research indicates that Seattle is a major center for earth energies. There are several places in the city that have the potential to become sacred places similar to, but not as large as, Stonehenge or the Great Pyramid.

- *Power-Center Markers.* Most of Seattle's power centers are located on private property or on places not appropriate for a full-scale sacred space. A limited edition of round cast-brass markers will be constructed for people's yards or to be inset in an interior floor.

- *Standing Stones.* A number of power centers located in parks and on beaches are ideal for a standing stone.

- *Stone Circle.* A lookout in wooded Interlaken Park is ideal for a small stone circle with viewpoints and astronomical alignments.

- *Earth Mound and Chamber.* In Roanoke Park, there is a power center next to a children's playground where a small earth mound covering a large concrete culvert with openings at each end would work well.

- *Beacon Buoys.* There are several power centers located over water for which we propose metalwork buoys patterned after the Delphi Oracle "seat" with lighted beacons at the apex (the Delphi Oracle was a position held by several women in succession in ancient Greece—the Oracle, a seer, advised world leaders on matters that affected world history).

Thinking About Making a Ley-Line Map for Your City?

There's more to dowsing a city than meets the eye. It's much more involved, complex, tiring, and dangerous than doing a small area like a house. I map-dowsed Seattle in Mike Sweeney's studio, using a four-by-eight-foot blueprint of the city. It took three months, working mainly on Saturdays. For protection and correct results, every dowsing session was preceded by meditation and a specific set of spiritual practices. The entire project was overseen and guided by the Seattle deva.

In any large city, there are weird things going on. Map dowsing is like flying over the entire city one section at a time and probing for places of power. Not all the power centers are positive and some may be harboring a bee's nest of entities. Also, as we discovered, even with good protection you can still be attacked by nonhuman and human entities.

One Saturday, I located a negative power center in southern Seattle and the entities came roaring into Mike's studio. This is where all the careful preparation and ideation paid off. The entities were successfully sent to where they belonged according to the will of the Supreme Consciousness. While this was happening, Mike (who was sculpting in another part of the room) experienced a debilitating headache, extreme shortness of breath, and nausea—later, he found out why. For the remainder of the project, special measures were taken to make the studio invisible to any entity.

Demon Attack

Here is Mike's account of the demon attack mentioned above:

> *Spiritual experience is not something I accept as easily as I accept solid objects. However, on several occasions while solving aesthetic problems in the presence of Chuck Pettis, I have had solid "knock you off your feet" supersensible experiences that made me giddy with spiritual convictions.*
>
> *In the fall of 1987, Chuck Pettis and I formed The Geo Group and received a grant to develop a project to identify Seattle's ley lines and*

power centers. One Saturday, Chuck came to my studio, we made our greetings, and he went to work dowsing his large map of Seattle. I was working on two pieces of sculpture; my mind was open and my antennae were out.

After a period of at least a half hour, I began to feel sick (flu-ish) and then, in very rapid succession, I felt weak, a pressure in my chest, headache, nausea and violently ill. I didn't want to bother Chuck, so I laid down on my couch thinking I had gotten some real strong twelve-hour flu or virus or something. I have a white light meditation I use to help me through many situations. At times I believe that I am actually soliciting energy from the infinite, and at other times, I am more inclined to think it works on the level of yoga in that I can focus on any part of my being and direct healing energy to that area in the form of blood, oxygen, nutrients, relax-ation, and encouragement.

I began the meditation, visualized the white light and directed it to the affected areas. After what seemed like one hour or so I realized that I was deep breathing at almost a panting level and that I had stopped sending light or thought to my head and stomach, but rather, I had formed a cocoon-like shell of white light around me and I was very intently keeping the light directed toward shielding me from negative influences.

This was happening without Chuck's awareness as he was, as usual, totally absorbed in his project and, for my part, I was so miserable, I had zero interest in what he was up to. I would have headed home if I wasn't so sick and disoriented.

After about one-and-a-half to two hours the illness began to subside and shortly it was totally gone except for a dry mouth and headi-ness. At this point, Chuck began to rustle around like one does at the end of a concentrated period. I went over to where he was working to tell him that I had just cured myself of some sort of flu attack in an hour-and-a-half of intense meditation, but before I had a chance to say anything, he looked up and said, "You're not going to believe what just happened."

He then told me of a point in his dowsing where he had passed over an area inhabited by what he thought were some kind of strong negative energy or entities and that it or they seemed to have channeled through his conscious connection, entered the studio, and for about an hour were affecting Chuck and everything in his vicinity in a very negative manner.

We swapped stories and realized that while coming from two different viewpoints, we had once again experienced something very powerful from outside ourselves which emanated from a nonphysical plane and confounded logic.

There are not many dowsers or people capable of handling a situation like this one. Therefore, I do not advise people to create ley-line maps for their own cities. It is simply too dangerous.

We later visited the source of these demons. This is one of the few places in my experience that reverted to negative after being neutralized. The feeling surrounding this house was so scary that the three people accompanying me would not even get out of the car and wanted to leave as soon as possible.

Happy Ending

All power centers found through map dowsing were checked on site. On a few of these trips, a water dowser joined us who related some interesting stories of the Callanish standing stones in northern Scotland. At the conclusion of the project, I was meditating and felt the presence of many ancient human entities from Callanish who felt it was time for them to pass over. As the last human entity crossed over, a ley line was born in Mike's studio.

Ley-Line Controversy

The line between religious art and spiritual art is a thin one. The Seattle Ley-Line Project received front page coverage in *The Seattle Times*.[2] Five years later, the April 1993 issue of *Seattle Arts* reported:

Some artworks start life in fiery controversy and eventually find enthusiastic acceptance. When in 1987 an artist working with individuals from other disciplines created an artwork tracking the invisible "ley lines" in the earth's surface—imposing a grid of lines over a satellite photo of the Seattle area and placing crystals at significant junctures,[3] then beautifully framing the whole thing to hang on the wall—it sparked a brief but nasty battle over the separation of church and state, art and faith. The (Seattle) Arts Commission was accused of funding a New Age pagan sect. Now the work hangs happily on the wall of a new home the DCLU (Department of Construction and Land Use in the Dexter Horton Building), where many visitors figure it must somehow relate to the City's zoning policies.

Secrets of Sacred Space
Revealed in This Chapter

♦ Dowsing a city is a dangerous process and is not recommended.

Notes

1 To answer a question I am regularly asked, I know of no ley-line maps for any other cities.

2 Dietrich, Bill. "The Coming of a New Age." *The Seattle Times*, January 18, 1987.

3 The crystals are actually placed on the ley-line power centers, not on ley-line crossings.

chapter eight

Designing a Sacred Space

You don't have to be a landscape architect to design and build a sacred space. All that is required is desire, time, and work. This chapter presents a simple approach to the design of sacred space using the Mutiny Bay Stone Circle, located in Washington state, as an example.[1]

Geomancy

Geomancy is the art of consciously changing, altering, and building upon the earth's surface in order to reveal, cooperate with, and evoke the earth spirit so as to facilitate spiritual experiences. Geomancy raises the level of consciousness in a particular area by bringing qualities of beauty, order, and harmony into the landscape. Simply put, geomancy is a set of techniques for creating an integrated sacred landscape based on spiritual values.

Geomancy is built upon number of important concepts:

- The earth is a divine being whose personality is manifested on its surface by topographic features, earth energies, and earth changes (including the daily changes of weather to the slow changes on the earth's surface as a result of erosion).

- The power of a space can be strengthened by the right combination of design elements and thought. Changing the earth's surface directly affects the health and well-being of the Earth Spirit and the living beings who dwell upon it.

- There is a direct relationship between idea (thoughts and visualizations) and manifestation. Every event in the manifested world is an expression of an idea in the unseen, unmanifested world. We are the link between heaven and earth.

- Geomancy is a way of perceiving, conceiving, and changing reality.

Geomancy literally means "earth divination." In this context, divination is an intuitional practice that harmonizes cosmic ideas and earth forms. Divination is, by definition, *divine*—that is, given or inspired by God. Divination or intuitional practice can be performed in many ways. It can be entirely internal as in meditation and contemplation, or may be partially externalized by the use of a pendulum and dowsing rod as well as "randomized" gestalt-type geomancies like the *I Ching*.

Two objectives of intuitional practice are:

- To become enlightened, to become a fully realized human being.

- To act in accordance with the divine will, the Tao, and the spiritual teachings, the dharma.

The concept of *oracle* is significant in the context of divine will. *Oracle* has roots from "oral" and "to speak." An oracle provides a medium for the divine will to communicate to the seeker of truth. Humans are the link between heaven and earth. By elevating our consciousness through spiritual practice, we can literally build a heaven on earth.

Feng shui (Chinese geomancy) is a direct application of these precepts. The earth is seen as the body of a living being. The life of this being is sustained and expressed by the yin and yang—currents of the universal life-giving principle (chi).

In Chinese, *feng shui* means "wind and water." It is so named because natural elements like wind and water and, indeed, life itself, cannot be grasped nor easily comprehended. Siddhartha became enlightened by living and meditating beside a river, a metaphor that can explain all of human existence. The basic aim of feng shui is to design a residence or a space of any kind so that it is in harmony with the earth spirit. Wind and water are the prime earth formers, thereby symbolizing the manifestation of the Tao—the will of God—on the earth's surface.

> Like water highest goodness flows:
> Without competing, it bestows
> In places men despise it plays;
> Thus on the loving road it stays [2]

> Who speaks with nature's tongue is seldom heard
> From morning's strongest winds by noon subside;
> And day time's hardest rains by night have died.
> Who makes these things? These things are nature's word. [3]

Feng shui is utilized by a geomancer to raise the level of consciousness in a particular locality by creating qualities of beauty, order, and harmony. Historically, the Chinese manifested their cosmology in the landscape, buildings, and tombs through the medium of feng shui. Aesthetically, scenes of the Chinese landscape are like microcosmic settings of the ideal blend of the landscape features. To achieve this, geomancers are consulted on the design and placement of any structure, tree, or road which affects the appearance and nature of the environment. The goals of this process are to provide a synthesis of ideology, cosmology, and spirituality with everyday life.

A detailed description of the practice of feng shui is beyond the scope of this book. The best practical and easy-to-put-into-practice book I've been able to find on feng shui is *Interior Design with Feng Shui* (New York: E. P. Dutton, 1990) by Sarah Rossbach.

A Step-by-Step Approach to Successful Sacred Space Design

♦ Locate a power center by dowsing, or pray that a power center be manifested in the area where you can build. The Mutiny Bay Stone Circle is located over a ley-line power center and an underground blind spring. There are four ley lines and one water line in the stone circle. Two ley lines came in while the stone circle was under construction.

♦ Develop an intuitional "oneness" with the site and explore design options. Examine, analyze, and inventory all elements of the site. This is a time of looking and *non-doing* at a time when one has a tendency to want to get on with it. Look at the site from many different angles and take photos. Give yourself a lot of time. What themes and images suggest themselves? What viewing points are present?

♦ Use meditation and divine inspiration to give you insight to the hidden potentials of the area. Meditate and tune in to Supreme Consciousness, the landscape angel, and specific devas that you feel comfortable with. Use their communications and guidance to direct your actions and design planning. Accept everything in this design stage as meaningful and significant. You will receive an inflow of creativity and ideas. The creation of sacred space is rare. Many forces will be eager to lend their help in many forms. Even small incidents or chance meeting of people may harbor tidings from the spiritual hierarchy. Let yourself be led. The more you can open yourself to this divine light, the more you will experience this as a sacred event.

♦ Develop a design plan. By now you probably have some general ideas on the theme of your space, potential forms for it to take and how all the elements of sacred space could be used in your design. Start drawing up sketches, geometry, astronomical alignments, and so on. Try out ideas on paper and then visit the site again. Make adjustments and finalize the design.

♦ Try building miniature versions of the ideas you are considering on the power center site. Use small stones or sticks to stake out the general area.

Step back and imagine that your initial ideas are already built. What will they look like? Will it work?

♦ If you have problems coming up with an idea, try *synectics*. This is the creative process of taking relationships from one situation and applying them to a new context. For example, if you like the forest, you could try and recreate the experience of being in the forest in your design. Stones could become trees. Wind chimes could simulate the sounds of the forest.

♦ Implement your design. Build it.

♦ Monitor the effects of your sacred space on yourself and others. Note what works and what could be better for your next creation. Evaluate your results. What have you learned? What could or should be changed?

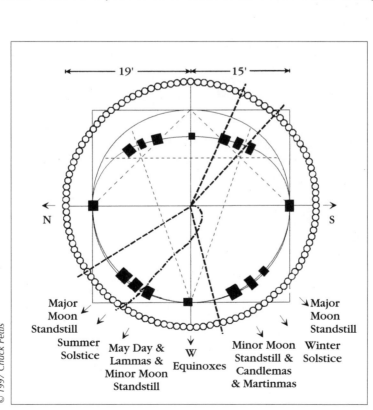

Figure 8.1—*The final design for the Mutiny Bay Stone Circle.*

The following members of the spiritual hierarchy were instrumental in the design and development of the Mutiny Bay Stone Circle: the Supreme Consciousness, the Landscape Angel, the Bodhisattva Chenrezi, Shrii Shrii Anandamurti, the Earth Spirit, the Ancient Ones (designers and builders of ancient monuments), and devas of ley, water, stone, sand, wind, ocean, and evergreen trees. Every stone was asked if belonged in the stone circle. I visualize an ascending pyramid of Buddhas and Bodhisattvas directly above the stone circle.

Figure 8.2—*Chuck Pettis directing the placement of stones at the Mutiny Bay Stone Circle.*

Photo © Janice Chieko Kato

Design Hints and Techniques

Use ancient monuments as models, as starting points and idea generators, not as ends in themselves. They're proof that the power of sacred space is real.

Numerology. Utilize symbolism. The Mutiny Bay Stone Circle consists of two outer henges or earth mounds, a circle of buried tree stumps, and an inner egg-shaped stone circle. There are 120 wood stumps (a multiple of twelve). Twelve is a number of wholeness. The diameter of the outer henges and the circumference of the stone circle is eighty-eight feet. Using numerology methods (number symbolism will be greater detailed in chapter thirteen), we can derive the following:

$$88 \rightarrow 8 + 8 = \mathbf{16} \qquad \rightarrow \qquad \textit{There are sixteen standing stones.}$$

$$16 \rightarrow 1 + 6 = \mathbf{7} \qquad \rightarrow \qquad \textit{Seven is the number of spiritual} \\ \textit{wholeness and perfection.}$$

Geometry. The sacred space is built around a squared-circle geometry such that the perimeter of the square that circumscribes the inner stone circle is the same length as the circumference of the outer circle of tree stumps: 120 feet. This symbolically unites the circle with the square, the irrational with the rational, and heaven with earth.

Astronomy. Astronomically, the stone circle is aligned to true north/south and east/west. Every stone marks an important astronomical alignment: true north, major moon standstills, Summer Solstice, May Day, Lammas, equinoxes, Candlemas, Martinmas, and Winter Solstice.

The Law of Correspondence. Balance opposites to create a transcendental space "on earth as in heaven." Use *syzygy* (*syn,* together + *zygon,* a yoke), the law of correspondence. Syzygy refers to two related things (alike or opposite) that are in balance. In astronomy, syzygy refers to the two points in the orbit of a heavenly body that are opposite one another. To put syzygy into practice here, balance or cancel out a feature by designing an opposite form. For instance, place a tall stone by a short, flat stone; select a tall hill beside a valley; raise a mound of earth or create a depression; put a wide, horizontal stone beside a thin, tall one; create a dark cave beside a stone facing the sunrise or sunset; combine a symmetric form with an asymmetric one; link a circular share with a square one; or unite geometric forms with natural settings.

Examples of balanced opposite forms at the Mutiny Bay Stone Circle include:

- Bilateral symmetry of the stone circle.
- Viewing the western horizon, the Olympic Mountains on one side and flat land and ocean on the other.
- Tall standing stones on the west side and smaller standing stones on the east side of the stone circle.

If the site has a yin (low-lying) spot, make a mound near it in such a way as to balance the concavity with convexity, the feminine with the masculine. If the site is near a road and the traffic is draining energy from the site, then plant a hedge, tree, or scrubs to enclose the area, muffle the sound, and prevent the feeling of being watched. If the area is too dense and dark, create open spaces of light.

Visual Choreography. Suppose one feature of the site is stealing attention or is unattractive. Plant flowers, make another large feature such as a mound, or make drawings or engraved symbols on other stones. This will spread the focus of attention and keep the viewer's eye moving, thus artistically building wonder and enchantment. Use sequence to lead people from lesser spaces to more important spaces. Create a visual climax, just as a composer or writer creates a climax in music or prose.

The Five Elements. Each of the five elements—solid, liquid, luminous, aerial, and ether (corresponding to earth, water, fire, air, and space)—should be considered in any sacred space. The use of stone, earth, and solid materials is easiest. The use of water is more involved. A basin or hollowed stone can catch rainwater. A small pool can be built. Depressions on a stone can create small pools and flows of water. Fires can be used ceremonially, and the luminous element can be included by a sundial or another means of directing light. Air can be witnessed with wind chimes, flags, or banners. Ethereal space can by symbolized by symbols of the Void—holes or balanced stone and earth arrangements which imply transformation to an empty state.

The Five Senses. Engage all the senses, not just sight. We can hear bells, singing, and speaking. We can touch textures, the wind, fog, and trees. We can smell flowers and vegetation. We can taste herbs, vegetables, and fruits.

Use repetition, hints, and miniaturization of ideas to build texture and richness. Start on a small scale. Be patient.

Secrets of Sacred Space Revealed in This Chapter

- Geomancy raises the level of consciousness in a particular locality by creating qualities of beauty, order, and harmony in the landscape.

- The earth is a divine being whose personality is manifested on the earth's surface by topographic features, earth energies, and earth changes.

- The power of a space can be strengthened by the right combination of design elements and thought. Changing the earth's surface directly affects the health and well-being of the Earth Spirit and the living beings on it.

- There is a direct relationship between idea (thoughts and visualizations) and manifestation. Every event in the manifested world is an expression of an idea in the unseen, unmanifested world.

- Humans are the link between heaven and earth. By elevating our consciousness through spiritual practice, we can literally build a heaven on earth.

- Accept everything in the design of a sacred space as meaningful and potentially significant.

- Balance opposites to create a transcendental space.

- Use sequence to lead people from lesser spaces to more important spaces.

Suggested Projects and Exercises

• Just about anywhere you live, you'll find examples of quality landscape design. Visit gardens and parks known for their beauty and study the ways that these places were designed. Try to identify some of the design tools used. Look for the use of proper placement, geometry, balance, and viewing points.

• Look up books on landscaping or landscape architecture at the library.

• Ask landscape designers to recommend some of their favorite and most outstanding examples of created landscape.

• Visit an ancient monument. Meditate on the geomancy of the space.

• Take a class on feng shui or read about it. Practice some of the principles in your own home or office.

Notes

1   See figure R in the color section of this book. Diana Graham's Eco-shrine in South Africa is a wonderful example of a successfully planned and executed contemporary sacred space.

2   Excerpted from "The Ways of Goodness," a poem from *The Bible of the Loving Road: Lao Tzu's Tao Teh Ching,* as translated by Robert Finley (Carbondale, IL: Bliss Press, 1972). Bliss Press is Chuck Pettis' private press.

3   Excerpted from "Speak Low," a poem from Finley, ibid.

Holiday Symbolism and Ceremony

Due to the tilt of the earth relative to the sun, we have seasons which vary in temperature, climate, and amount of sunlight and darkness. The slowly changing combinations of these conditions have a profound effect on our lives and how we feel and act.

The earth is a living being with great power and wisdom. The seasons reflect the many temperaments, emotions, and capacities of this incredible spirit on whom we live. To relate to this great consciousness, societies throughout history have ascribed to it the form of an earth goddess.

Season comes from roots meaning "to sow" and has parallels with "seed" and "semen." Each season is symbolized by a different manifestation of the earth goddess. She can take as many forms as the archetypal woman. The circular and rhythmic manifestation of herself in the various seasons has, of course, deep parallels to the growth of ourselves as individuals and as a society. Each of the stages of life has an obvious parallel time of the year in the seasons:

Equivalence of Earth and Human Seasons.

EARLY SPRING	→	INFANCY
SPRING	→	CHILDHOOD TO PUBERTY
SUMMER	→	MARRIAGE, MATURITY, AND PARENTHOOD
FALL	→	OLD AGE
WINTER	→	DEATH

Different types of monuments reinforce the symbolism of each season. Avenues and stone rows are suggestive of processions, uniting the male and female energies in the generative springtime. Earth mounds work well with the harvest festival time, symbolizing the abundance of food for the winter hardship to come. Underground chambers are often oriented to the midwinter solstice sunrise, when the usually dark interior is lit on the day when longer daylight begins.

The whole idea is to live in harmony and balance throughout the seasons by celebrating festivals. Celebrations and ceremony bring power and deep psychological impact to the psyche. The uncommon acting out of cosmic ideas with a group on a festival day, along with all its implied symbolic meanings, is a special experience and one easily remembered.

In ceremony, we participate in the acting out of deep, intuitive fantasies relating ourselves to the Great Spirit and Supreme Consciousness. Held at intervals throughout the year, ceremony facilitates the gradual assimilation of spiritual values into one's life. Of equal importance to our improved well-being is the healing of the earth. Offering our love to the earth is one of the most positive and beneficial acts we can perform.

As we think, so we become. See the world in harmony—and it is. Our monuments and celebrations reflect our own perceptions of harmony, not only for the now, but for the future, as well. Monuments are, by their nature, long lasting. So, what we build today has the potential to pass our wisdom and spiritual ideas on to future generations.

Spiritual experiences can be induced by ceremony and ritual. Ceremony brings power and deep psychological comfort to the soul. Sacred rites reveal the continuity of life through transformation and renewal, and uplift the quality of our thinking. In short, ceremony helps us keep thinking clearly and positively, not crudely and negatively.

How to Plan a Ceremony

+ Work with a small group of people, and get them involved right at the beginning. Involvement is the key to a successful ceremony. Explain the parts of the ceremony and give each person an activity such as reading a poem, smudging, lighting candles, or placing flowers. Ask all to have an open mind, as this kind of ceremony may be new to them.

+ Pick a special calendar time of the year. Research the history, background, and tradition of that day.

+ Choose a single leader to integrate everybody's ideas into a cohesive program. This person should write up and distribute copies of the meaning and symbolism of the day as well as a simple description of the ceremony itself. Hand this program out as people arrive so they can read and assimilate it.

+ The real power of ceremony is what people are thinking and feeling *during* the ceremony. Use offerings as symbolic gifts to the higher self and the deities. These can include candles, incense, semiprecious stones (like quartz, obsidian, or lapis), bones, flowers, fruit, and so on.

+ Involve the kids. They'll love it and their happiness is contagious!

+ If possible, include live music. Poetry is also extraordinarily effective.

+ Have food and drink afterward.

+ Make it a yearly tradition—do it every year at about the same time.

The Traditional Calendar Holidays and their Meanings

The *ideal* dates for each of the following calendar holidays are based on a subdivision of the year into eight parts (this is done to achieve certain astronomical efficiencies as described in Appendix II: The Table of Astronomical Alignments). The *conventional* dates are the days that the holiday is generally recognized and celebrated in communities today.

Because I have a predisposition and affinity for the traditional Celtic calendar and because I eagerly look forward to spring and the advent of the high-mountain hiking season, you will note that I refer to Candlemas as "the first day of spring" (rather than March 21). Feel free to use the conventional dates for the beginning of the seasons, if you prefer.

Candlemas

Held: the first week of February
Conventional Date: February 1 or 2
Ideal Calendar Date: February 5

Candlemas marks the first day of spring, the rebirth of nature and the return of the Goddess from the Underworld. It is traditionally associated with female puberty rites and is held on the waxing or full moon, if possible. The Goddess is reborn as a young girl reaching the point of puberty when it is first possible to beget or bear children, the time of the first menstruation. It is best celebrated in the early morning with a lighted torch procession by stone rows or avenues.

The name *Candlemas* comes from a ceremony of the Church of Rome, where candles are blessed by the clergy and distributed among people who then carry them lighted in a solemn procession designed to commemorate the purification of Mary.

Possible Ceremonial Themes: returning of the light, rebirth, childhood, puberty, purification, transition, growth, blessing, kindness, and omens (Groundhog Day).

Spring Equinox

Held: March 21–23
Conventional Date: March 21
Ideal Calendar Date: March 23

The spring equinox is a time of harmony and balance. Day and night are equal; the equinox is the halfway point between the Summer and Winter Solstices. The Equinoxes and the Solstices are the four primary times of the year which form the cosmic cross (a circle with vertical and horizontal lines crossed inside it)—a symbol of wholeness.

Possible Ceremonial Themes: birth, resurrection, lively coloration, balancing the male and female within, bringing balance into one's life, creating wholeness, envisioning harmony, or claiming a renewal of self to go forth in the world in a different and better way.

May Day

Held: the first week of May
Conventional Date: May 1 or 14
Ideal Calendar Date: May 6

May Day, also referred to as *Beltane*, marks the first day of summer and is the time for the planting of crops. May Day is traditionally associated with fertility and sexual energy. It is a day for communing with nature and things of beauty.

The well-being and survival of the community depends on the success of the planting done at this time of year. Plowing symbolizes the preparation of the seed bed. This is a time of procreation and lovemaking on all levels, and phallic and vaginal symbols abound. Traditionally, May Day has included lovemaking in the fields, circular dances, serpent images, the meeting of processional lines of men and women, and the lighting of bonfires on hilltops (Beltane). This festival is held on the full moon, if possible.

The maypole tradition is an acting-out of union, fertility, and the joy of love. Some communities have a May Queen, a flower-crowned "maid" who acts as a living representation of the goddess Flora. This young girl is situated near the pole as an object of admiration.

> *The outbreak into beauty which Nature makes at the end of April and beginning of May executes so joyful and admiring a feeling in the human breast, that there is no wonder the event should have at all times been celebrated in some way. The first emotion is a desire to seize some part of the profusion of flowers and blossom which spreads around us, to set it up in decorative fashion, pay it a sort of homage, and let the pleasure it excites find expression in dance and song. A mad happiness goes abroad over the earth, that Nature, long dead and cold, lives and smiles again. Doubtless there is mingled with this, too, in bosoms of any reflection, a grateful sense of the Divine goodness, which makes the promise of seasons so stable and sure.*

—The Book of Days[1]

Possible Ceremonial Themes: beauty, the holy union of male and female, the divine marriage within, fertility, celebration of beauty, planting, love and light, joy, good fortune, flowers, song, dance, happiness, and energy.

Summer Solstice

Held: June 20–June 23 (northern hemisphere)[2]
Conventional Date: June 21
Ideal Calendar Date: June 22

The Summer Solstice is one of the most important days of the year. It is the time when the northern hemisphere of the earth is pointed directly at the sun. It is the longest day of the year. The sun rises in the northeast, its northernmost sunrise point of the year. From now until the Winter Solstice in late December, the days will get shorter and the nights will get longer. Fires are lit to renew the sun and give it strength and energy.

The night *before* the Summer Solstice has been celebrated by Christians as St. John's (the Baptist) Eve. This is the night when the souls of all people leave their bodies and wander to the place where death will finally separate them from this world. Hence, people stay up all night with fires burning to "keep watch," avoiding confrontation with death.

Possible Ceremonial Themes: energy, abundance, vitality, fire, light, strength, fulfillment, and happiness.

Lammas

Held: end of the first week of August
Conventional Date: August 1
Ideal Calendar Date: August 7

Lammas marks the early harvest and is celebrated by a "first fruits ceremony" on the full or waning moon. This is the time of pregnancy and birth. Traditionally, a fair is held on top of a sacred mountain, hill, or mound. This is a time to worship the divine torso—the belly filled with life, sustenance, and fulfillment of labor. A community ceremonial meal of the first fruits and vegetables marks the beginning of the harvest.

The festival is usually held on a Sunday and is a time for communal expression of joy. This is the original "fair" with booths, picnicking, and music. Rituals are held to ensure the safe delivery of the harvest child. Everyone wears a flower to the top of a hill or mound. On the summit, all the flowers are put into a specially dug hole and covered with earth—a sign that summer has ended and fall has begun. A Lammas tower of stones and earth can be built in a conspicuous place during the month prior to the festival. The whole community should care for and attend to its creation and construction. On the festival day, colorful handmade flags are placed on top of the tower to the sound of blowing horns.

Possible Ceremonial Themes: harvest, gifts of the land, fair, picnics, music, joy, flowers, and flags.

Fall Equinox

Held: September 20–22
Conventional Date: September 23
Ideal Calendar Date: September 21

The fall equinox is a time of balance, with equal days and nights. Autumn has always been an important time in the life of a farmer—it represents the harvesting of crops, reaping the benefits of all the hard work earlier in the year. The harvest moon, the full moon nearest the fall equinox, appears after sunset for several days, allowing harvest work to continue into the night. Now is the time to give thanks for the fruits of summer and make provision for the coming winter.

Possible Ceremonial Themes: bringing balance into one's life, creating wholeness, envisioning harmony, preparation, and caution with resources.

Martinmas/Hallowmas

Held: end of the first week of November
Conventional Date: October 31 or November 1
Ideal Calendar Date: November 7

Martinmas, also known as *Hallowmas, Halloween,* and *Samhain,* marks the beginning of winter. A fire festival is held to ward off hardship in the coming months of cold and darkness. It should coincide with the new moon, if possible, to deepen the feeling of darkness. This is the time of death and old age with the Goddess taking the form of a squatting hag, symbolizing the Great Destroyer or Devourer. Ceremonies are usually held in long barrow tombs or mound chambers. At this time, the Great Mother merges with the earth to receive the dead.

This time of year, commonly called Halloween, is the time when supernatural influences prevail. It is the night set apart in the year for the spirits to return and walk the earth.

Possible Ceremonial Themes: death of the old self (old habits, behaviors, and beliefs), protection from entities, divination, night, fire, aging, death, impermanence.

Winter Solstice

Held: December 21–22 (northern hemisphere)
Conventional Date: December 22
Ideal Calendar Date: December 22

The Winter Solstice marks the shortest day of sunlight in the year in the northern hemisphere. The sun is at its southernmost declination. But, from this day on, the days will become longer, and so, warmer days are foretold. The lighting of the Christmas tree acts as a beacon to guide the sun back.

On the Winter Solstice, the sun's rays enter the inner chamber of the Newgrange passage tomb (see figure C in the color insert section) through the upper opening (the "roofbox"). Hugh Kearns[3] postulates that in Neolithic times a revolving reflector, hung from a tripod in the corbelled chamber, reflected the sun's light out through the entrance passage (the lower opening in figure C) down to the River Boyne, creating the world's first laser-light show!

Possible Ceremonial Themes: a well-deserved rest, conservation, focus on the family, leaving the past where it belongs (behind you), putting new energy into a project that has been lagging, darkness, death, acceptance, resurrection, and self-examination.

Secrets of Sacred Space Revealed in This Chapter

- Different types of monuments reinforce the symbolism of each season.
- Seasonal celebrations facilitate the gradual assimilation of spiritual values into one's life.
- Spiritual experiences can be induced by ceremony and ritual.

Notes

1   Chambers, R., *The Book of Days* (Philadelphia: J. B. Lippincott & Co., 1863), 570–571.

2   In the southern hemisphere, the Summer Solstice happens on December 21–22 (which is the date of the *Winter* Solstice in the northern hemisphere), and vice versa.

3   Kearns, Hugh, *The Mysterious Chequered Lights of Newgrange* (Dublin: Elo Publications, 1993).

© 1998 Chuck Pettis

Figure A—*A left-handed (first turn is to the left) classical three-circuit labyrinth constructed by Chuck Pettis. The labyrinth, a spiritual maze with a single path to the center, is an archetype of wholeness, representing the path of life, and an ancient tool for contemplation and deep access to the inner self.*

Figure B—*Thousands of standing stones at Carnac, France, form a fanlike matrix—miles long—marking ley lines and astronomical alignments.*

© 1996 Chuck Pettis

Figure C—*Many of the mounds and barrows throughout the British Isles were originally brilliant white and conspicuous against the landscape. The most famous of all Irish prehistoric monuments, the beautifully refurbished Newgrange passage tomb, is about 280 feet (85m) in diameter and 44 feet (13.5m) high. Surrounding the base of the mound are no less than 97 large horizontal stones, many of which are beautifully carved with spirals, zigzags, and other symbols: not only have they been carved on the visible side of the stone, but often on the inside, hidden part too.*

Figure D—*Sacred spaces are artworks which experience continuous change and evolution. Once a sacred space is built, the desire also arises to make it "bigger and better." For example, at Newgrange, a stone circle about 340 feet (104m) in diameter was added about 1,000 years after the initial construction of the mounded passage tomb. Today, only a few stones from the original circle remain.*

Figure E—*Entrance to the Newgrange passage tomb leading to a magnificent internal corbelled chamber. On the Winter Solstice, the Sun's rays enter the inner chamber through the upper opening (the "roofbox"). Hugh Kearns postulates that, in Neolithic times, a revolving reflector was hung from a tripod in the corbelled chamber: this reflected the Sun's light out through the entrance passage (lower opening in the photo) down to the River Boyne, creating the world's first laser-light show!*

Figure F—*Enclosing a womblike space, dolmens (literally "stone table") symbolize the feminine principle. "Le dolmen de Kercadoret à Locmariaquer" is one of the most beautiful and peaceful dolmens in the region of Carnac, France.*

© 1996 Chuck Pettis

© 1975 Chuck Pettis

Figure G—*The Cherhill White Horse in southern England was "cut" in 1780 by Dr. Christopher Alsop through the process of removing a layer of topsoil and exposing the chalk subsoil underneath. The figure stands out strikingly, in white relief against the surrounding countryside. Earth figures are kept free of grass by a "scouring," traditionally performed every seven years by the local people.*

© 1995 Chuck Pettis

© 1996 Chuck Pettis

Figure H—The Mutiny Bay Stone Circle, located on Whidbey Island in Washington State, is a contemporary sacred space specially designed for meditation and spiritual practice. Incorporating the same design elements and techniques used in most of the world's ancient monuments, this circle is sited over a power center (there are four ley lines and one water line within the stone circle). It was also designed so that sun- and moonsets will be framed by the Olympic Mountains.

Figure I—White ceremonial scarf (kata), placed on the large standing stone by His Holiness Jigdal Dagchen Sakya, head Lama of the Sakyapa Order of Tibetan Buddhism, at the consecration ceremony for the Mutiny Bay Stone Circle.

© 1996 Chuck Pettis

Figure J—*A spiral of small stones marks the underground water line and ley-line power center at the center of the Mutiny Bay Stone Circle. The rice, red flower, and green evergreen twig are from the Tibetan Buddhist consecration ceremony led by His Holiness Jigdal Dagchen Sakya.*

© 1998 Chuck Pettis

Figure K—*This stone sundial by Mike Sweeney marks the point where a ley line enters the earth at my home. Sundials can easily be integrated into any landscape to remind us of our place in a much larger and magnificently ordered universe.*

Figure L—*The Neolithic Irish site of Loughcrew, located west of Kells in the Mountains of the Witch, remains one of the best-kept megalithic secrets on the planet. Loughcrew consists of numerous cairns, each aligned to an important holiday to create a true megalithic calendar. At dawn on the Spring Equinox, the sun's rays frame one of the sun symbols on stone 14 in "Cairn T."*

© Tim O'Brien

Figure M—*The peaceful and ancient Lundin Farm "Four-Poster" (four-stone) stone circle in central Scotland today has an oak tree growing in its center.*

Figure N—*A five-stone circle, forming part of the very beautiful and magical Kealkill Stone Circle in southwestern Ireland.*

© 1998 Chuck Pettis

Figure O—*Monks circumambulating the Mahabodhi Temple. The sacred places of Buddhism differ from most other ancient monuments because many people not only visit them, but also perform spiritual practices there. This adds greatly to the power felt at the site.*

© 1998 Chuck Pettis

© 1998 Chuck Pettis

Figure P—*In the central chamber of the Mahabodhi Temple lies this circular black stone, marking the power center. A monk explained, "This is point zero." It is said that this is the only place on the planet stable enough to withstand the energy from the enlightenment of the Buddha.*

Figure Q—*The Mahabodhi Temple, a nine-storied pyramid in Bodhgaya, India, marks the place of the Buddha's enlightenment.*

Figure R—Diana Graham's Eco-shrine was created in Hogsback, a small tourist village in South Africa. As a place of common worship and reverence for nature and the Creator, the Eco-shrine captures the spirit of many sacred spaces throughout the world. Using sculpture, paintings, mosaics, a central fishpond with fountain, along with many other elements, the shrine provides a stunning example of contemporary sacred art placed in a breathtaking setting amidst mountains, forests, and waterfalls.

Creating Astronomical Alignments

There's something magical about watching the sun or moon rise or set over a standing stone, above a far mountain peak, or on one of the traditional holidays of the year. It is a bonding experience with the heavens, and a perfect time to meditate.

The word *origin* comes from roots meaning "to rise," especially referring to the sun and moon. The moment of sunrise and moonrise is the time of all beginnings and rebirths. It is a time when we are very aware of the moment— indeed, a very good time for meditation.

The movements of the heavenly bodies have been observed with great interest throughout human history. Celestial patterns are the writing of God upon the heavens. They bring light to the dark void of space. They fill the sky with the master testament of cosmic beauty.

Astronomical Alignments

There are many excellent books on astronomy and an increasing number of books dealing with *archeoastronomy*, the study of astronomical alignments at ancient sites and monuments (see bibliography).

The purpose of this chapter is not to embark on the scientific study of astronomy or even to examine the use of astronomy in ancient monuments. Its purpose is to *utilize* what has been learned about the use of astronomy in ancient monuments in order to design, lay out, and build stone and earth monuments *today,* celebrating astronomy in the landscape. My approach is primarily practical, but does involve some astronomical theory to explain how alignments may be obtained and checked. Of course, all the diagrams in the world cannot take the place of actually observing how the sun and moon move through the sky.

I've provided time-honored techniques for sun and moon observation, to which you should add your own common sense. For instance, don't look directly at the sun—as we all know, it could cause blindness.

Another valuable resource to help you to check for astronomical alignments at your sacred space location is the table in Appendix II, which provides compass readings on where the sun and moon will rise and set on the horizon on key holidays.

The Sun and the Earth

The earth revolves around the sun in an elliptical orbit (near-circular). Viewed from a vantage point above the North Pole, all the planets and the moon orbit in a counterclockwise direction. We call the time period it takes for the earth to make one complete revolution around the sun one year. During the earth's revolution, it rotates counterclockwise on its axis approximately 365.25 times.

The axis of the earth is an imaginary line through the globe around which the earth rotates. This axis is inclined at an angle of approximately 23.44 degrees from a line perpendicular to the plane of the earth's orbit around the sun. This imaginary plane is called the *ecliptic*. It is this inclination that produces the seasons and regulates the earth's climate.[1]

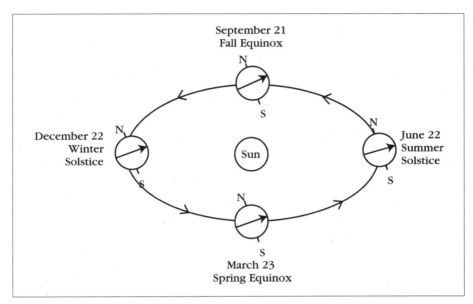

Figure 10.1—*The relationship of the earth and sun and the seasons.*

The Sun From the Earth's Point of View

As the earth rotates on its axis, the sun rises over the eastern horizon, moves overhead through the day and sets behind the western horizon in the evening. On the equinoxes, day and night are equal. Another special feature of the equinoxes is that the sun rises exactly in the east and sets exactly in the west, regardless of the lati-

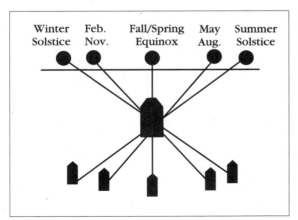

Figure 10.2—*Placing stones in alignment with the sun to mark the traditional holiday sunsets.*

tude. On the Summer Solstice, the sun rises in the northeast and sets in the north-west after a long movement across the sky. On the Winter Solstice, exactly the opposite is true—the sun rises in the southeast and sets in the southwest after a relatively short distance across the southern sky.

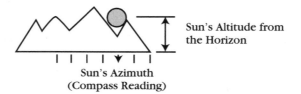

Figure 10.3—*Locating the point where the sun rises or sets by measuring the sun's altitude from the horizon and its azimuth (compass reading).*

Sun's Altitude from the Horizon

Sun's Azimuth (Compass Reading)

The Horizontal Coordinate System. When defining the position of the sun, there are two basic coordinate systems in use. The one we will use is called the horizontal coordinate system. It locates the sun, moon, or any other celestial object by two variables called *azimuth* and *altitude*. Azimuth is the angular distance (a compass reading) between the point in question on the horizon and true north, as measured clockwise (eastward) from true north. Altitude is the angular distance (in degrees) of the object as measured up from the horizon (as in a distant mountain range).

Monument Sundials

A sundial is an instrument that uses light and shadow to tell time. In doing so, it translates solar or lunar motions into easy-to-see visual patterns. Marking the points on the horizon where the sun rises or sets will create, in effect, a sundial.

The traditional sundial offers an easy-to-understand vehicle for communicating the passing of daily time, the passing of the seasons, and the sun's paths through the sky. It can be integrated into any monument where it seems appropriate.

There are several ways that sundial technology can be integrated into a monument to achieve a heightened awareness of the harmony and beauty of the universe. Most simply, use the shadow of a standing stone or obelisk to mark noon on one of the traditional holidays. To do this, on the day in question, note the location of the shadow at noon and install a stone or marker of some kind at the point of the standing stone's shadow.

The Analemma

The *analemma* can also be used to create a more sophisticated sundial. The analemma is a chart which shows both the sun's declination (the angle of the sun relative to the celestial equator or the path of the sun on the equinox at noon) and the equation of time. The equation of time is the daily difference between apparent "sun" time and clock time. There is a difference because the earth's

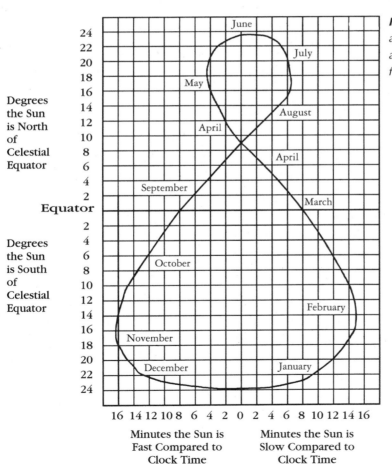

Figure 10.4—A sample analemma chart. An analemma looks like a funny-shaped "8."

orbit around the sun is an ellipse, which causes the speed of the earth around the sun to vary slightly depending on its position on this ellipse.

An analemma looks like a funny-shaped "8." An analemma can be constructed for any time of day, but noon is best because it calls attention to the meridian—the invisible line drawn from the North to South Poles. When the sun crosses the meridian, it is directly overhead.

How to Make an Analemma or "Noon Solar Calendar."

* Use a standing stone with a pointed tip or a pole as the noon-time "sighter." At noon, the tip's shadow can be used to mark the noon position.

* Align the stone and the ground where you will "map" the sun's noontime position to true north and south.

* Each day at noon (clock time) mark the point and date where the sun spot falls on the ground. If you mark the spot every sunny day, over a one-year period you will create the analemma shape quite precisely. You could also just mark the noon position on special calendar days. Be sure to mark noon at *standard time* (during daylight savings time, make your mark at 1:00 P.M., not 12:00 P.M.). Remember, it is important to be exact about "noon" because even a minute or two difference can throw the analemma off.

Variations on the Analemma Theme.

* Align stone structures to use the dramatic effect of sun (and moon) light and shadows. Design and construct an underground chamber that is lit by the sun on one of the Celtic holidays. Place sun symbols on the lit back stone to mark where the sun's beam hits the stone before, during, and just after the holiday.

* Place a large stone slab in the ground, mark the analemma on it for a year (or more, if necessary). Then, take it to a monument (grave) or stone dealer who does sandblasting. Have the analemma inscribed with dates or symbols for the dates you want specially noted.

The Moon and the Earth

The moon is the earth's natural satellite—the largest satellite in the solar system in relation to its planet. The relationship of the moon to the earth and sun is truly remarkable. From earth, the moon and sun have approximately the same angular size in the sky, resulting in perfect or near-perfect[2] solar and lunar eclipses. Not only that, if we could place the moon on top of the earth, as shown in Figure 10.5, the moon fits perfectly into a squared circle diagram—the earth squares the circle of the moon.

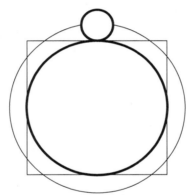

Figure 10.5—*The earth (bold center circle) squares the circle of the moon (small circle on top).*[3]

The moon has a diameter of about 2,163 miles and revolves around the earth in an elliptical orbit, counterclockwise as seen from above the North Pole. Its average distance from the earth is 238,866 miles.

The moon turns on its axis in the same time it takes to complete one orbit around the earth. This means that the same hemisphere (or side) is always facing the earth. To see what I mean, get a friend and try a little demonstration. Pretend that you are the earth and your friend is the moon. Hold hands and have your friend, the moon, move around you in a circle. Don't let your hands loose! Just as your friend always faces you, the same half of the moon is always facing the earth. Note that your friend actually turned around once while "orbiting" you.

The moon has no light of its own; the moonlight we see is actually a reflection of the sun's light off of the surface of the moon. Furthermore, the phases are not caused by the earth's shadow. If you shine a bright light into a room and hold a tennis ball up to the light, one half of that ball is lit, no matter how you spin the ball. However, if you "orbit" the ball around your head and turn with it, you will notice that it appears to be less lit or more lit depending on where it is and where you are looking. This kind of scenario is what causes the phases of the moon.

When the moon is between the earth and the sun, we can see no part of the

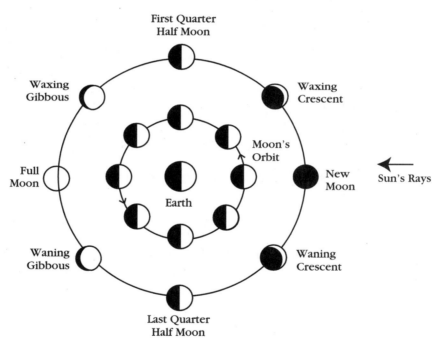

Figure 10.6—The Moon's Phases. The inner circle depicts the sidereal period, the time (27.3 days) it takes for the moon to travel once around its orbit. The outer circle depicts the synodic month, the time (29.5 days) it takes for the moon to go through one complete period of phases.

First Quarter
Half Moon

Waxing Gibbous

Waxing Crescent

Moon's Orbit

Full Moon

New Moon

Sun's Rays

Earth

Waning Gibbous

Waning Crescent

Last Quarter
Half Moon

moon illuminated. We call this the *new moon*. The moon is said to be *waxing* as it changes phases from the new to the *full moon* (fully illuminated) and is said to be *waning* as it changes from the full moon back to the new moon. A few days after the new moon, the moon is in the *waxing crescent* phase. This is the familiar horned shape you see just after sunset. The horns of the crescent moon always point away from the sun. About a week after the new moon comes the *first quarter half moon*. In this phase, the moon has completed one quarter of its monthly orbit and half of it is illuminated. After ten days, the moon is almost completely full, with only a portion of it in shadow. This is called the *waxing gibbous* phase. Then, about two weeks after the new moon, the moon is full, having completed one-half of its orbit. During the second half of its orbit, the moon goes through the *waning gibbous, last quarter half moon,* and *waning crescent* phases, finally returning to the new moon phases when the cycle begins all over.

As the moon orbits around the earth, its movement can be seen in the apparent eastward shift of twelve to thirteen degrees of the moon from night to night. That is, if you look at the sky each night at the same time, the moon will appear to have moved eastward a noticeable amount. And, of course, as its position in the sky shifts, its phases change. Another effect of the moon's orbiting is that moonrise is approximately fifty minutes later each night than it was the previous night.

Symbolism of the Moon and its Phases

The word *moon* comes from roots meaning "to measure." This is undoubtedly because of its obvious cyclic nature and its historic use as a measure of time. This cyclic nature is the center of the moon's symbolism.

The moon has always been closely connected with water. Tides are caused by the moon (as well as the sun—and some would include Jupiter also). The crescent moon is symbolic of water, perhaps because it seems to emerge from and fall into the waters just before or after the sun. This gravitational pull is not restricted to the oceans. If the moon can distort the oceans so dramatically, surely its effect on people, animals, and plants is significant—hence the term *lunatic*. Having worked as a supervisor in a sheltered workshop for mentally and physically handicapped people, I can personally testify as to the effect of the full moon on people's emotions. Most grand mal epileptic seizures seemed to happen around the time of the full moon each month. The parallels of the moon to the feminine principle are also well known as, for example, the coinciding of the lunar month with women's menstrual cycles.

The Moon's Movements Through the Sky

One of the easiest ways to get acquainted with the movements of the moon through the sky is to compare it to the sun. In general, the moon's monthly path is approximately the same as the sun's path in a year. We know that the sun is low in the sky in winter and high in the sky in summer. This change in declination results in the sun's rising positions at the horizon to move—risings are southeast in the winter, east in the fall and spring, and northeast in the summer, completing one complete cycle in one year. Similarly, the moon goes through one complete declination cycle in twenty-seven to twenty-eight days. It follows the same pattern as the sun, but does so thirteen times as fast.

Whereas the sun has only four limiting positions (sunrise and sunset on the Summer and Winter Solstices), the moon has eight, (moonrise and moonset on

Figure 10.7—*The variation of the moon's declination over 18.61 years.*[4]

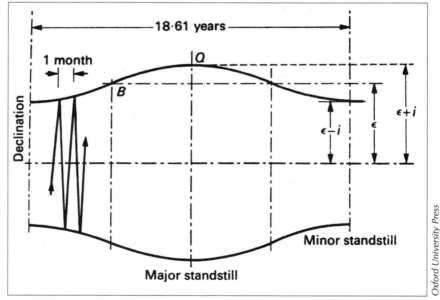

the major and minor standstills). By *limiting position* (or more precisely, *limiting declination*), I refer to the point on the horizon where the sun's risings or settings during the course of a year stop and reverse direction. When we are referring to the moon, we call this limiting declination a *major* or *minor standstill*—so termed because the limiting declinations vary by no more than twenty arc minutes.

Major and Minor Standstills. During the course of a complete year, the sun's declination oscillates between the limits of $+\varepsilon$ and $-\varepsilon$ where ε is the *obliquity of the ecliptic*, or the declination of the sun at the solstices. The *ecliptic* is the plane of the earth's orbit around the sun (23.5 degrees, the tilt of the earth). The obliquity of the ecliptic (i.e., the tilt of the earth) describes the deviation from the ecliptic—which is currently approximately 23.44 degrees. The moon's orbit around the earth intersects the plane of the ecliptic at angle i ($\angle i$), or approximately 5.14 degrees. If the moon's orbit was not inclined to the ecliptic, it would go through the same cycle only in the period of a month rather than a year like the sun. However, because the moon's orbit is inclined to the ecliptic, its declination limits vary between $+/-(\varepsilon+i)$—a major standstill—and $+/-(\varepsilon-i)$—a minor standstill. A major standstill of the moon occurs when the moon's orbit is inclined at $(\varepsilon+i)$ to the equator (that is, when the moon's declination is approximately 28.58 degrees), which results in the moon rising or setting either quite north or quite south on the horizon. A minor standstill occurs when the moon's declination is approximately 18.3 degrees $(\varepsilon-i)$.

As seen in figure 10.7, the moon takes 18.61 years to go through a complete cycle of limiting declinations, from $(\varepsilon-i)$ to (ε) to $(\varepsilon+i)$ to (ε) to $(\varepsilon-i)$. There are 9.3063 years between these major and minor moon standstills. Bear in mind that each month the moon's declination makes a complete cycle—that is, (using a major standstill as an example), in one month the moon's declination changes from $+(\varepsilon+i)$ to $-(\varepsilon+i)$ and back to $+(\varepsilon+i)$. In each of the 9.3-year time periods between major and minor standstills, the moon's limiting declinations change slowly between approximately $(+/-)29$ and $(+/-)18$ degrees from the ecliptic.

Times of the Major and Minor Moon Standstills.

Major Standstills	Minor Standstills
March, 1969	*July, 1978*
November, 1987	*Early March, 1997*
June, 2006	*Late September, 2015*

In summary, the moon's movements through the sky in one month make the same movements the sun makes in a year, but are also a part of another cycle that takes place over a period of 18.6 years. The moon's movements are complex to all sky watchers—it is a fast-changing and fascinating celestial dancer, changing phases, moving throughout the sky, low to high, in a back-and-forth monthly swing.

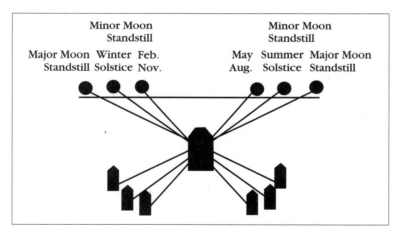

Minor Moon Standstill

Major Moon Winter Feb.
Standstill Solstice Nov.

Minor Moon Standstill

May Summer Major Moon
Aug. Solstice Standstill

Figure 10.8—
Placing stones to mark the major and minor moon standstills. Relative horizon points shown for sun- and moonsets in the Seattle area.

How to Indicate Sun and Moon Alignments

- Use two or more stones to form a sighting line. The master of megalithic observatory science is A. Thom, who wrote a number of books on the subject including *Megalithic Sites In Britain*.[5]

- Use one specially shaped stone or two stones together to point to a horizon notch or the slope of a hill that runs parallel with the rising or setting sun or moon. Compared to the use of two aligned stones pointing to any

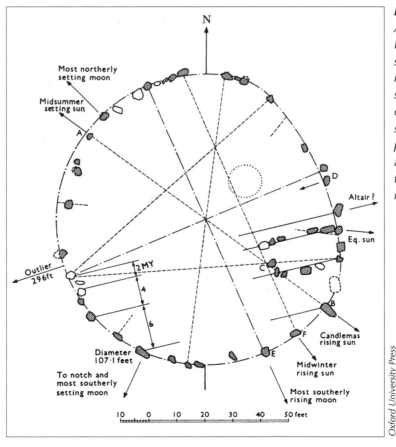

Figure 10.9—
A. Thom's Castle Rigg stone circle survey. Each pairing of standing stones on the circumference of the stone circle marks particular rising and setting point of the sun and moon.[6]

point on the horizon where the sun or moon happens to rise or set, the use of a distant horizon notch or prominent feature is by far the more accurate for astronomical purposes; it is possible to detect changes of declination of only a few seconds of an arc. I suggest the use of a specially-shaped or marked stone for this use to reinforce the alignment to the prominent feature on the horizon, making it more obvious. When only mystical or symbolic aspects are desired, then the use of two stones to indicate a general direction is totally adequate.

Figure 10.10*—Winter Solstice sunset stone looking back at the center of Mystery Hill.*

Photo ©1976 Chuck Pettis

♦ Use a passageway, tube, pipe, or sighting arrangement to point to the sun, moon, the North Star, Venus, or other celestial object at a significant time of day or year.

How to Observe Solar and Lunar Risings and Settings

♦ Mark a line (see line formed by A, M, and A in figure 10.11) on the ground approximately parallel to the horizon (a general north/south line will do fine) where you will make your observations. Have a supply of stakes and rods handy to plot the movement of the sun or moon over a period of time.

♦ Observe the sun or moon on successive days before and after the special calendar day (such as the Summer Solstice) you wish to highlight. This is much easier with two people. To do this, use two rods close enough together to be used as a sighting point to the horizon (see the rod on point T and the dotted rod in front of it). If you are sighting on a notch, hilltop, or hillside, the sighting line can be formed by the distant point and one rod.

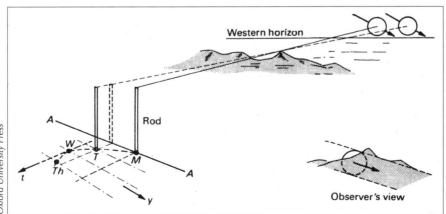

Oxford University Press

Figure 10.11—*Using stakes to observe and mark alignments with the sun and moon.*[7]

- On each day, locate and set a stake on the north/south line (AMA) so as to make every rising and setting appear in the notch or the more distant fixed rod (in this illustration, the dotted rod) in the same manner.

- As you can see in the illustration, each day, as the solstice or monthly maximum nears, the sun or moon will set further to the right (or rise further to the left) on the horizon.

- Using stakes as markers on the ground, you can keep track of the changing positions of the stakes. When tracking the Solstice sunset, for example, the stake at the furthest point south on the north/south line (point W in the illustration) marks the correct Summer Solstice (or other calendar day) sunset alignment.

The above method is excellent for locating and precisely marking solar alignments. It also fine for locating and indicating the maximum declinations of the moon, but is not accurate enough to precisely locate and mark it. This is because the moon moves very quickly relative to the horizon during its monthly movements. There are a number of methods for extrapolating the actual maximum point from the observed moon risings and settings. If you get to the point of actually creating lunar alignments, you will need to go further than this book (an overview) can take you. While the advanced methods are not terribly complex, they are lengthy to describe. If you're interested in learning more, take a look at *Megalithic Lunar Observatories* (London: Oxford University Press, 1973) by A. Thom and *Sun, Moon, and Standing Stones* (Oxford: Oxford University Press, 1978) by John Edwin Wood.

The Table of Astronomical Alignments

I have collected a few dozen books on archeoastronomy and astronomy in general over the years and, amazingly enough, none of them give handy tables to help one get a close idea of where the sun will rise and set on the key traditional holidays or where the moon will rise on the major and minor standstills—so I created one.

Using the table and directions provided in Appendix II, you can use a compass, a pocket transit, transit, or theodolite to measure the apparent altitude of the horizon. Then, knowing your latitude from survey maps, you can get a good approximation of where the sun and moon will appear on the horizon at your site. For the best accuracy, you should calculate your latitude to one hundredth of a degree. The "Table of Astronomical Alignments" is also available for use in an interactive version (responsive to your personal latitude, which you can enter into the spreadsheet) on The Geo Group's web site (www.geo.org).

Secrets of Sacred Space Revealed in This Chapter

+ The moment of sunrise and moonrise is the time of all beginnings, a perfect time to meditate.

+ The marking of solar and lunar rising and setting horizon points is, in effect, a sundial marking the various holidays of the year.

Suggested Projects and Exercises

+ The best and easiest way to locate astronomical alignments is by using a pocket transit. I have a Lietz pocket transit and it works just fine. It's definitely not transit- or theodolite-accurate, but it's a start. Alternatively, you could find a friend with a transit or theodolite to help you do some field work.

+ Try making an analemma. Or, using a stake, mark the position of the sun at noon on the Celtic holidays.

+ Visit some sites with known astronomical alignments and put yourself in the designer's place. How did they do, in your opinion?

Notes

1   All unattributed diagrams in this chapter are based on drawings © 1999 Chuck Pettis.

2   When the moon is an apogee, or its farthest distance from the earth, its angular size is slightly smaller. So, eclipses at these times are annular, or ring-like, because the moon does not cover the entire disk of the sun. This is worst time to look directly at the sun.

3   Diagram after Martineau, John. A *Book of Coincidence* (Wales: Wooden Books, 1995), 31. If you have any interest in sacred geometry, you'll love this book.

4   Reproduced by permission of Oxford University Press from A. Thom's *Megalithic Lunar Observatories*, 1973.

5   In the illustration of A. Thom's survey of Castle Rigg (figure 10.9), note the many pairings of standing stones on the circumference of the stone circle mark rising and setting points of both the sun and the moon. Note, as well, the elegance of the geometry of the egg-shaped stone circle. What, at first glance, appears to be a random placement of stones is actually a sophisticated megalithic observatory.

6   Reproduced by permission of Oxford University Press from A. Thom's *Megalithic Sites in Britain*, 1967.

7   Reproduced by permission of Oxford University Press from A. Thom's *Megalithic Lunar Observatories*, 1973.

Coding and Decoding Sacred Spaces

Sacred spaces are built to keep ideas and cosmologies alive through the language of symbolism, the universal language which touches the innermost self of all people. They are receptacles of universal knowledge.

Cosmology

Let's begin with some definitions. The universe (*unus*, one + *versus*, turned) is the totality of all things that exist. It is the wholeness of existence, turned and viewed from all around. The *cosmos* is a conceptualization of the universe as an orderly and harmonious system. Cosmology is the study of theories, laws, and relationships concerning the nature of this holistic, ordered universe. Here's an example of a personal cosmology (contributor name withheld):

> *We are all part of an ever-changing universe. From the beginning of time, we have tried to explain the workings of this universe.*

While the interpretations vary, there is a resemblance in general attribution to divine origin, and frequently to a beginning in sound, or Word. The idea that all began in sound, and that all matter is differentiated sound is not completely at variance with modern science which has discovered smaller and smaller universes whirling in smaller and smaller space, deep within matter.

Important also is light, which came out of darkness and constantly alternates with darkness. As one becomes older, one is more aware not only of night and day but of the seasons and how they constantly follow in their ordered way, represented by the growth of trees (and tree rings) and every living thing.

Asian artists have expressed the flowing, ever-changing qualities of life in their representations of plants, of dragons, and of masses of people all gracefully related. I have sometimes tried to show this in painting, by using dots of interpenetrating color, blue dots of sky and brown dots of earth, for instance, mixed in with the green dots of a tree, and yellow dots of light in all.

For a symbol I shall choose two adjoining double spirals with a small circle in the center, a representation of transformation and regeneration taking place about a quiet center.

And another:

My cosmology is represented by the ancient and familiar symbol of the cross within the circle. [Within this symbol,] the circle is the universe, the vertical bar is spirit, the horizontal bar is matter.

The universe is an orderly system formed from the Void by the Supreme Entity, whom I call the Allness and who is also the Void as well as the universe and everything within it. It is composed of cosmic energy that takes on countless manifestations, is operated under cosmic law and within the divine plan, which is based on light, love, and wisdom.

Every part of the universe, no matter how small, is part of the Allness, of the Whole, and progresses downward through the various energy levels into matter, and then back up to the source, the Allness, of Whom it is a part, having experienced everything during its endless journeys.

Symbolism

Symbols are very important in the design of sacred space. A symbol is something that represents another thing or idea. The word *symbol* is derived from the Greek word *sumbolon* which means "to throw together." A symbol joins two or more concepts together, thereby establishing a relationship.

The true symbol is effective on all levels: visually, emotionally, intellectually, and spiritually. It reveals underlying realities, ideally pointing to real, immutable, and sacred truths. Indeed, it has the capacity to express aspects of ultimate reality that can be expressed in no other way.

Symbols reveal and conceal at the same time. To one not aware of the higher meaning associated with a particular symbol, the symbol seems to only be a simple figure or picture, without apparent meaning. But to those aware of the meaning and potency of symbolism, the same symbol can be filled with bountiful wisdom.

Archetypes and the Collective Unconscious

Symbols are created and formed from archetypes within the collective unconscious. The concepts of *archetype* and the *collective unconscious* are very relevant to the use of symbolism in sacred space. An archetype (*arche*, first + *typos*, mark of the blow) is the original pattern from which all other things of the same type are made. It is a prototype or source image of a symbolic form or principle that exists within the collective unconscious.

The collective unconscious is a common psychic foundation that is present in everyone. It is a reservoir of common associations of images and psychological states. It is a collective self to which everyone is attuned, of which everyone is a part. Archetypes spring from the collective unconscious as primordial images or thought forms.

Imagine it this way: if the collective unconscious is the prepared garden bed, archetypes are the major plant groups that can grow in the garden (like carrots, tomatoes, and beans) Within this model, *symbols* are the different species of the major plant groups—like *green* beans, *lima* beans, and *wax* beans.

Archetypes exist for all major roles and human experiences—mother, father, and rebirth are examples. Each archetype defines essential characteristics of a thing. For instance, the mother archetype consists of three essential aspects: *sattva* (the mother's cherishing, nourishing, and goodly nature), *rajas* (the mother's emotional, passionate nature), and *tamas* (the mother's dark side). The Sanskrit word *prakrti* (*pra*, the proper way + *kri*, to do + *ti*, feminine suffix) describes the mother archetype.

It is important to stay in touch with primordial life, just as it is important to stay in touch with the earth and its energies and rhythms. In the spirit of understanding this, try to go outside regularly in all types of weather. Visit different natural settings. If we cut ourselves off from our fountain of inner images and desires by segregating ourselves from nature, then reason alone becomes the arbiter of right and wrong. We become *whole* beings only when our internal forces of intuition and reason are in equilibrium. Our goal is self-integration and self-realization.

Synchronicity

* Nothing is meaningless.
* Everything is significant.
* Nothing is independent.
* Everything is related to something else.

These basic precepts have important significance for the designer of sacred space. If one accepts that everything is significant and related to everything else, then it becomes very important to pay close attention to even the smallest detail. Everything within a particular design must be properly expressed in relation to the surrounding (natural and design) elements.

The idea of everything being significant is closely related to the concept of *synchronicity* as propounded by C. G. Jung. He defines synchronicity as an acausal connecting principle or, in more basic terms, a meaningful coincidence.

Synchronicity happens to me on a daily basis. Two or more independent things will happen close enough together (or with enough similar conditions) that they appear to be connected. For example, some friends brought over some lilies. We have never had lilies in our house before. That same evening we played a record by Moondog, a musician who looks like a Viking and wears a bull horn hat. The next day, a book arrived entitled *The Lily and the Bull* (New York: Hill and Wang, 1979) by Moyra Caldecott, which was just the right book, at the right time, for me to read.

It is these kinds of events that make life truly inspiring. It is a secure feeling to have events occur that directly relate to and help your inner growth emotionally, intellectually, and spiritually.

Events, people, and things are drawn to us by the harmony of their corresponding vibrations. Likewise, things and situations are repelled from us by discordance between our own vibrations and the vibration of the potential event. Here is one of the secret teachings: if you think what happens to you is what is *supposed* to happen to you, then you move in harmony with the flow of events, positively and constructively. Obviously, this is not an excuse for immoral behavior.

Building sacred space is an attempt to put as many compatible events and ideas together as possible and thus encourage the synchronous moment—the moment when everything seems to fit together.

Sympathetic Vibration

Sacred space works on the principle of *sympathetic vibration*. Here's an example that demonstrates how sympathetic vibration works: there are two guitars in a room. If a chord or a single string is played on one guitar, then the other guitar will begin to vibrate, too. The same analogy can be applied to the interaction of symbolic art (sacred space) and the person viewing it. By achieving a condition of coinciding rhythms, an exchange of information can take place.

Symbols have multiple, simultaneous meanings. A *mandala* is a circular image or pattern, which may be drawn, painted, sculpted, or carved in a variety of materials. A psychological symbol that expresses wholeness and the totality of the self, a mandala typically consists of a circular pattern of concentric rings surrounding a central point (the self) to which everything in the symbol is related.

Most sacred spaces and monuments are mandalas. Although they are not all circular, they are always center-oriented. When visiting monuments, naturally the first place people tend to go to is the center or the top of the monument, the focal point of attention and feeling.

The Symbolic Formulas of Synthesis

I have visited and studied hundreds of ancient monuments. All these places share a common set of visual patterns that are symbolic representations of one universal and elementary cosmology. Five important concepts are included in this cosmology: wholeness, transformation, duality, the Void, and transcendence.

Wholeness

The universe viewed as a whole is the cosmos. This wholeness is recognized by all cultures and religions of the world as God. By getting close to or at one with God, we realize true happiness.

In many Eastern religions, God is called Brahma, the One Who is uniquely great, Who has the power to make others part of Him. He is Supreme Consciousness, eternal, pure, indescribable. She is shapeless, without blemish, all-blissful. He is the center of all mandalas and all expression, the fountainhead and depository for all matter, energy, and consciousness.

In Buddhism, wholeness is the attainment of enlightenment in order to provide the highest good for all living beings. What is *enlightenment?* Enlightenment is the purpose of human existence. Since it is entirely experiential, it is not something that can be described other than with words like emptiness of mind, nondual clarity, and ultimate reality. To attain enlightenment, there are several requisite factors and methods: giving and helping others, moral conduct, patience, avoidance of anger, effort, meditation, and wisdom. I cannot encourage you enough to take advantage of your human birth and seek out the teachings of enlightenment.

Admittedly biased, I recommend Tibetan Buddhism as a path for enlightenment. I am a member of the Sakya Monastery in Seattle, Washington. Tibetan Buddhist teachings come from a long lineage of teachers (Lamas). Based on my very modest experience, their methods are effective.[1]

Transformation and Symbols of Duality

Most cosmologies begin with a description of the creation of the universe. The first transformation of the one into two (the great primal beginning) has entranced mankind since the beginning of thought. What is the great primal beginning? It is the very first manifestation of duality in the Void. Here are some basic symbols of duality:

Yin-Yang. The yin/yang figure ☯ is symbolic of the first act of creation in the cosmos. The One's initial transformation into *two*, the dual, results in a severed circle. The resultant halves are mirror images of each other, identical yet opposite, like the bilateral symmetry of the human body. These opposites are described in the *I Ching* archetypally as "cloudy/overcast" (yin) and "banners waving in the sun/shone upon," (yang). Further binary aspects of yin and yang are: dark and light, shadow and bright, female and male, yielding and firm.

Centrifugal-Centripetal. Virtually everything in the universe is rotating around some central object: electrons around the nucleus of an atom, moons around planets, planets around the sun, solar systems around galaxies. Centrifugal force makes a rotating body move *away* from the center of rotation. Centripetal force makes rotating bodies move *toward* the center of rotation.

Shakti-Shiva. A Tantric text, *Ánanda Sútrum*, says "Shiva-shaktyátmakam Brahma" ("Brahma is composed of Shiva and Shakti"). Brahma is the Supreme Being, Shiva is the archetypal Supreme Consciousness, and Shakti is the archetypal operative principle—the substantiation of consciousness in the form of energy and matter. Shiva and Shakti are described as being like two sides of a piece of paper: inseparable from one another, yet distinct in and of themselves. Together they are the elemental underlying forces of all creation—everything is composed of consciousness and energy. Their reciprocal interaction is the basis for all manifestation and life throughout the cosmos. Similarly, when brought together under the proper conditions, they can fuse and become one: Brahma.

Division-Union. In simplest terms, all of these forms of expressing duality can be reduced to the division-union transformation. Change and transformation is a characteristic of everything. Change can always be viewed as a division or union process. Division is any sort of separation or partitioning. Union is a uniting, a fusion or combining process. Consider any object—the processes of division and union will play a part in its existence. From the atom to cellular growth to galactic processes, *everything* is in the process of being divided, eroded, and broken up *or* being united with other objects, growing into new wholeness.

The division-union duality is closely related with *entropy* and *anti-entropy.* Entropy is the tendency for a system to become randomized, disordered, and broken down. Anti-entropy is the tendency for a system to become ordered and whole. In a forest, these processes are easily observed. The process of decay gradually reduces organic materials into a homogenous humus, which in turn is the fertile material on which new growth emerges and is sustained.

Manifested-Unmanifested. When dealing with sacred ideas and symbols, there is a constant interplay between what is apparent to the senses and what is not. Something evident, near at hand, plain, clear, and demonstrable is said to be manifest (*manus*, a hand + *fendere*, to strike). That which is hidden, coded, non-physical, and beyond the obvious is unmanifested.

In yoga, the manifest universe is termed *Saguna* (*sa,* with + *guna*, bondage). The unmanifested universe is *Nirguna* (*nir,* without + *guna*, bondage). The thought of no form, time, or space is scary, but on the other hand, this is a state that transcends such concepts. Imagine being one with God—a wholeness so complete it cannot even be expressed in form, much less words. This feeling is what yogis yearn for—*samadhi*, a perfect absorption or union with Brahma. The best thing about *samadhi* on any level is that it is accompanied by a feeling of beautiful, peaceful happiness.

The Void

All things arise from the Void. All cosmologies and tales of creation begin at the beginning. The Void is what precedes all beginnings. It is the source of life and manifestation. Every spoken or written word must have a silence or empty space before and after the word.

The Void, as utter emptiness, is a state beyond the apprehension of the intellect and represents what is unknown to us. The Void is the unconscious part of ourselves that makes itself known in our dreams, sleep, meditation, or during moments of sudden change or crises when our subconscious and unconscious are revealed to us.

The Symbolic Formula of Union and Division

The relationship between wholeness, transformation, and duality can be summarized in two simple symbolic equations. The first is expressed as ●❸●● and symbolizes division. With the solid circle symbols replaced by words, this equation reads: wholeness ● is transformed ❸ into duality ●●. It symbolizes the division of one into two, the transformation of unity into diversity. Monuments that only have one primary element ●, such as a mound or a single standing stone, express ●❸●●.

The second equation is expressed as ●●❸● and symbolizes the transformation ❸ of duality ●● into wholeness ●, the joining of two into one, and the transformation of diversity into unity. ●●❸● also stands for paired similars—the technique of putting similar images side by side to reinforce a central concept. A few examples of paired similars include:

- The use of like stones in a stone circle.
- The multiplicity of passage cairns at a site like Loughcrew.
- Two stone circles placed side by side.
- The use of a common number throughout a sacred space.

The repetition of stones, cairns, or a common number reinforces the importance of that element and calls attention to it. For example, the numerous cairns grouped together at Loughcrew imply that the cairns are connected, work together, and have a common meaning.

The Symbolic Formula of Creation and Transcendence

The expression $\bigcirc \, \circledcirc \, \odot$ can be read as "All things $\odot$ are created $\circledcirc$ from the Void $\bigcirc$. The empty circle stands for the Void and $\odot$ stands for ordered form. The Void is an unmanifested symbol. Ideally, it would have no representation other than empty space. The manifestation of objects (from the Void) is the ordered form, symbolized here as a point inside a circle $\odot$. Monuments that have a symbolic depiction of the Void, such as a dark passage, chamber, or a hole in the ground or a stone, express $\bigcirc \, \circledcirc \, \odot$.

Transcendence

The expression $\odot \, \circledcirc \, \bigcirc$ can seen as a symbolic representation of transcendence (*trans*, over + *scandere*, to climb). Transcending is the process of going beyond a limited state of mind by understanding completely, by becoming one with. It is a point of clarity, an instant when an idea or object is wholly comprehended (encircled). In psychology, transcendence is a significant self-experience or self-realization. It describes all great discoveries, when true insight is attained—the *Eureka*, the *Ah-ha!* It is iridescence, the ability to see oneness in duality. In the spiritual sense, it is when the self merges with God, becoming one with all existence.

Transcendence is the basis for understanding and surmounting problems, for creating theories for all of science, the basis of the most sophisticated calculus in mathematics,[2] as well as the fountainhead of all cosmology and religious thinking.

The equation $\odot \, \circledcirc \, \bigcirc$ can be used to create sacred spaces with great symbolic power through the use of paired opposites $\odot$. The technique of putting opposite images side by side, the art of *syzygy*, to create a wholeness is nicely illus-

Figure 11.1—
Stone chamber and large boulder in Connecticut.

trated by the juxtaposition of the large boulder and the dark chamber in figure 11.1. Another dramatic illustration of this equation is in the creation of life. Two separate forms, the sperm and the egg, unite into one for a split second, resulting in a new form—a new life. Then, the process of cellular division ●❂●● and growth ●●❂● begins, resulting in a new human being.

To create a sacred space that enables transcendental, altered states of consciousness (the feeling of being spiritually "high"), we must go beyond the duality of the world. To do this, we place opposite forms next to each other. Opposite forms create an ordered form, which creates the potential for a transcendental experience, the creation of a new reality. This technique is used extensively in one form or another in almost all ancient monuments. Examples of paired opposites include:

+ A stone circle surrounding a passage cairn (Newgrange).

+ A ditch next to a bank or henge (Avebury).

+ A stone circle made of large stones next to a stone circle made with small stones.

+ A stone circle surrounded by a henge.

+ A central stone surrounded by a circular stone circle or henge.

The use of paired opposites creates a balancing force that facilitates transcendental experience.

How to Most Effectively Express Your Cosmology

The symbolic formulas of synthesis provide the grammar or structure for expressing symbolic cosmologies in monument form. For those who like an analytical approach to design, here are two tables that can be used to help design symbolically effective sacred spaces.

The Tables of Symbolic Communication

The Tables of Symbolic Communication are your handy guide to quickly solve difficult problems of how to express spiritual ideas most effectively. They summarize each of the symbolic formulas, including primary central concept, type of transformation (change) taking place, secondary ideas, and, most importantly, the proper sculptural form to use for maximum effectiveness.

Symbolic Communication Table One.

FORMULAS/EQUATIONS	●❓●●	●●❓●
CENTRAL CONCEPT	DIVISION	UNION
TYPE OF TRANSFORMATION	EXTROVERSIAL	INTROVERSIAL
SECONDARY IDEAS	FORMATION, RELATIONSHIP, GROWTH	JOINING, ONENESS, SIMPLIFICATION
SCULPTURAL EXPRESSIONS	SINGLE DOMINANT FORM	PAIRED SIMILARS
EXAMPLES	MOUND, HENGE, LARGE STANDING STONE, CAIRN, EARTH PYRAMID	TWO OR MORE SIMILARLY RELATED STRUCTURES LOCATED CLOSE TOGETHER, STONE LINE, STONE CIRCLE

Symbolic Communication Table Two.

FORMULAS/EQUATIONS	○◑⊙	⊙◑○
CENTRAL CONCEPT	CREATION	TRANSCENDENCE
TYPE OF TRANSFORMATION	EXTROVERSIAL, CENTRIFUGAL	INTROVERSIAL, CENTRIPETAL
SECONDARY IDEAS	MANIFESTATION, DEVELOPMENT, GROWTH	BALANCING, HEALING, SIMPLIFICATION
SCULPTURAL EXPRESSIONS	PASSAGE, CHAMBER, HOLE	PAIRED OPPOSITES
EXAMPLES	CAIRN, MOUND, OR BARROW WITH PASSAGE, OR CHAMBER/DOLMEN, STONE WELL/HOLE IN STONE	TWO OR MORE OPPOSITELY RELATED STRUCTURES LOCATED CLOSE TOGETHER, STANDING AND RECUMBANT STONES TOGETHER, MEDICINE WHEEL

Using the Tables

Decide what idea, image, or cosmology you want to express in your sacred space. Analyze your cosmology. What is the central idea? Some examples might be earth goddess, spiritual wholeness, or earth healing. Next, if it's appropriate, develop your central idea a little fuller. Try expressing it as a sentence, adding a verb (transformation) and an object (result of the transformation). Here are some examples:

+ "All begins in sound."
+ "Everything in life is gracefully related."
+ "The universe is formed from the Void by the Supreme Entity."

Compare your idea or sentence to the tables of symbolic communication. Us them to decide if the central concept of your idea is division, union, creation, or transcendence. Here are some examples:

Defining Your Central Concept.

CENTRAL CONCEPT	→	TYPE OF TRANSFORMATION
EARTH GODDESS	→	CREATION
SPIRITUAL WHOLENESS	→	TRANSCENDENCE
EARTH HEALING	→	UNION
ALL BEGINS IN SOUND	→	CREATION
THE UNIVERSE IS FORMED FROM THE VOID	→	CREATION

Read off the corresponding sculptural expression for your idea. Here's how it works. In each formula, you are making your monument form in the image of the first part of the formula—the part to the left of ☯. Your goal in this is to *imply* the central concept—the part to the right of ☯. The viewer naturally finishes the "unspoken" (not physically manifested) part of your idea.

Figure 11.2—*Underground chambers (covered dolmens) are symbolic of the Void and the womb which imply transcendence and new life: "From the womb emerges new life."*

Figure 11.3—*The Knowth Mounds, Ireland, are an excellent example of mounds that symbolize the Great Mother and Her children.*

Photo ©1997 Chuck Pettis

Let's say you want to express the generative aspect of the Great Mother. Your central idea might be: "From the Great Mother is generated new lives." *Generative* implies creation, birth, and new life. This concept could be visually expressed with a large mound, implying the figure of a pregnant woman.

Summary

We have outlined the essential elements of a simple cosmological model which can serve as a preliminary representation or plan of all cosmologies. This model includes the concepts of wholeness, transformation, duality, Void, and transcendence. The universe is created when the original whole is transformed into a minimum of two constituent parts. The ideal goal of the designer is to place the parts of a sacred space together in such a manner so as to create a harmonious form that facilitates the transcendental union of the parts into wholeness, providing meaningful spiritual experiences.

Secrets of Sacred Space Revealed in This Chapter

- Sacred spaces are receptacles of universal knowledge.

- Symbols are very important in the design of sacred space. A symbol reveals underlying realities pointing to real, immutable, and sacred truths.

- Nothing is meaningless. Everything is significant. Nothing is independent. Everything is related to something else. Sacred space is an attempt to put as many compatible events and ideas together as possible—and thus encourage the synchronous moment when everything seems to fit together.

- If you think what happens to you is what is *supposed* to happen to you, then you move in harmony with the flow of events, positively and constructively.

- Sacred space works on the principle of sympathetic vibration.

- Places of power share a common set of visual patterns, which are symbolic representations of one universal and elementary cosmology. Five important concepts are included in this cosmology: wholeness, duality, transformation, the Void, and transcendence.

- To create a sacred space that enables transcendental or altered states of consciousness, use the art of *syzygies*—the creation of paired opposite forms.

Suggested Projects and Exercises

- On one side of a piece of paper write your own cosmology. Use only one piece of paper. That'll keep it simple and focused on the important points. On the other side, draw a symbol of your cosmology.

- Look through some books with pictures of ancient monuments. Find one or two you really like. Study them. Look for key features, paired opposites, paired similars, symbols, materials, and alignments. What's the message?

- Use the paired opposites technique. Pick a message or key sentence from your cosmology statement. Then, look for monuments that seem to express your idea. Why do they work? That is, why are the designs successful? What features are the ones that really carry out your idea?

- Go to an art museum. Look through it, noting pieces that you particularly like or are attracted to. Revisit your favorites and look at them carefully. Look at them up close and at different angles and distances until you find the best viewing place. What feelings come to your mind as you look? What vibrations are you picking up on? What artistic devices seem to create the most positive feelings for you?

- Look through monument picture books. Look for single dominant forms, paired similars, and paired opposites.

- Pick one monument and "decode" its cosmology based on its geometry, monument type, and the arrangement of the earth and stones.

Notes

1 Recommended introductions to Tibetan Buddhism: *The Beautiful Ornament of the Three Visions* (New York: Snow Lion Publications, 1991) by Ngorchen Konchog Lhundrub and *The Three Levels of Spiritual Perception* (Boston: Wisdom Publications, 1995) by Deshung Rinpoche.

2 For an elegant and comprehensive presentation of this metaphysical arithmetic of logic, read G. Spencer Brown's *Laws of Form* (New York: The Julian Press, 1972).

chapter twelve

Cosmic Geometry

Geometry and number have been used since the beginning to encode and represent secret knowledge. With symbolism as their vehicle, geometry and measure use the *principle of correspondence*—the "as above, so below principle"—to connect our secular individualistic world with the spiritual holistic world. Uniting opposites causes an alchemical wedding to occur, inducing transcendental experiences. Let's delve into how this is accomplished.

Geometry is the science of space, and the building block of space is *distinction*. The simplest distinction is a circle drawn on a blank sheet of paper. The circle creates three new spaces on the paper: the line or set of points that is the circle, the space inside the circle, and the space outside the circle.

Look around you now and see all the distinctions. Every object and person you see—the chair, the lamp, the window, a tree, and this book—are all distinctions.

Einstein defined the aim of science to be the comprehension of all experience by the use of a minimum number of primary concepts and relations. *Science,*

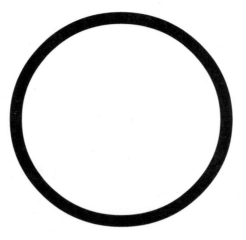

Figure 12.1—*The building block of space is distinction. The simplest distinction is a circle.*

being derived from roots meaning "to know" and "to cut through," is fundamentally based on the concept of distinction. Mathematics is a special science because it seeks to say less and less about more and more. Mathematics puts things in their place and causes things to be or become. These are exactly the activities we undertake when we create a sacred space.

The building of a monument is a very deliberate and thoughtful use of space. A monument is a special sacred space in which all design elements relate to each other and to a central cosmology. The monument is a cosmic distinction, a conscious definition of inside and outside, a demarcation of space. A stone circle or underground chamber is an invitation to step inside to see what is there. Everyone who steps inside is affirming the existence of wholeness, transformation, and duality.

The space created by the monument is receptive, like a vessel. The visitor is the active force entering and filling the vessel. In this simple way, the purpose of the vessel is fulfilled. What is a vessel without the filling substance? What is the egg without the sperm, the yin without the yang, light without darkness? Every time people enter the monument, they are acting out, physically and symbolically, the process of two becoming one, the process of unification.

The monument is an elementary temple. A minimum number of forms are used to create a very important distinction. In fact, monuments are like science books, trying to summarize important experiences and knowledge with a minimum of primary concepts.

> Sacred space, in the form of a temple, represents, in this world, a paradigmatic prototype which pre-exists in archetypal space, "in the beginning" and therefore originates outside existent space; in a similar way sacred time is "controlled" by the correct— "timely"—exercise of rites within those boundaries.[1]

—Keith Critchlow

The word *temple* comes from *templum*, meaning a space that is "cut off" or demarcated as being consecrated to the gods. A temple is a sacred edifice and a place of religious worship. *Temple* is also related to the words *tempus* and *temperare*, bearing the connotation of doing things at the right time—at the suitable season. Finally, *temple* is derived from *contemplare*, meaning to view intensely or for a long time. So, the sacred space—the temple—is actually the basis for all existence because it includes time (*tempus*), space (*templum*), and self (*contemplare*).

Geometric Forms and Their Symbolism

Geometry is the purest and simplest way to construct sacred-space-as-temple. Here is a summary of the variety of geometric forms and their symbolism.[2]

The Void

Creation begins with the Void. The Void is an empty or unmanifested form which is not representable in space. The Void is the precreation universe, the blackboard on which we draw and make manifest our creations. It is the womb of creation, the entrance to existence and form. The Void may be represented by a hole in the ground, a tunnel, or a hole in a stone (see figures 12.2 and 12.3).

Figure 12.2— *Angled passage-grave of Kerners in Bono (Carnac, France area).*

Photo ©1979 Stephen Miller

Figure 12.3—Reconstructed stairs in the Mané-er-Hroeh Tumulus in Locmariaquer. Chambered mounds are literal depictions of the Void.

Photo ©1979 Stephen Miller

The Line

Lines *"de-line-eate"* space. Using a line as a design element can serve to mark earth energies. It can also be used to direct a viewer's eye toward celestial events. This is the purpose of the diagrams in figure 12.4, which are intended to direct a viewer's attention to the midwinter sunset alignment at Ballochroy, Kintyre.

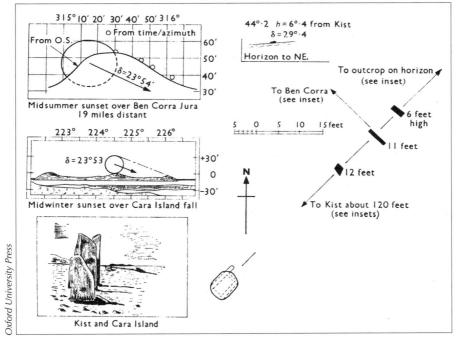

Figure 12.4—Using a line to direct the view toward the midwinter sunset at Ballochroy, Kintyre.[3]

The Plane

A plane is formed by the intersection of two lines and is characterized by being level and flat (all points on both lines exist on the plane). The primary symbol of the plane is the cross, which is formed by the intersection of two lines, as in an *X*. An *X* on the earth has been used by several male earth artists.[4] In 1968 and 1969,

Richard Long created two *X* earthworks—one in Kenya created by walking through dust-covered grass and one in Bristol, England formed by decapitating daisies in a field. In 1969, Dennis Oppenheim created *Directed Seeding: Cancelled Crop* by designing the seeding plan of a wheat field that was subsequently harvested in the form of an *X*. Processing was symbolically withheld. In 1978, Dennis Oppenheim again used the *X* motif in an earthwork entitled *Relocated Burial Ground* constructed of black asphalt primer and located in El Mirage Dry Lake, California. In 1974, Robert Morris in the Grand Rapids (Iowa) Project made two eighteen-foot-wide asphalt ramps in the form of a large *X* that led to a central platform.

The most elementary expression of the plane in sacred space is a platform or carefully leveled space. Many monuments have obviously been built upon leveled ground or a plane. In these cases, the plane is literally the foundation—a place for activity, ritual, and dramatic performance.

Proportion

> *The senses delight in things duly proportional.*
>
> —Thomas Aquinas (1224–1274)

Proportion is the harmonious relationship between the length and width or length and height of a rectangular structure. If two lengths are placed at right angles to one another to form a rectangle, certain relationships will be more visually pleasing than others. These harmonious rectangles are usually based on the mathematical ratios $1:\sqrt{2}$, $1:\sqrt{3}$, $1:2$, $1:\sqrt{5}$ and $1:1.618$ (the *Golden Section*[5]). These proportions are very important because they produce naturally pleasing forms. For instance, from the Golden Section, we can derive the Golden Rectangle (figure 12.5).

Deriving the Golden Rectangle From a Square.

1. Start with a square.

2. From the midpoint of the bottom edge of the square (E) to one of the upper vertices of the square (C), draw an arc of equal radius to the midpoint down to the intersection of the bottom line (G). The new line segment formed (line AG) is equal to 1.618 (1 + Φ). The resulting Golden Rectangle is shown as rectangle ADFG.

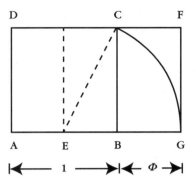

Figure 12.5—*Deriving the Golden Section and the resulting Golden Rectangle from a square. The distance from E to C is equal to the distance from E to G.*

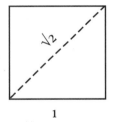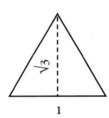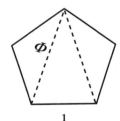

Figure 12.6—*The* √2, √3, *and the Golden Section (**Φ**) proportions.*

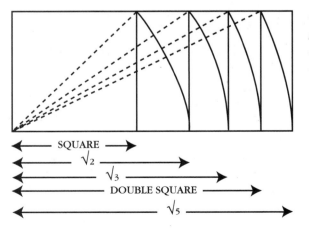

Figure 12.7—*The root (√) rectangle proportions and their construction. From the square, you derive √2. From √2, you derive √3, and so on.*

The Circle

With neither a beginning nor an end, the circle symbolizes transformation and all cyclic processes. The circle is perfection itself since all points on it are equidistant from the center. It symbolizes equilibrium and balance since it is omni-symmetric.

The circle is used constantly in monument design because it is so easily identified with, so innately understood, and is associated with beauty. The most prevalent monument forms—the stone circle and the mound—are both elemental circular forms.

A circle can be easily constructed on the ground with a central stake and a string or wire held at a fixed length. A pointed stick can then be held or positioned at the end of the wire and rotated all around.

Figure 12.8—
View of the Avebury Stone Circle restored.

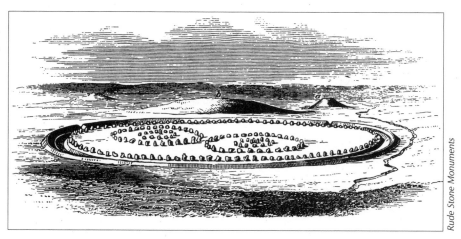

Rude Stone Monuments

The Squared Circle

The squared circle is the most important geometric form for the designer of sacred space. Many significant properties and relations are revealed by the squared circle. The name for the squared circle comes from not only the circumscribing of the circle by the square, but also from the ability to geometrically construct a unique square and circle such that the square's perimeter is equal to the circle's circumference to within 1.82 percent accuracy.

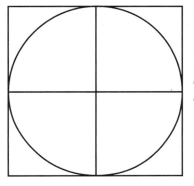

Figure 12.9—
The squared circle. The circle's circumference is equal to the square's perimeter (within 1.82 percent).

The squaring of the circle unites the symbolic image of the square with that of the circle together in a balanced symbolic form. It represents the manifestation of heaven on earth and the reconciliation of the rational (square) and irrational (circle).

Many significant proportions and relationships are revealed by the squared circle. For example, the eight-pointed star, easily derived from the squared circle, can be used to subdivide the square's edge into two to ten equal parts.[6]

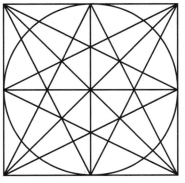

Figure 12.10—
Construction of the squared circle eight-pointed star.

The Great Pyramid and the Squared Circle. The Great Pyramid epitomizes the effective application of cosmic geometry. Its plan view (figure 12.11) and a combined plan/section view (figure 12.12) are represented below. In figure 12.12, the Pyramid's base is defined by DDDD and the section by CBC. The square of the pyramid's height (AB) is equal to the area of each of its faces (CBC).

Figure 12.11—*Plan of the* Great Pyramid *in the squared circle.*

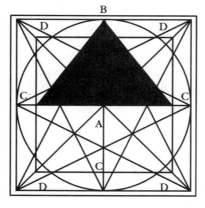

Figure 12.12—*CBC is the section view of the* Great Pyramid *in the squared circle. DDDD represents the Pyramid's base.*

The Great Pyramid contains many significant proportions within its geometry. If half the length of its base (DC) is 1, then the *apothem*[7] (CA) is 1.618 (the Golden Section), and the height (AB) is 1.272 (the square root of the Golden Section). Note also that 4.00 divided by 1.272 equals 3.14 or *pi*. The perimeter of the Pyramid's square base (DDDD) is equal to the circumference of a circle whose radius is the Pyramid's height (AB), hence the term *squared circle*.

The Ellipse

The ellipse is most easily envisioned as a circle with two centers. An ellipse is formed from a curved line, with each point on the line located such that the sum of the distances from two fixed points (or foci) is constant.

An ellipse can be marked out on the ground with two stakes stuck in the ground at the foci (see F1 and F2 in figure 12.13). Affix a string of length 2c (that is, of length *c + c)* fixed at both ends to stakes F1 and F2. Then, take a pointed stick, stretch out the string, and walk all around.

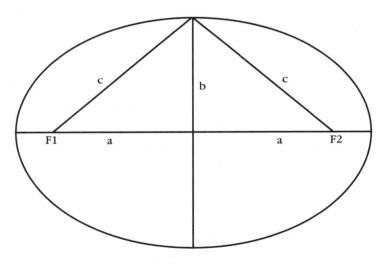

Figure 12.13—
Marking an ellipse on the ground can be done with two fixed stakes (at F1 and F2) and a string of length c + c.

Pythagorean Triangles

Ideally, the ellipse is based on a Pythagorean triangle (in Figure 12.13, for instance, $a^2 + b^2$ would equal c^2) to best incorporate number symbolism in the sacred space. The Pythagorean triangle allows circumferences to approximate whole numbers.

Figure 12.14—
3.5 by 12 by 12.5
(or in whole numbers,
7 by 24 by 25). This is
the Pythagorean trian-
gle used in the Ellis
Hollow Stone Circle to
create a circumference
of seventy-seven feet.
The major axis of this
ellipse is twenty-five
feet and the minor axis
is twenty-four feet.

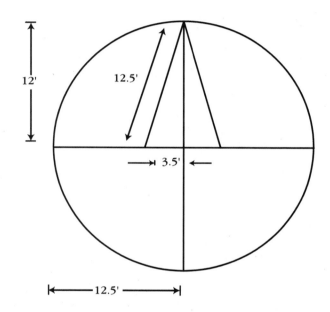

Many ancient monuments, when geometrically analyzed, show that a great deal of effort went into the design of the monument in order to have the circumference and as many internal dimensions as possible come out as whole, rational numbers. This concern for whole numbers is another design element in which the symbolism for wholeness is emphasized.

A. Thom, a well-known authority on British megalithic monument geometry and metrology, has found that many of the stone circles are not perfect circles at all, but ellipses and egg-shaped figures (based on Pythagorean triangles) which distort the circle to obtain integral values (that is, whole numbers—numbers with no fractions, like seventy-seven) for the minor and major axes, and the circumference.

The Pythagorean triangle is characterized by having a right angle and side lengths such that the sum of the squares of the two sides forming the right angle equals the square of the hypotenuse. There are an infinite number of Pythagorean triangles whose three sides are whole integral numbers, but only a small number of these serve the needs of the monument designer.

Some Useful Pythagorean Triangles ($a^2 + b^2 = c^2$).

A	B	C
3	4	5
5	12	13
8	15	17
7	24	25
12	35	37
20	21	29

The Egg (Flattened and Egg-Shaped Circles)

The words *egg, ovum,* and *oval* are all etymologically related. An egg is an oval body laid by a female animal. It consists of an enclosing shell or membrane containing the rudimentary form and food from which a new organism develops. So, the egg is a literal symbol of creation and fertility.

There are many flattened or egg-shaped circles that can be constructed to fit a particular site or idea. Flattened circles are usually formed by connecting circular arcs with varying radii. Circles, ellipses, and flattened circles make up over ninety percent of the existing stone circles. The following illustrations describe the construction of the most popular Type A and Type B flattened circles, as well as the Type I and Type II egg-shaped circles discovered by Professor Thom.[8]

Type A Flattened Circle.

1. Draw a circle with a center point A. Draw a line from A to the bottom of the circle (point B). Use point B as a reference point for an arc that starts from A and swings counterclockwise until it hits the circle. Mark that intersection as point C. Lines from A, B, and C should form an equilateral triangle.

Figure 12.15—*Step 1.*

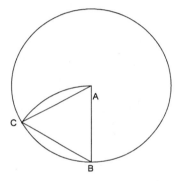

2. From point C, use the same technique as above to find point G on the circle: draw an arc starting from A that swings counterclockwise to the circle. Mark that as point G. Lines from C, A, and G should form an equilateral triangle.

Figure 12.16—*Step 2.*

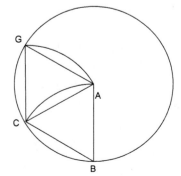

3. Use the same technique from steps 1 and 2 to find points D and H, but on the opposite side of line AB.

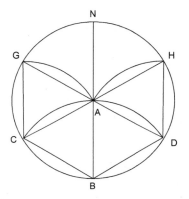

Figure 12.17 — Step 3.

4. Find point N by extending the line from point B to A straight to the top of the circle.

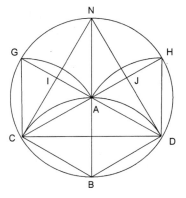

Figure 12.18 — Step 4.

5. Draw a triangle using points N, C, and D (see figure 12.18). Where line CN and GA intersect, mark point I. Where line ND and HA intersect, mark point J. From point J, draw a circle using line JH as the radius. Similarly, from point I, draw a circle using line IG as the radius.

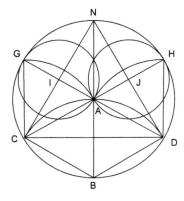

Figure 12.19—*Step 5.*

6. Finally, draw a line from B to I. Extend the line until it hits the circle of which I is the center point. Mark that intersection as point K. Draw a line from B to J. Extend the line until it hits the circle created by J. Mark that point L. Complete the flattened circle perimeter by drawing an arc from point K to L using B as the vertex.

Figure 12.20—*Step 6.*

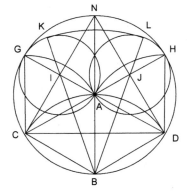

The perimeter of the Type A flattened circle is thus defined as LHDBCGK. The ratio of the diameter of the circle (CAH) to the flattened circle perimeter (LHDBCGK) = 1:3.0591.

Type B Flattened Circle.

1. Draw a square and connect the four corners with lines. Mark the intersection of those lines as point A. Mark the corners B, C, E, and D. Draw a circle with the distance from point A to point B (or another corner of the square) as the radius.

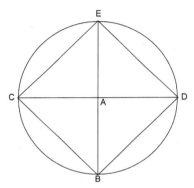

Figure 12.21 — Step 1.

2. Divide the diameter CD into three equal parts. To do this, use E as the vertex and draw a circular arc from A until it intersects the circle on both sides. Mark those points F and G. Draw a line between F and G. Mark the intersection of FG with the square's sides ED and EC with points H and I, respectively.

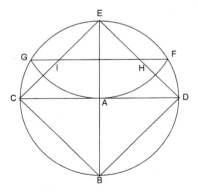

Figure 12.22 — Step 2.

3. From B, draw lines BH (and beyond) and BI (and beyond) to divide the diameter CD into thirds: CJ, JK, KD.

Figure 12.23—*Step 3.*

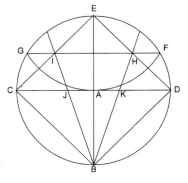

4. From the vertices J and K, draw the short circular arcs CL and DM, respectively. Points L and M are located where the circular arcs intersect with lines BI and BH. Finally, from B, complete the flattened circle outline by drawing the circular arc LM.

Figure 12.24—*Step 4.*

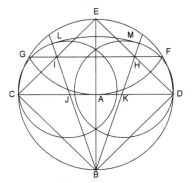

The perimeter of the Type B flattened circle is thus defined as FDBCGLM. The ratio of the diameter of the circle (DC) to the flattened circle perimeter = 1:2.9572.

Type I Egg-Shaped Circle.

1. Draw Pythagorean triangle (e.g., 3 by 4 by 5) AIE. Mirror it on the longest leg side (IA) to create the Pythagorean triangle AIF. Extend the line EAF on both sides to create the circle radius of your choosing (radius = 4 in this example). From point A, draw the semi-circle DBC.

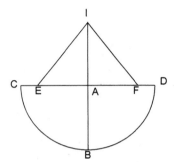

Figure 12.25—*Step 1.*

2. With F as the vertex, draw a circular arc from point C clockwise. Extend the line FI until it crosses the arc from C and mark that intersection as point G. Similarly, with E as the vertex, draw a circular arc from point D counterclockwise. Extend the line EI until it crosses the arc from D and mark that point as H.

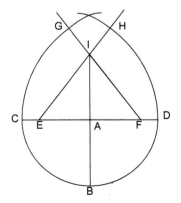

Figure 12.26—*Step 2.*

3. Finally, from the vertex I, complete the Type I egg-shaped circle by drawing the circular arc GH. The perimeter of the Type I egg-shaped circle is
   thus defined as HDBCG.

Figure 12.27—Step 3.

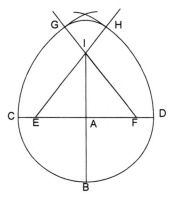

4. Clean and trim edges to get an egg shape (see figure 12.28). The shape and
   size of egg perimeters for Types I and II vary depending on the circle's radius
   chosen in step 1. Calculate the perimeter by using a rope or tape measure, or
   else use a protractor and the formula C = 2πR.

Figure 12.28—Step 4.

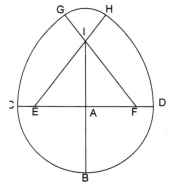

Type II Egg-Shaped Circle.

1. Draw Pythagorean triangle (e.g., 3 by 4 by 5) AIB with angle ABI being the right angle. Mirror it on the hypotenuse (IA) to create the Pythagorean triangle AIC with ACI being the right angle.

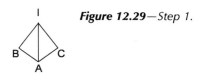

Figure 12.29—*Step 1.*

2. Extend the lines AC and AB until they equal the length you would like for the radius of the larger end of the egg shape (radius = 10 in this example). Mark the ends as D and E, respectively. With A as the vertex, draw a circular arc from E clockwise to point D.

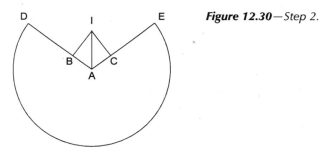

Figure 12.30—*Step 2.*

3. From point I, create a straight line parallel to and the same length as line BD, ending at point F. The length of BD should equal IF (BD and IF = 7 in this example). Join the points D and F creating a line parallel to BI. The length of DF should equal BI. Similarly, again from point I, create a straight line parallel to and the same length as line CE, ending at point G. The length of CE should equal IG. Join the points E and G creating a line parallel to CI. The length of EG should equal CI (see Figure 12.31).

Figure 12.31—*Step 3.*

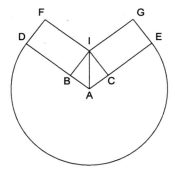

4. Finally, from the center point I, draw a circular arc from F to G (radius of the arc = 7 in this example).

Figure 12.32—*Step 4.*

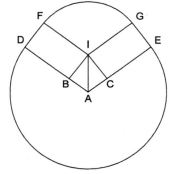

The perimeter of the Type II egg-shaped circle is thus defined as GEDF. Note the emphasis on the Pythagorean triangle dimensions in the egg-shaped circles.

The Spiral

The spiral (*spira*, a coil) is a curved line that circles around a central point in such a manner that the distance from the center to the curve is constantly increasing or decreasing. The spiral is a natural form symbolizing growth, change and transformation. It encapsulates both the extroversial, generative force as well as the introversial, transcendental force in one form.

The spiral is found in the "cup and ring" patterns that are carved in many megalithic stones, such as the ones at Newgrange. These ancient marks are an expression of the *omphalos*—the invisible umbilical cord connecting the earth and the heavens.

Rude Stone Monuments

Figure 12.33—*The spiraling "cup and ring" symbol from Newgrange, Ireland.*

Photo ©1997 Chuck Pettis

Figure 12.34—*Spirals on stone at Newgrange, Ireland.*

Summary

Viewed with insight, geometric symbols form the basic foundation of all creative, artistic, and uplifting experience. Symbolic geometry—and particularly the squared circle—are an integral part of most of the world's great sacred spaces. The important geometric and symbolic forms in this chapter make sacred space design easier as well as more effective and visually pleasing.

Secrets of Sacred Space Revealed in This Chapter

◆ Monuments are cosmic *distinctions*—a conscious definition of inside and outside, a demarcation of space. Everyone who steps inside consecrated space is affirming the existence of wholeness, transformation, duality, emptiness, and transcendence.

◆ Monuments summarize knowledge with a minimum of primary concepts.

◆ Geometry is the purest and simplest way to construct sacred-space-as-temple.

◆ The 1:√2, 1:√3, 1:2, 1:√5 and 1:1.618 (the Golden Section) proportions produce naturally pleasing forms.

◆ The squared circle is the most important geometric form for the designer of sacred space.

◆ When designing a sacred space, use *whole number* dimensions.

Suggested Projects and Exercises

◆ Play with the important squared-circle shape. With graph paper, ruler, colored magic marker, and pens, make patterns, stars, and proportions. See your geometric drawing as a visual meditation.

◆ Use a ruler, compass, and pencil to draw each of the geometric forms. Get a feel for the actual simplicity inherent in geometry. Draw the Type A and Type B flattened circle shapes. Or, design your own shape based on Pythagorean triangles.

Notes

1   Critchlow, Keith. *Time Stands Still* (London: Gordon Fraser, 1979), 150.

2   All unattributed diagrams in this chapter are based on drawings © 1999 Chuck Pettis.

3   Reproduced by permission of Oxford University Press from A. Thom's *Megalithic Sites in Britain*, 1967.

4   Lippard, Lucy R., *Overlay: Contemporary Art and the Art of Prehistory* (New York: Pantheon Books, 1983), 52–54.

5   The Golden Section is the division of a line such that the ratio of the whole to the greater part is the same as the ratio of the greater part to the smaller part.

6   For an in-depth treatise on the squared circle, see *The Secrets of Ancient Geometry and Its Use, Volumes 1 & 2* by Tons Brunes (Copenhagen: Rhodos, 1967).

7   The apothem is the perpendicular line from the side of a polygon to its center.

8   Thom, A. and A.S. Thom, *Megalithic Remains in Britain and Brittany* (Oxford: Clarendon Press, 1978), 18.

The Symbolism of Number and Measure

Number is a very fundamental part of all sacred space. The number of stones in a stone circle, the number of major elements in the space, and their relationship to one another are all important decisions to be made. This brief presentation on number symbolism provides a base upon which to make decisions regarding number in your own sacred space.

Number is a symbol of the creation and development of the universe and all rhythmic evolutions. The word "number" derives from:

- The Indo-European root *nem* and the Greek word *nemein*, both meaning "to divide" and "to distribute."
- The Sanskrit word *nama* meaning "name."
- The Egyptian roots *khefr* meaning "to make a form."

Isn't it amazing how the concepts of form, geometry, metrology, number, and cosmology are all so interrelated?

The Symbolism of Numbers

Number helps, probably more than anything else, to bring order into the chaos of appearances. The numbers from one to ten symbolize the quantum levels of creation, beginning with the ideal form (one) and ending in the material form (ten). The following is a listing of each number from one to ten and each number's traditional and esoteric meanings and symbolism.[1]

One: The Monad (1, I)

The monad is whole, indivisible. It is the first discreet quantity that is self-generating (1 x 1 = 1), and it includes all numbers. The monad is the beginning of all things; all numbers are derived from it. The further a number is from unity, the more deeply it is involved in the world.

Figure 13.1— *The author in front of Le Géant, the tallest (19.7 feet) standing stone still in the Morbihan area around Carnac, France. The "Quadrilateral" rectangular stone circle lies nearby.*

Photo ©1996 Chuck Pettis

The monad is symbolized by a point, having no magnitude yet including everything within it. It is also symbolized by the circle, the essence of form.

Figure 13.2—*The monad is represented by the point and circle.*

The monad is God, Brahma, the mystic center, the all-including *one*. It is the beginning and end of all, itself having neither a beginning nor end. The monad is *Purusa*—the witnessing consciousness that lies quiescent in everything—eternal, pure, and indescribable. The monad is essentially spiritual in nature.

Two: The Dual (2, II)

The dual is plural, divided, and *two* in nature. The basic characteristic of the dual is polarity. It is the first dimension, or length, as represented by a line. Its dualistic nature is manifested as the positive/negative, yang/yin, and male/female aspects. In the cosmic creation, the monad finds its substantiation in the dual. The causative action of the *one* (monad) results in an accompanying reaction, resulting in *two:* thesis and antithesis. The monad is spirit, the dual is body. The monad is spirit, the dual is matter. The monad is the causative essence, the dual is the formative essence. The monad is *Purusa* (consciousness), the dual is *Prakrti* (the operative principle).

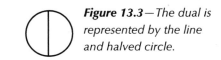

Figure 13.3—*The dual is represented by the line and halved circle.*

The dual creates diversity; it is plastic and moldable. The purpose of polarization and division is growth, the manifestation of consciousness in a myriad of forms. Everything is composed of consciousness (the life principle) and energy (substance) just as every cell has a nucleus and an enclosing membrane. Hence, in Buckminster Fuller's words, "unity is plural and at minimum two."

Three: The Triad (3, III)

The triad is the sum of the monad and the dual. It is the synthesis of thesis and antithesis. The triad is symbolized by the triangle, the only two-dimensional figure that has innate structural integrity. There is no stability without the triangle. Try this experiment. Get some pieces of wood. For simplicity, make them pieces

Figure 13.4—*The triad is represented by the triangle.*

of equal lengths. Now, nail them together into a triangle and push on any side of the form. It will hold together without disfigurement or collapse. Try the same thing with a square. The square will collapse if you push on it and take on funny shapes if you pull on it. It will only return to its original shape with careful rearrangement. Every polygon *except the triangle* will respond like this. Only the triangle will hold its shape.

The dual, as the archetypal operative principle, is composed of three basic and universal forces known in Sanskrit and Eastern philosophy as *Satva* (sentient), *Ragas* (mutative), and *Tamas* (static). At a sacred space, a *sentient* person will comment that it is a holy place, a *mutative* person will say it is a beautiful place, and the *static* person will think that it is a good-for-nothing place.

The table on page 201 shows how these basic principles of the triad are manifested in a number of systems:

Principles of the Triad.

SYSTEM	SENTIENT	MUTATIVE	STATIC
NUMBER	MONAD	DUAL	TRIAD
TIME	FUTURE	PRESENT	PAST
SPACE	LENGTH	WIDTH	BREADTH
COORDINATE	X	Y	Z
LIFE	CREATION	PRESERVATION	DEATH
MIND	INTUITION	INTELLECT	INSTINCT
COLOR	WHITE	RED	BLACK
LENGTH	BEGINNING	MIDDLE	END
TRIANGLE	EQUILATERAL	ISOSCELES	SCALENE
ANGLE	RIGHT	ACUTE	OBTUSE
HARMONY	DIAPASON (2:1)	DIAPENTE (3:2)	DIATESSERON (4:3)
NOTE	DO (I)	MI (III)	SOL (V)
TRINITY	FATHER	SON	HOLY GHOST

Four: The Tetrad (4, IV)

The tetrad is the fountain of all natural phenomena. It is the number of earth, of rational organization, and of terrestrial order.

The tetrad is symbolized by the square and the cross (see figure 13.5). The square represents solidity, firmness, materiality, and the earth element. The square and cross, both consisting of two vertical and horizontal elements, symbolize a reunion of the dual tendencies in a materialistic form.

The tetrad is the first depth, resulting in the first solid—the *tetrahedron*. The tetrahedron is to three dimensions what the triangle is to two dimensions. The tetrahedron is the minimum system necessary to form a distinction in space, dividing the universe into a microcosm (inside) and macrocosm (outside).

The tetrad is quaternary in nature. The following table shows a number of examples that show how fourness is part of our social consciousness.

Figure 13.5—*The tetrad is represented by the square and cross.*

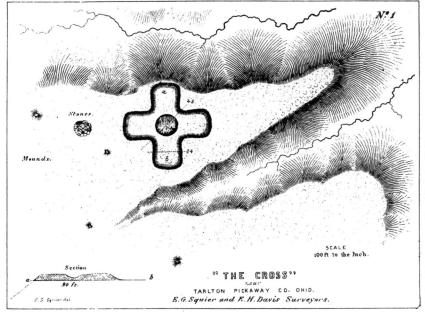

Figure 13.6— The Cross Mound in Pickaway County, Ohio.

Ancient Monuments of the Mississippi Valley

Principles of the Tetrad.

CONCEPT	1	2	3	4
CARDINAL DIRECTIONS	EAST	SOUTH	WEST	NORTH
SEASONS	SPRING	SUMMER	AUTUMN	WINTER
ELEMENTS	AIR	FIRE	WATER	EARTH
AGE	INFANCY	YOUTH	MIDDLE AGE	OLD AGE
TIME	DAWN	MIDDAY	EVENING	NIGHT
MOON	CRESCENT	FULL	WANING	NEW
CONSCIOUSNESS	SEEING	FEELING	THINKING	INTUITION
SECONDARY COLORS	ORANGE	GREEN	INDIGO	VIOLET
SECONDARY NOTES	RE	FA	LA	TI

Five: The Pentad (5, V)

The pentad is the number of harvesting, being the union of the triad (symbolizing natural order) and the dual (symbolizing the feminine principle). The pentad is half of the decad and is a number of completion and marriage, being the union of odd and even numbers.

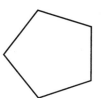 

Figure 13.7—*The pentad is represented by the pentagon and the five-pointed star.*

The pentagon and pentagram are the geometric symbols of the pentad, representing quintessence, the most perfect embodiment of a quality or thing.

Principles of the Pentad.

CONCEPT	*1*	*2*	*3*	*4*	*5*
SENSES	HEARING	SMELL	TASTE	TOUCH	SIGHT
PLATONIC SOLIDS	OCTA-HEDRON	ICOSAHEDRON	TETRAHEDRON	CUBE	DODECA-HEDRON
COLORS	BLACK	YELLOW	RED	BLUE	WHITE
ELEMENTS	EARTH	LIQUID	LUMINOUS	AERIAL	ETHER
PROPERTIES OF MATTER	INERTIA	DISSOLUBILITY	DIVISIBILITY	INTERPRET-ABILITY	FORM

Six: The Hexad (6, VI)

The hexad is the number of equilibrium, balance, and wholeness. Its primary symbol is Solomon's Seal, the six-pointed star, consisting of two oppositely overlapping equilateral triangles (see figure 13.8). These two trinities are joined in this omnisymmetrical symbol to represent the union of life and form, spirit and matter, meditation and service, and the marriage of man and woman.

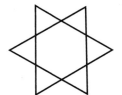 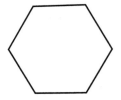

Figure 13.8—*The hexad is represented by the hexagon and the six-pointed star.*

The hexad is firmly bound to the realm of space—it takes a minimum of six vectors to define a three-dimensional space. So, the tetrahedron is also associated with the hexad since it has six lines (or vectors). Three-dimensional space has six directions: up, down, right, left, back, and front.

Seven: The Heptad (7, VII)

The heptad symbolizes perfect order—a complete period or cycle. The musical octave has seven notes, the color spectrum has seven colors, and the week has seven days. The human body has seven *chakras,* or subtle energy centers. The heptad represents

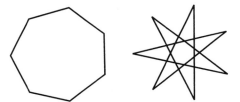

Figure 13.9—*The heptad is represented by the heptagon and seven-pointed star.*

the spiritual and mystical nature of humanity, our threefold spiritual body and fourfold material body. These attributes make the heptad the sacred number of spirituality and religion.

Eight: The Ocdoad (8, VIII)

The ocdoad is symbolized by the eight-pointed star, which consists of overlapping, omnisymmetrical squares. As a means of higher spiritual attainment practiced in several Asian religions, the Eight-Fold Path[2] describes the eight practices forming the foundation of enlightenment and self-realization. The figure-eight (∞) reinforces this concept by being a vertical sign of the infinite and by being the only completely enclosed simple number.

Figure 13.10—*The ocdoad is represented by the octagon and eight-pointed star.*

Nine: The Ennead (9, IX)

The ennead is the limit of the numerical series before returning to unity. It is the horizon that the decad rises from. Nine signals the vanguard of completion. It is the sign that the work of creation is nearing its completion and a change is due.

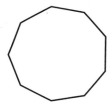

Figure 13.11—*The ennead is represented by the enneagon and the nine-pointed star.*

Ten: The Decad (10, X)

The decad is the number of completion. It contains all things in itself and marks a return to unity as well as the potential for rebirth. The decad is the number of perfection and spiritual achievement. It comprehends all the arithmetic and harmonic proportions, especially as revealed through the *tetractys*.

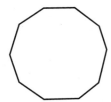

Figure 13.12—*The decad is represented by the decagon and the ten-pointed star.*

Figure 13.13—A tetractys is has three vertice points (spiritual, mental, physical) and seven inner points.

Figure 13.14—The six-pointed star in a tetractys represents two-dimensional manifested reality.

Figure 13.15—The cube in a tetractys represents three-dimensional manifested reality.

The shape (figure 13.12), a triangle of ten points, is a symbol of the creation. The three points that are the vertices of the triangle symbolize the three aspects of the creation: spiritual, mental, and physical. The seven points in the center of the figure represent the seven levels of manifested creation expressed two-dimensionally as a six-pointed star (figure 13.14) and three-dimensionally as a cube (figure 13.15).

The six-pointed star symbolizes the union of the introversial and extroversial aspects of human nature. The cube defines the three-dimensional (x-y-z) coordinate system. The sides of the cube form three planes corresponding to the three axes of rotation (roll, pitch, and yaw) that all objects, from atoms to stars, are subject to.

Figure 13.16—*Pascal's triangle.*

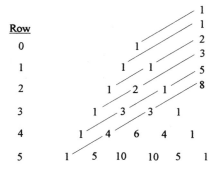

Pascal's Triangle. Pascal's triangle (see figure 13.16) is a numeric expansion of the tetractys. The triangle begins with one at the apex. Then, each other number is the sum of the two numbers directly above it. Both the tetractys and Pascal's triangle can be expanded infinitely. They are bilaterally symmetric. In contradistinction to this static symmetry, the sums of the diagonal lines in Pascal's triangle form the *Fibbonacci* series: 1, 1, 2, 3, 5, 8, 13, 21, . . . , a classic example of dynamic symmetry. The Fibbonacci series is a sequential expansion of numbers that form a "growth spiral" (the foundation of everything from DNA to a spiral nebula) and give a pleasing proportion. The series is created by adding each number in sequence to its sum, as follows: $1 + 1 = 2$; $1 + 2 = 3$; $2 + 3 = 5$; $3 + 5 = 8$; and so on into infinity.

Pascal's triangle condenses a wealth of mathematical information into a very simple array. For example, each horizontal row of the array gives the coefficients of the binomial expansion: $(x + y)^n$. To find the coefficients of $(x + y)^n$ in correct order, just look at the triangle's n^{th} row. For example: $(x+y)^2 = x^2 + 2xy + y^2$. This can also be expressed as $(x+y)^2 = 1x^2 + 2xy + 1y^2$. The coefficients 1, 2, 1 are the numerals in the second row ($n = 2$) of Pascal's triangle.

Other Numbers and the Decad. All numbers are contained within the decad:

1. The monad is spirit, wholeness.
2. The dual is polarization of wholeness, the first distinction.
3. The triad is the first stability that allows form to become manifest.
4. The tetrad is the foundation of matter on earth.
5. The pentad is the expression of matter.
6. The hexad is matter and spirit in equilibrium.
7. The heptad is spiritual wholeness.
8. The ocdoad is the perfect expression of order in space.
9. The ennead is the nearing of completion.
10. The decad is the completion of the creation and opens the way for the cosmic creative process to begin all over again.

Using Number in Sacred Space

There are many ways that number can be used symbolically in sacred space. The use of number can be literal (as in the number of stones used in a stone circle) or "hidden" (as in the the measure of the circumference of the stone circle). For example, sixteen (16) stones were used in the Mutiny Bay Stone Circle. The circumference is eighty-eight (88) feet. **88** → 8 + 8 = **16**, and 16 → 1 + 6 = **7**, the number of spiritual wholeness. This is a hidden use of number symbolism.

Consider using one special number as a theme in your space. For example, in the Ellis Hollow Stone Circle, we used the number seven in several significant ways. First, the shape of the stone circle was an ellipse, designed so that the distance between the two foci of the ellipse was seven feet and the circumference was seventy-seven feet. Then, since the stone circle was built in 1977, seventy-seven 1977 pennies were put underneath one of the stones. Finally, the stone circle was expanded in 1997.

Metrology: Using Earth-based Measures in Sacred Space

Another way to use number in sacred space is to use sacred measures. Historically, monument dimensions have been chosen with the utmost care. In sacred space, each component of the whole design should be multipurposed. Similarly, the monument should communicate a maximum of information and ideas with a minimum of indication.

An ideal measurement system should be elementary, simple enough for all to understand, have a geometric basis, and synthesize the concepts of space and time on which all measurements are based. In the study of ancient metrology, most is known about the Egyptian, Greek, and Roman systems. A. E. Berriman, in his book, *Historic Metrology* (New York: Greenwood Press, 1969), presents his conclusions on these and other cultures' systems of measurement. His study reveals that ancient metrology was geodetic (*geo*, the earth + *daiein*, to divide) in origin and was based upon a sexagesimal ($1/60$) division of the earth's circumference.

The Egyptian, Greek, and Roman metrologies are similar and related. They are all logical and elegant metrologies in which human microcosmic dimensions are consciously linked to geodetic macrocosmic dimensions. Put another way, these measurement systems relate the dimensions of the human body and the earth's circumference in terms of significant proportions. Rather than the inch, foot, and mile, they use the units of the *stade, cubit, foot,* and the *digit*.

- The *stade* is derived from the length of a stadium. Our modern stadium is derived from the Olympic stadium of six hundred Greek feet.

- The *cubit* is the distance from the elbow (from the Greek word *kubiton*) to the tip of the middle finger.

- The *foot* is self-apparent.

- The *digit* is the width of the "pointer" finger.

The Earth's Circumference in the Context of Metrology

The circumference of the earth is first divided into 360 degrees, then each degree into sixty minutes and then each minute into sixty seconds; the circumference is thus divided into 360 (or 360 x 1); 21,600 (or 360 x 60); and then 1,296,000 (or 21,600 x 60) equal sections of degrees, minutes, and seconds, respectively. Now, look at how the human and earth measurements fit together numerically:

Stades. There are 216,000 stades in the earth's circumference, 600 stades to a degree, ten stades to a minute, one stade to a tenth of a minute (one tenth of a minute = six seconds) and one sixth of a stade to a second. Remember that the measures of second, minute, and degree all relate to a specific subsection of the length of the earth's circumference.

Cubits. There are 86,400,000 cubits in the earth's circumference. Note that there are 86,400 seconds to a day, from which we can derive that in one second the earth rotates one thousand cubits. In this way, the cubit synthesizes time and space, as well as earth and human dimensions.

Foot. There are 129,600,000 feet in the earth's circumference. This means that there are 360,000 feet per degree, 6,000 feet per minute, 600 feet per tenth of a minute and one hundred feet per second.

This sexagesimal (1/60) subdivision is truly apparent throughout this metrology. It is also interesting to see the interaction of the sexagesimal and decimal (1/10) number systems. For example, there are 10,000 digits to a stade. There is also the correlation between the number of subdivisions of the earth's circumference and the corresponding number of stades, feet, and digits. For example, one second is 1/1,296,000 of the earth's circumference. There are 129,600,000 feet to the Earth's circumference.

All the basic relationships of the stade, cubit, foot, and digit are neatly summarized in the following table.

Comparative Measure for Subdivisions of the Earth's Circumference.

COMPARATIVE MEASURE		CIRCUM-FERENCE	DEGREE	MINUTE	.1 MINUTE	SECOND
STADE	→	216,000	600	10	1	$1/6$
CUBIT	→	86,400,000	240,000	4,000	400	66.6
FOOT	→	129,600,000	360,000	6,000	600	100
DIGIT	→	2,160,000,000	6,000,000	100,000	10,000-	1,666.6

The metrological system just enumerated is how the Egyptian and Greeks sub-divided the Earth's circumference to obtain numerologically related units. The Roman units are very similar to this system. For example, the Romans used the Greek stade of six hundred Greek feet, but rated it as six hundred twenty-five Roman feet. Greek and Roman foot measurements are therefore related in a 24:25 ratio (600:625).

There is a certain amount of discrepancy among metrologists as to the "exact" length of the Roman, Greek, and Egyptian feet. For example, depending on the sources used to determine the length, estimates of the Greek foot can range from 12.13 to 12.17 of our U.S. inches (0.3081–0.3091 meters) or a little over one-eighth inch larger than the foot we work with today.

The connection of measures to the earth's circumference was gradually lost after the decline of the Greek and Roman civilizations until the origination of the metric system in 1795. The metric system was an attempt on France's part to adopt a new universal metrology based on a natural unit of length. The meter was orig-inally defined as one ten-millionth of the earth's meridian quadrant extending through Dunkirth and Barcelona. It was based on the decimal system and dis-carded the traditional degrees and minutes of angular measurement.

Needless to say, although the system was based on an earth measurement, the new metrology was popularly disregarded. Traditions die hard. And, since then, the length of the meter has been gradually refined to its present value of 39.370 inches or, more specifically, 1,650,763.73 vacuum wavelengths of the orange-red light radiation emitted under specific conditions by the krypton atom of mass 96.

Naturally, I am a proponent of foot-based measurements that relate to the earth's circumference.

Secrets of Sacred Space
Revealed in This Chapter

Number is a very fundamental part of all sacred space. The number of stones in a stone circle, the number of major elements in the space, and their relationship to one another are all-important.

+ Number helps, probably more than anything else, to bring order into the chaos of appearances. The numbers from one to ten symbolize the quantum levels of creation.

+ Historically, monument dimensions have been chosen with the utmost care. In sacred space, each component of the whole design should be multipurposed. Similarly, the monument should communicate a maximum of information and ideas with a minimum of indication.

Suggested Projects and Exercises

+ Make a poster showing all the numbers and symbols of each number—you could make a collage using illustrations cut out from magazines and pasted on poster board.

+ Look at pictures of ancient monuments and do some counting! How many stones are used? How many mounds? How is number used in the monument design?

+ Think about what makes an ideal measurement system. If you were in ancient times and were commanded by your ruler to devise a set of measurements that would please the gods and please the people, what would you come up with?

Notes

1 All unattributed diagrams in this chapter are © 1999 Chuck Pettis.

2 The Eight-Fold Path of Buddhism includes:

right understanding, right thoughts, right speech, right action, right livelihood, right effort, right mindfulness, and right concentration.

The Eight-Fold Path of Yoga includes:

yama, niyama, asanas, pranayama, pratyahara, dharana, dhyana, and samadhi.

Epilogue

Secrets of Sacred Space presents the best information and techniques I know of to understand, find, and create sacred spaces. I have two final suggestions on how you can use this information for your spiritual well-being and growth:

1. Go on a sacred space pilgrimage.
2. Create your own sacred space.

The impulse to travel and see new places is as old as humankind. A pilgrimage is a journey to a holy and sacred place. Plan a vacation or holiday to visit ancient monuments and holy places that attract and interest you. I have gone on sacred space pilgrimages to: southern England; the Peak District in England; Scotland; Ireland; Carnac, France; New England; Ohio; the Yucatán; and most recently, India.

The pilgrimage to the sacred spaces of Buddha's life in India was the best I have experienced for one important reason: those places are revered, respected and, most importantly, used daily for spiritual practices by both monks and visiting pilgrims. The power of most ancient monuments is being "withdrawn" and depleted by visitors who come to experience and see the site, but don't "deposit" and add to the power by meditation, prayer, and other spiritual practices.

The sites where Buddha was born, enlightened, taught, performed miracles, and passed away are different from other sacred sites I have visited because of the great amount of spirit, emotion, and devotion that people feel at these sites. You see monks and visitors doing prostrations, circumambulating *stupas*, lighting candles and incense, meditating, and praying. You can't help but feel the growing power of these special places.

Pilgrimages take you off the beaten path. They take you to places you haven't gone before. Each day is an adventure and an exploration. Old habits and patterns fall away. You meet new people.

Pilgrimages provide inspiration and ideas for your own personal spaces. They inspire us to shape our life with a profound sense of affection and spirit rather than pursuit of profit and material gain.

Ultimately, sacred space is about emptiness, worshipping without roofs. Our days are filled with one activity after another, one word after another, and one thought after another. Sacred spaces are the places where we can take refuge, where we can go completely within to "silence the mind."

> Thirty spokes we unite for our wheels;
> Yet a wheel always turns on a hole.
>
> We mold clay into cleverest forms;
> Yet the use is the space not the bowl.
>
> For our homes we build the sturdiest walls;
> Yet the windows and doors are most enjoyed.
>
> The most solid and tangible things
> Are but servants unto what is void.[1]

Fortunately, increasing numbers of people are creating sacred spaces, stone circles and labyrinths. Join this wonderful group of people in the noble cause to help heal the planet and bring about world peace. Through the feeling of sacred space, go deep into your inner silence and find happiness and freedom from sorrow. Through the service of sacred space, inspire others to their own spiritual path.

Notes

1   Finley, Robert (translator). *The Bible of the Loving Road: Lao* *Tzu's Tao Teh Ching* (Carbondale, IL: Bliss Press, 1972).

More information is available from the author on the ideas discussed in *Secrets of Sacred Space* at The Geo Group's Web site at http://www.geo.org. If you would like information on Geopathic Survey services, send a stamped, self-addressed envelope to: The Geo Group, P.O. Box 602, Medina, WA 98039. All other correspondence should be sent to The Geo Group at the address above.

Appendix I:

The Solar Calendar

The calendar is our system of regulating time by determining the beginning, length, and divisions within the year. The word *calendar* comes from the root *calendarium*, meaning an account book, and from *kalends*, meaning to call or proclaim.

The year has traditionally been divided into four and eight parts, which is a natural way of creating harmonic periods. Each of these time periods is distinguished by season, temperature, weather, and plant and animal growth cycles.

The division of the year into four gives us the summer and winter solstices and the autumn and spring equinoxes. The division of the year into eight adds the important Candlemas, May Day, Lammas, and Martinmas holidays.

To divide the year into eight "ideal" times, there are four things to consider:

1. The sun's declination should be at its maximum deviation from the ecliptic at the summer and winter solstices.

2. The sun's declination at May Day and Lammas should be as close as possible so that only one horizon marker may be used for both dates. The same goes for Martinmas and Candlemas.

3. The time from the spring equinox to the autumn equinox and from the autumn equinox to the next spring equinox should be equal. The same

applies to the time from May Day to Martinmas, from Lammas to Candlemas, and from summer to winter solstice.

4. The time periods between each of the eight calendar times should be as equal as possible and still maximize the above requirements.

The calculation of the eight ideal calendar times would be much simpler if the earth's orbit around the sun was circular. If this was the case, the graph of the sun's declination would be a perfect *sine curve* and all the conditions listed above would be easily satisfied.

In actuality, the earth's orbit is an ellipse and a number of complications therefore come into play. The determination of the exact dates for the eight time periods becomes ambiguous and requires compromise to achieve a "best fit."

Determining the Eight
Ideal Calendar Days

A resource called *Astronomical Phenomena for the Year* is published each year by the U.S. Government Printing Office. It gives comprehensive and very accurate data on the sun, moon, and other planets—much more accurate than anyone other than a specialist could obtain or calculate from the standard formulas available in astronomical textbooks.

I used this guide's data from the sun tables to obtain the sun's declination for each day of the year and made a large graph of it. To compensate for the effect of the leap year, I referenced declination data that was listed for 1977–1980 and 1989–1992 for the days around the *estimated* eight calendar days. I averaged those declination values, then calculated the sun's azimuths (compass readings). The maximum difference between azimuths from each of the two four-year periods was 0.02 degrees, close enough for most purposes. Serious and professional astronomers may want to do their own calculations.

The following tables are based on 1989-1992 data.

Holiday Date and Declination Data.

HOLIDAY	DATE	DECLIN-ATION	AVG. DEC-LINATION	DECLINATION RANGE
CANDLEMAS	FEB. 5	-15.7998	-15.8282	0.2195
EQUINOX	MARCH 23	0.00	0.00	0.00
MAY DAY	MAY 6	16.7175	16.75703	0.21103
SOLSTICE	JUNE 22	23.44048	N/A	0.00386
LAMMAS	AUGUST 7	16.79656	16.75703	0.20814
EQUINOX	SEPT. 21	0.00	0.00	0.00
MARTINMAS	NOV. 7	-15.8565	-15.8282	0.232
SOLSTICE	DEC. 22	-23.4408	N/A	0.0034

Holiday Date and Day Data.

HOLIDAY	DATE	DAYS TO NEXT HOLIDAY
CANDLEMAS	FEB. 5	44
EQUINOX	MARCH 23	44
MAY DAY	MAY 6	47
SOLSTICE	JUNE 22	46
LAMMAS	AUGUST 7	45
EQUINOX	SEPT. 21	47
MARTINMAS	NOV. 7	45
SOLSTICE	DEC. 22	44

Another very good resource as you pursue further study of the solar calendar is chapter nine ("The Calendar in Megaligthic Sites") of *Megalithic Sites In Britain* (Oxford, England: Oxford University Press, 1967) by A. Thom. He provides his own methodology and historical calendar declination data.

Appendix II:

The Table of Astronomical Alignments

The purpose of this table is to enable you to determine if there are any sun or moon alignments at your sacred space site. If so, it will help you locate the points where the sun will rise or set on the horizon on the traditional solar holidays—and where the moon will rise or set on the horizon at the major and minor standstills.

This is not an easy subject to understand or explain. There are many circumstances that can affect the results. Therefore, if you are faced with a complex situation, need extremely accurate fieldwork, or you just want peace of mind, you should consult a professional archaeoastronomer or astronomer. Additionally, all alignments should be checked on-site before making permanent construction decisions—that is, don't install anything permanently until you've checked and confirmed the specific astronomical alignments on-site.

Assumptions

The mathematics of astronomical alignment is complex and involves a number of complicating factors that arise as you get into the mathematical details of sun and moon risings and settings. For example, if you are on a mountain, you can see further than someone at the base of the mountain, and the apparent altitude of the point where the sun rises or sets is quite different than it would be if seen from below.

Therefore, a number of assumptions had to be made in order to provide readers with generalized direction. Please note the following table parameters:

The table assumes that you are in a location of the point where the sun or moon rising or setting is between -0.33 and +5.0 degrees of the true horizon. The true horizon is defined as the plane tangent to the sphere of the earth at the point where you are standing. Consequently, this table won't work if you are on a tall mountain or have a tall mountain in front of you.

You must have a very good compass and pocket transit. You should also have a transit or a theodolite. If you aren't using a transit or theodolite, you will need a *clinometer* (or a protractor with a weighted line attached to the central spot). A clinometer is used to measure vertical angles such as the altitude of a nearby hill or mountain. I use a pocket transit that has a simple, built-in clinometer to measure the horizon's altitude. In addition, you will need a topographic map of the area to determine the site's exact latitude and to get the degrees of magnetic deviation for your locality. For simplicity, from here on out, we will assume you *don't* have a transit or theodolite but you *are* using a pocket transit or a very accurate compass.

The *Table of Astronomical Alignments* includes constants, formulas, and declination assumptions used in the calculations. The table, actually a spreadsheet, lists individual tables for selected latitudes that provide the azimuths (i.e., corrected compass readings) to find the point on the horizon where the sun or moon rise on the date selected. To get the azimuth for the point on the horizon where the sun or moon <u>sets</u> on the date selected, use this simple formula: sunset or moonset azimuth = 360 degrees – sunrise or moonrise azimuth. For example, to get the azimuth for sunset on the summer solstice at 45 degrees latitude and 0 degrees apparent altitude, subtract 55.06 degrees from 360 degrees to get 304.94 degrees.

The actual azimuth will vary depending on whether:

1. The sun or moon is just barely appearing above the horizon—the first or last glimpse azimuth;

2. Half of the sun or moon is visible above the horizon; or

3. The sun or moon is completely visible and just touching (that is, tangent to) the horizon. This is termed the contact azimuth.

The azimuths provided in this table are for option 2, above, or when half of the sun or moon is visible above the horizon. If you want the azimuth for first flash at sun or moon rising or setting (option 1), subtract 0.25 degrees from the apparent altitude. If you want the azimuth for sun or moon when its full circular shape is visible and just touching (tangent to) the horizon (option 3), add 0.25 degrees to the apparent altitude.

The azimuths provided in this table assume that the horizon is nearby, for example, the sun rises over a nearby low hill. For distant horizons, a correction for the earth's curvature must be subtracted from the apparent altitude for both the sun and moon. This correction factor is 0.00724 degrees-per-mile of distance from the site to the horizon. For example if the sun sets forty miles from the site, the correction factor would be 40 miles x 0.00724 (or 0.29 degrees). In this case, the apparent altitude used to determine the azimuth should be reduced by 0.29 degrees.

Instructions

First, determine the latitude of your site and the magnetic deviation for your locality from a topographic map.

Next, look up your latitude on the *Table of Astronomical Alignments* and the azimuths of the alignments you are studying. For example, the June 22 sun azimuth for 45 degrees latitude and 0 degrees apparent altitude is 55.06 degrees. More than likely, due to space limitations, your exact latitude isn't listed on the table. Therefore, it is necessary to go through a few extra steps and calculations, outlined below.

The Table of Astronomical Alignments was created in a Microsoft Excel spreadsheet. At the time of the writing of this book, the spreadsheet file could be obtained and downloaded from The Geo Group web site (www.geo.org). With the spreadsheet loaded into Microsoft Excel, you can go to the listing for any latitude, insert your exact latitude, and reference all the values for that latitude.

Practically speaking, if you only need an approximate azimuth location, you can get close enough by interpolation of the data provided in the table below.

Here is an example of how to use interpolation to find the summer solstice sunrise azimuth for 44 degrees latitude (north) and 0 degrees horizon altitude using the 45 degree and 42.5 degree latitude tables:

* $^1/_{2.5}$ = x/100 (i.e., 1 degree (45 - 44 = 1) is to 2.5 degrees (45 - 42.5 = 2.5) as x is to 100. This calculation determines the correction factor for the azimuth at 44 degrees latitude based on the azimuth at 45 degrees.

* x = 40. Therefore, use a correction factor of 40%.

* 56.71 - 55.06 = 1.65 degrees. Summer Solstice azimuth at 42.5 degrees minus the azimuth at 45 degrees.

* 40% x 1.65 degrees = 0.660 degrees. Applies the correction factor to the azimuth.

* 55.06 + 0.66 = 55.72 degrees or the approximate azimuth at 44 degrees. The azimuth as calculated by the spreadsheet is 55.75 degrees, so the interpolation is "off" 0.03 degrees, more than adequate for an approximate reading with a compass.

Now you'll need to correct your azimuth reading to account for magnetic deviation. The amount of magnetic deviation correction needed is located at the bottom of most USGS maps (geodetic survey maps in the U.S.). In the eastern United States, *magnetic north* is west of *true north*, so you have to subtract the deviation to get true north. In the western United States, magnetic north is east of true north, so you have to add the deviation to get true north. For example, the latitude in Seattle is approximately 47.5 degrees, so the summer solstice azimuth at 0 degrees apparent horizon altitude is 53.14 degrees. Magnetic deviation is 21 degrees. So, we add 21 degrees to 53.14 degrees to get a compass reading of 74.14 degrees.

Set up your compass on a tripod or small table to avoid needle movement and "wiggle." Compasses are very sensitive, so you may also have to remove any ferrous metal on you that may affect the compass needle. Take your compass readings to find if you have any possible clear views to the horizon for the astronomical alignments you are interested in.

Measure the apparent altitude of the horizon for possible astronomical alignments. This is a very important step. Except for people on the equator, the sun doesn't rise straight up. North of the equator, the sun appears to rise up and to the right from where it emerges from the horizon. The actual angle of sunrise relative to the horizon can be calculated as 90 degrees minus your latitude.

To measure the apparent altitude of the horizon, you can use your pocket transit or construct a homemade clinometer using a protractor and a thin weighted line attached to the center point of the protractor. From the same location as your compass bearing, take a sighting along the flat side of the protractor from your site to the horizon. A second person is needed to take the apparent horizon reading, which means reading where the suspended weighted line intersects the hash marks along the circular edge of the protractor.

Now that you know the apparent altitude of the horizon, go back to the table and find the azimuth for the altitude you just measured. For Seattle, the June 22 azimuth at 2 degrees apparent altitude is 56.18 degrees. Add 21 degrees to 56.18 degrees to correct for magnetic deviation and you have 77.18 degrees. Now, with your compass, locate the horizon point. If the horizon varies due to mountains, it may be necessary to remeasure the altitude and azimuth a few times until you are confident you are close. Put a stake in the ground at a convenient distant point from your viewing point to mark the alignment for future reference.

Finally, check the alignment on-site at the appropriate time.

Appendix II — Table of Astronomical Alignments

Azimuth (Corrected Compass) Readings for Important Solar and Lunar Events

© 1998 Charles R. Pettis, III All Rights Reserved.

Constants

Degree: Radians	0.017453
Radian: Degree	57.29583

Formula to determine Azimuth reading

$$\text{Azimuth} = \text{ACOS}\frac{\text{SIN(declination)} - \text{SIN(latitude)SIN(altitude)}}{\text{COS(latitude)COS(altitude)}}$$

Declination

	Jun 22	May 6 / Aug 7	Mar 23 / Sep 21	Nov 7 / Feb 5	Dec 22	Major +(ε+i)	Minor +(ε-i)	Minor -(ε-i)	Major (ε+i)
Declination	23.44048	16.75703	0	-15.8282	-23.441	28.58	18.3	-18.3	-28.58

SUN Close Horizon / MOON Close Horizon

Apparent Altitude Degrees	Refraction Degrees	Parallax (1/2 disk)	Corrected Altitude Degrees	Apparent Altitude Degrees	Refraction Degrees	Parallax (1/2 disk)	Corrected Altitude Degrees
-0.33	0.67	0	-1.00	-0.33	0.67	0.95	-0.05
0.00	0.58	0	-0.58	0.00	0.58	0.95	0.37
0.33	0.61	0	-0.28	0.33	0.61	0.95	0.67
0.67	0.45	0	0.21	0.67	0.45	0.95	1.16
1.00	0.41	0	0.59	1.00	0.41	0.95	1.54
2	0.31	0	1.70	2	0.31	0.95	2.65
3	0.24	0	2.76	3	0.24	0.95	3.71
4	0.20	0	3.80	4	0.20	0.95	4.75
5	0.17	0	4.84	5	0.17	0.95	5.79

Note: it is assumed that the horizon is nearby. For distant horizons, subtract an altitude correction for the Earth's curvature of 0.00724 degrees per mile distance from the site to the horizon. (0.0045 degrees per kilometer)

Note: values assume 1/2 of sun or moon is visible above the horizon. For last flash of sun or moon as it dips below the horizon, subtract 0.25 degrees from the apparent altitude. For sun/moon to be tangent to the horizon, add 0.25 degrees.

Latitude Degrees	Apparent Altitude	Sun's Azimuths					Moon's Azimuths				Major Standstill
							Major Standstill	Minor Standstill			
		June 22	May 7 August 6	March 23 Sept 21	Nov 6 Feb 6	Dec 22	+(ε+i)	+(ε-i)	-(ε-i)	-(ε+i)	-(ε+i)
0	-0.33	66.56	73.24	90.00	105.83	113.44	61.42	71.70	108.30	118.58
0	0.00	66.56	73.24	90.00	105.83	113.44	61.42	71.70	108.30	118.58
0	0.33	66.56	73.24	90.00	105.83	113.44	61.42	71.70	108.30	118.58
0	0.67	66.56	73.24	90.00	105.83	113.44	61.42	71.70	108.30	118.58
0	1.00	66.56	73.24	90.00	105.83	113.44	61.42	71.70	108.30	118.58
0	2	66.56	73.24	90.00	105.83	113.44	61.42	71.70	108.30	118.58
0	3	66.56	73.24	90.00	105.83	113.44	61.42	71.70	108.30	118.58
0	4	66.56	73.24	90.00	105.83	113.44	61.42	71.70	108.30	118.58
0	5	66.56	73.24	90.00	105.83	113.44	61.42	71.70	108.30	118.58

Latitude Degrees	Apparent Altitude	Sun's Azimuths					Moon's Azimuths				Major Standstill
							Major Standstill	Minor Standstill			
		June 22	May 7 August 6	March 23 Sept 21	Nov 6 Feb 6	Dec 22	+(ε+i)	+(ε-i)	-(ε-i)	-(ε+i)	-(ε+i)
10	-0.33	65.98	72.79	89.82	105.90	113.63	60.93	71.40	108.58	119.05
10	0.00	66.06	72.87	89.90	105.97	113.71	61.01	71.48	108.66	119.14
10	0.33	66.12	72.93	89.95	106.03	113.77	61.07	71.53	108.72	119.20
10	0.67	66.22	73.02	90.04	106.12	113.87	61.17	71.62	108.81	119.30
10	1.00	66.29	73.09	90.10	106.19	113.94	61.25	71.69	108.88	119.37
10	2	66.50	73.29	90.30	106.39	114.15	61.47	71.90	109.09	119.60
10	3	66.71	73.48	90.49	106.59	114.36	61.68	72.10	109.28	119.81
10	4	66.91	73.68	90.67	106.78	114.56	61.89	72.29	109.48	120.03
10	5	67.10	73.87	90.85	106.97	114.76	62.10	72.48	109.67	120.23

Latitude Degrees	Apparent Altitude	Sun's Azimuths					Moon's Azimuths				Major Standstill
							Major Standstill	Minor Standstill			
		June 22	May 7 August 6	March 23 Sept 21	Nov 6 Feb 6	Dec 22	+(ε+i)	+(ε-i)	-(ε-i)	-(ε+i)	-(ε+i)
20	-0.33	64.55	71.75	89.64	106.49	114.65	59.38	70.46	109.50	120.58
20	0.00	64.72	71.91	89.79	106.65	114.81	59.55	70.62	109.66	120.76
20	0.33	64.84	72.03	89.90	106.77	114.93	59.68	70.74	109.78	120.89
20	0.67	65.04	72.21	90.08	106.95	115.13	59.89	70.93	109.97	121.10
20	1.00	65.19	72.36	90.22	107.10	115.28	60.05	71.07	110.12	121.26
20	2	65.63	72.78	90.62	107.52	115.73	60.51	71.50	110.54	121.73
20	3	66.06	73.18	91.00	107.93	116.16	60.95	71.91	110.96	122.18
20	4	66.47	73.58	91.38	108.32	116.58	61.38	72.30	111.36	122.63
20	5	66.88	73.97	91.76	108.72	117.00	61.81	72.70	111.77	123.08

Latitude Degrees	Apparent Altitude	Sun's Azimuths					Moon's Azimuths				Major Standstill
							Major Standstill	Minor Standstill			
		June 22	May 7 August 6	March 23 Sept 21	Nov 6 Feb 6	Dec 22	+(ε+i)	+(ε-i)	-(ε-i)	-(ε+i)	-(ε+i)
25	-0.33	63.45	70.96	89.54	107.03	115.52	58.11	69.71	110.25	121.83
25	0.00	63.66	71.17	89.73	107.23	115.73	58.34	69.91	110.45	122.06
25	0.33	63.82	71.31	89.87	107.38	115.89	58.51	70.06	110.60	122.23
25	0.67	64.08	71.56	90.10	107.62	116.15	58.78	70.31	110.85	122.50
25	1.00	64.27	71.74	90.28	107.81	116.34	58.98	70.49	111.04	122.71
25	2	64.84	72.28	90.79	108.35	116.92	59.58	71.04	111.59	123.32
25	3	65.39	72.80	91.29	108.87	117.48	60.15	71.56	112.12	123.92
25	4	65.92	73.31	91.77	109.38	118.03	60.71	72.07	112.65	124.51
25	5	66.45	73.81	92.25	109.89	118.57	61.26	72.58	113.17	125.09

	Sun's Azimuths						Moon's Azimuths			
							Major Standstill		Minor Standstill	Major Standstill
Latitude Degrees	Apparent Altitude	June 22	May 7 August 6	March 23 Sept 21	Nov 6 Feb 6	Dec 22	+(ε+i)	+(ε-i)	-(ε-i)	-(ε+i)
30	-0.33	62.01	69.94	89.42	107.75	116.70	56.44	68.71	111.23	123.50
30	0.00	62.28	70.20	89.67	108.01	116.97	56.72	68.97	111.49	123.79
30	0.33	62.47	70.38	89.84	108.19	117.16	56.93	69.16	111.67	124.00
30	0.67	62.79	70.68	90.12	108.49	117.48	57.27	69.46	111.98	124.34
30	1.00	63.04	70.92	90.34	108.72	117.73	57.53	69.70	112.22	124.61
30	2	63.75	71.59	90.98	109.39	118.45	58.28	70.37	112.91	125.38
30	3	64.44	72.23	91.59	110.04	119.15	59.00	71.02	113.57	126.14
30	4	65.10	72.87	92.19	110.69	119.84	59.70	71.66	114.23	126.89
30	5	65.75	73.49	92.79	111.32	120.53	60.38	72.28	114.88	127.63

	Sun's Azimuths						Moon's Azimuths			
							Major Standstill		Minor Standstill	Major Standstill
Latitude Degrees	Apparent Altitude	June 22	May 7 August 6	March 23 Sept 21	Nov 6 Feb 6	Dec 22	+(ε+i)	+(ε-i)	-(ε-i)	-(ε+i)
32.5	-0.33	61.14	69.33	89.37	108.20	117.43	55.41	68.11	111.83	124.52
32.5	0.00	61.44	69.62	89.63	108.48	117.72	55.73	68.40	112.11	124.84
32.5	0.33	61.66	69.82	89.82	108.68	117.94	55.96	68.60	112.32	125.08
32.5	0.67	62.01	70.15	90.14	109.01	118.30	56.34	68.94	112.66	125.46
32.5	1.00	62.29	70.41	90.38	109.27	118.57	56.63	69.20	112.92	125.76
32.5	2	63.08	71.16	91.08	110.01	119.37	57.46	69.95	113.68	126.63
32.5	3	63.83	71.87	91.76	110.74	120.16	58.26	70.67	114.43	127.48
32.5	4	64.57	72.57	92.42	111.45	120.93	59.04	71.37	115.16	128.32
32.5	5	65.29	73.25	93.08	112.15	121.69	59.80	72.06	115.80	129.16

	Sun's Azimuths						Moon's Azimuths			
							Major Standstill		Minor Standstill	Major Standstill
Latitude Degrees	Apparent Altitude	June 22	May 7 August 6	March 23 Sept 21	Nov 6 Feb 6	Dec 22	+(ε+i)	+(ε-i)	-(ε-i)	-(ε+i)
35	-0.33	60.15	68.65	89.30	108.71	118.26	54.23	67.43	112.50	125.69
35	0.00	60.48	68.96	89.59	109.02	118.59	54.59	67.74	112.82	126.05
35	0.33	60.72	69.18	89.80	109.24	118.83	54.84	67.97	113.05	126.31
35	0.67	61.12	69.55	90.15	109.61	119.22	55.26	68.34	113.42	126.74
35	1.00	61.42	69.84	90.42	109.89	119.53	55.59	68.63	113.71	127.08
35	2	62.30	70.66	91.19	110.71	120.42	56.52	69.45	114.56	128.05
35	3	63.13	71.44	91.93	111.51	121.29	57.41	70.24	115.38	129.00
35	4	63.95	72.21	92.66	112.30	122.15	58.27	71.02	116.19	129.94
35	5	64.75	72.97	93.38	113.08	123.00	59.11	71.78	116.99	130.89

	Sun's Azimuths						Moon's Azimuths			
							Major Standstill		Minor Standstill	Major Standstill
Latitude Degrees	Apparent Altitude	June 22	May 7 August 6	March 23 Sept 21	Nov 6 Feb 6	Dec 22	+(ε+i)	+(ε-i)	-(ε-i)	-(ε+i)
37.5	-0.33	59.02	67.87	89.24	109.30	119.21	52.87	66.65	113.28	127.04
37.5	0.00	59.39	68.21	89.56	109.64	119.58	53.27	66.99	113.62	127.44
37.5	0.33	59.66	68.46	89.79	109.88	119.85	53.56	67.24	113.88	127.73
37.5	0.67	60.10	68.87	90.16	110.28	120.28	54.03	67.65	114.29	128.21
37.5	1.00	60.43	69.18	90.46	110.59	120.62	54.39	67.97	114.61	128.58
37.5	2	61.40	70.08	91.30	111.50	121.61	55.42	68.88	115.54	129.67
37.5	3	62.32	70.95	92.12	112.38	122.57	56.40	69.75	116.45	130.74
37.5	4	63.22	71.79	92.92	113.25	123.53	57.36	70.60	117.35	131.80
37.5	5	64.10	72.62	93.71	114.11	124.48	58.29	71.43	118.24	132.87

		Sun's Azimuths						Moon's Azimuths			
Latitude	Apparent		May 7	March 23	Nov 6		Major Standstill	Minor Standstill			Major Standstill
Degrees	Altitude	June 22	August 6	Sept 21	Feb 6	Dec 22	+(ε+i)	+(ε-i)	-(ε-i)	-(ε+i)
40	-0.33	57.73	66.99	89.16	109.97	120.31	51.31	65.76	114.15	128.59
40	0.00	58.14	67.36	89.51	110.34	120.72	51.75	66.14	114.54	129.04
40	0.33	58.44	67.64	89.77	110.61	121.01	52.07	66.42	114.82	129.37
40	0.67	58.92	68.08	90.18	111.05	121.49	52.59	66.87	115.27	129.91
40	1.00	59.30	68.43	90.50	111.39	121.87	52.99	67.21	115.63	130.32
40	2	60.37	69.42	91.42	112.39	122.96	54.14	68.21	116.65	131.55
40	3	61.39	70.37	92.32	113.36	124.03	55.24	69.17	117.66	132.75
40	4	62.38	71.29	93.19	114.31	125.10	56.29	70.10	118.65	133.95
40	5	63.35	72.20	94.06	115.26	126.16	57.32	71.02	119.63	135.16

		Sun's Azimuths						Moon's Azimuths			
Latitude	Apparent		May 7	March 23	Nov 6		Major Standstill	Minor Standstill			Major Standstill
Degrees	Altitude	June 22	August 6	Sept 21	Feb 6	Dec 22	+(ε+i)	+(ε-i)	-(ε-i)	-(ε+i)
42.5	-0.33	56.26	65.98	89.09	110.73	121.58	49.49	64.75	115.16	130.40
42.5	0.00	56.71	66.40	89.47	111.14	122.02	49.99	65.17	115.58	130.90
42.5	0.33	57.04	66.70	89.74	111.44	122.35	50.35	65.47	115.89	131.27
42.5	0.67	57.58	67.19	90.20	111.92	122.89	50.93	65.97	116.39	131.87
42.5	1.00	57.99	67.57	90.54	112.30	123.30	51.38	66.35	116.78	132.34
42.5	2	59.17	68.66	91.55	113.39	124.52	52.66	67.44	117.92	133.72
42.5	3	60.30	69.70	92.53	114.46	125.71	53.87	68.49	119.02	135.08
42.5	4	61.40	70.71	93.48	115.51	126.89	55.05	69.52	120.12	136.45
42.5	5	62.46	71.71	94.43	116.56	128.08	56.19	70.52	121.21	137.84

		Sun's Azimuths						Moon's Azimuths			
Latitude	Apparent		May 7	March 23	Nov 6		Major Standstill	Minor Standstill			Major Standstill
Degrees	Altitude	June 22	August 6	Sept 21	Feb 6	Dec 22	+(ε+i)	+(ε-i)	-(ε-i)	-(ε+i)
45	-0.33	54.55	64.84	89.00	111.61	123.04	47.36	63.59	116.31	132.51
45	0.00	55.06	65.30	89.42	112.06	123.54	47.93	64.05	116.78	133.08
45	0.33	55.43	65.63	89.72	112.39	123.90	48.33	64.38	117.11	133.49
45	0.67	56.02	66.17	90.21	112.92	124.49	48.99	64.93	117.67	134.17
45	1.00	56.48	66.59	90.59	113.33	124.95	49.49	65.35	118.10	134.71
45	2	57.79	67.78	91.70	114.54	126.31	50.92	66.55	119.35	136.28
45	3	59.04	68.93	92.76	115.71	127.64	52.28	67.71	120.58	137.84
45	4	60.25	70.04	93.80	116.88	128.97	53.58	68.83	121.80	139.41
45	5	61.43	71.13	94.84	118.04	130.31	54.85	69.92	123.01	141.02

		Sun's Azimuths						Moon's Azimuths			
Latitude	Apparent		May 7	March 23	Nov 6		Major Standstill	Minor Standstill			Major Standstill
Degrees	Altitude	June 22	August 6	Sept 21	Feb 6	Dec 22	+(ε+i)	+(ε-i)	-(ε-i)	-(ε+i)
47.5	-0.33	52.57	63.53	88.91	112.63	124.74	44.85	62.25	117.64	135.01
47.5	0.00	53.14	64.04	89.37	113.12	125.29	45.49	62.76	118.15	135.66
47.5	0.33	53.55	64.40	89.69	113.48	125.70	45.95	63.13	118.52	136.13
47.5	0.67	54.21	65.00	90.23	114.07	126.36	46.69	63.73	119.14	136.91
47.5	1.00	54.72	65.45	90.65	114.52	126.88	47.26	64.19	119.61	137.52
47.5	2	56.18	66.77	91.85	115.85	128.40	48.87	65.52	121.01	139.33
47.5	3	57.57	68.02	93.01	117.15	129.89	50.40	66.79	122.37	141.14
47.5	4	58.91	69.25	94.15	118.43	131.39	51.85	68.02	123.72	142.99
47.5	5	60.21	70.44	95.28	119.72	132.91	53.27	69.22	125.08	144.89

		Sun's Azimuths					Moon's Azimuths			
							Major Standstill	Minor Standstill		Major Standstill
Latitude	Apparent		May 7	March 23	Nov 6					
Degrees	Altitude	June 22	August 6	Sept 21	Feb 6	Dec 22	+(ε+i)	+(ε-i)	-(ε-i)	-(ε+i)
50	-0.33	50.24	62.01	88.81	113.80	126.74	41.82	60.70	119.18	138.01
50	0.00	50.88	62.57	89.31	114.35	127.36	42.56	61.26	119.75	138.76
50	0.33	51.34	62.98	89.67	114.74	127.81	43.09	61.67	120.16	139.30
50	0.67	52.09	63.63	90.25	115.39	128.56	43.94	62.34	120.84	140.21
50	1.00	52.66	64.14	90.71	115.89	129.14	44.59	62.85	121.37	140.93
50	2	54.30	65.59	92.02	117.36	130.85	46.43	64.31	122.92	143.06
50	3	55.84	66.97	93.29	118.80	132.55	48.15	65.71	124.44	145.22
50	4	57.33	68.32	94.53	120.22	134.26	49.80	67.06	125.96	147.46
50	5	58.77	69.63	95.77	121.65	136.00	51.38	68.39	127.49	149.81

		Sun's Azimuths					Moon's Azimuths			
							Major Standstill	Minor Standstill		Major Standstill
Latitude	Apparent		May 7	March 23	Nov 6					
Degrees	Altitude	June 22	August 6	Sept 21	Feb 6	Dec 22	+(ε+i)	+(ε-i)	-(ε-i)	-(ε+i)
60	-0.33	34.34	52.64	88.27	121.02	139.95	16.63	50.99	128.80	162.82
60	0.00	35.60	53.55	89.00	121.87	141.08	18.99	51.92	129.73	165.46
60	0.33	36.48	54.19	89.52	122.48	141.92	20.53	52.57	130.41	167.69
60	0.67	37.89	55.24	90.37	123.50	143.33	22.84	53.64	131.54	172.72
60	1.00	38.95	56.03	91.03	124.29	144.44	24.48	54.46	132.43	—
60	2	41.90	58.31	92.94	126.64	147.87	28.74	56.77	135.07	—
60	3	44.59	60.45	94.78	128.97	151.52	32.36	58.94	137.74	—
60	4	47.10	62.50	96.60	131.33	155.57	35.59	61.02	140.49	—
60	5	49.49	64.49	98.39	133.75	160.32	38.54	63.04	143.38	—

		Sun's Azimuths					Moon's Azimuths			
							Major Standstill	Minor Standstill		Major Standstill
Latitude	Apparent		May 7	March 23	Nov 6					
Degrees	Altitude	June 22	August 6	Sept 21	Feb 6	Dec 22	+(ε+i)	+(ε-i)	-(ε-i)	-(ε+i)
-10	-0.33	66.37	73.16	90.18	106.26	114.02	60.95	71.42	108.60	119.07
-10	0.00	66.29	73.08	90.10	106.19	113.94	60.86	71.34	108.52	118.99
-10	0.33	66.23	73.03	90.05	106.13	113.88	60.80	71.28	108.47	118.93
-10	0.67	66.13	72.94	89.96	106.04	113.78	60.70	71.19	108.38	118.83
-10	1.00	66.06	72.87	89.90	105.97	113.71	60.63	71.12	108.31	118.75
-10	2	65.85	72.66	89.70	105.77	113.50	60.40	70.91	108.10	118.53
-10	3	65.64	72.47	89.51	105.57	113.29	60.19	70.72	107.90	118.32
-10	4	65.44	72.27	89.33	105.38	113.09	59.98	70.52	107.71	118.11
-10	5	65.24	72.08	89.15	105.19	112.90	59.77	70.33	107.52	117.90

		Sun's Azimuths					Moon's Azimuths			
							Major Standstill	Minor Standstill		Major Standstill
Latitude	Apparent		May 7	March 23	Nov 6					
Degrees	Altitude	June 22	August 6	Sept 21	Feb 6	Dec 22	+(ε+i)	+(ε-i)	-(ε-i)	-(ε+i)
-20	-0.33	65.36	72.51	90.36	107.25	115.45	59.42	70.50	109.54	120.62
-20	0.00	65.19	72.35	90.21	107.09	115.28	59.24	70.34	109.38	120.45
-20	0.33	65.07	72.24	90.10	106.98	115.16	59.11	70.22	109.26	120.32
-20	0.67	64.87	72.05	89.92	106.79	114.96	58.90	70.03	109.07	120.11
-20	1.00	64.72	71.91	89.78	106.65	114.81	58.74	69.88	108.93	119.95
-20	2	64.27	71.48	89.38	106.23	114.37	58.27	69.46	108.50	119.49
-20	3	63.84	71.07	89.00	105.83	113.94	57.82	69.04	108.10	119.05
-20	4	63.42	70.67	88.62	105.43	113.53	57.37	68.64	107.70	118.62
-20	5	63.00	70.28	88.24	105.05	113.12	56.92	68.23	107.31	118.19

| | Sun's Azimuths | | | | | | Moon's Azimuths | | | |
Latitude Degrees	Apparent Altitude	June 22	May 7 August 6	March 23 Sept 21	Nov 6 Feb 6	Dec 22	Major Standstill +(ε+i)	Minor Standstill +(ε-i)	-(ε-i)	Major Standstill -(ε+i)
-30	-0.33	63.30	71.16	90.58	108.97	117.99	56.50	68.77	111.29	123.56
-30	0.00	63.03	70.91	90.33	108.71	117.72	56.21	68.51	111.03	123.28
-30	0.33	62.84	70.73	90.16	108.53	117.53	56.00	68.33	110.84	123.07
-30	0.67	62.52	70.42	89.88	108.23	117.21	55.66	68.02	110.54	122.73
-30	1.00	62.27	70.19	89.66	108.00	116.96	55.39	67.78	110.31	122.47
-30	2	61.55	69.51	89.02	107.33	116.25	54.62	67.09	109.63	121.72
-30	3	60.85	68.86	88.41	106.69	115.57	53.86	66.43	108.98	121.00
-30	4	60.16	68.21	87.81	106.06	114.90	53.11	65.77	108.34	120.30
-30	5	59.47	67.57	87.21	105.44	114.25	52.37	65.12	107.72	119.62

| | Sun's Azimuths | | | | | | Moon's Azimuths | | | |
Latitude Degrees	Apparent Altitude	June 22	May 7 August 6	March 23 Sept 21	Nov 6 Feb 6	Dec 22	Major Standstill +(ε+i)	Minor Standstill +(ε-i)	-(ε-i)	Major Standstill -(ε+i)
-40	-0.33	59.69	68.79	90.84	111.76	122.27	51.41	65.85	114.24	128.69
-40	0.00	59.28	68.42	90.49	111.38	121.86	50.96	65.46	113.86	128.25
-40	0.33	58.99	68.14	90.24	111.11	121.56	50.63	65.18	113.58	127.93
-40	0.67	58.51	67.70	89.82	110.67	121.08	50.09	64.73	113.13	127.41
-40	1.00	58.13	67.35	89.50	110.33	120.70	49.68	64.37	112.79	127.01
-40	2	57.04	66.35	88.58	109.34	119.64	48.45	63.35	111.79	125.86
-40	3	55.97	65.37	87.68	108.40	118.61	47.25	62.34	110.83	124.76
-40	4	54.90	64.40	86.81	107.48	117.62	46.05	61.35	109.90	123.71
-40	5	53.84	63.44	85.94	106.58	116.65	44.84	60.37	108.98	122.68

| | Sun's Azimuths | | | | | | Moon's Azimuths | | | |
Latitude Degrees	Apparent Altitude	June 22	May 7 August 6	March 23 Sept 21	Nov 6 Feb 6	Dec 22	Major Standstill +(ε+i)	Minor Standstill +(ε-i)	-(ε-i)	Major Standstill -(ε+i)
-50	-0.33	53.26	64.67	91.19	116.43	129.76	41.99	60.82	119.30	138.18
-50	0.00	52.64	64.12	90.69	115.87	129.12	41.24	60.25	118.74	137.44
-50	0.33	52.19	63.72	90.33	115.48	128.66	40.70	59.84	118.33	136.91
-50	0.67	51.44	63.07	89.75	114.83	127.91	39.79	59.16	117.66	136.06
-50	1.00	50.86	62.56	89.29	114.33	127.34	39.07	58.63	117.15	135.41
-50	2	49.15	61.07	87.98	112.90	125.71	36.94	57.08	115.69	133.57
-50	3	47.45	59.61	86.71	111.53	124.16	34.78	55.56	114.29	131.85
-50	4	45.74	58.10	85.47	110.20	122.67	32.54	54.04	112.94	130.20
-50	5	44.00	56.70	84.24	108.90	121.2	30.19	52.51	111.61	128.62

| | Sun's Azimuths | | | | | | Moon's Azimuths | | | |
Latitude Degrees	Apparent Altitude	June 22	May 7 August 6	March 23 Sept 21	Nov 6 Feb 6	Dec 22	Major Standstill +(ε+i)	Minor Standstill +(ε-i)	-(ε-i)	Major Standstill -(ε+i)
-60	-0.33	40.05	56.87	91.73	125.14	145.66	17.18	51.20	129.01	163.37
-60	0.00	38.92	56.01	91.00	124.27	144.40	14.54	50.27	128.08	161.01
-60	0.33	38.08	55.38	90.49	123.64	143.52	12.31	49.59	127.43	159.47
-60	0.67	36.67	54.33	89.63	122.62	142.11	7.28	48.46	126.36	157.16
-60	1.00	35.56	53.52	88.97	121.84	141.05	—	47.57	125.54	155.52
-60	2	32.13	51.11	87.06	119.62	138.11	—	44.93	123.23	151.26
-60	3	28.48	48.70	85.22	117.52	135.41	—	42.26	121.06	147.64
-60	4	24.43	46.25	83.40	115.51	132.90	—	39.51	118.98	144.41
-60	5	19.68	43.73	81.61	113.55	130.51	—	36.62	116.96	141.46

Glossary

In addition to definitions I drafted for specific use in this book, some of the following list of definitions are from these references:

- *The Concise Oxford Dictionary* (Oxford University Press, New York, 1999).
- *Webster's New World Dictionary of the American Language* (The World Publishing Company, Cleveland and New York, 1966).
- *Megalithic Sites in Britain* (Oxford University Press, London, 1967) by A. Thom.
- *Sun, Moon, and Standing Stones* (Oxford University Press, Oxford, 1978) by John Edwin Wood.
- *Laws of Form* (The Julian Press, New York, 1972) by G. Spencer Brown.
- *Is Enlightenment Possible?* (Snow Lion Publications, Ithaca, 1993) by Roger R. Jackson.

alignment—Stones, avenues, passages, mounds, etc., arranged in a straight line, usually to mark a ley line or astronomical alignment.

altitude—The *apparent altitude* of the sun, moon, or a terrestrial object, like a distant horizon, is the observed angle of elevation to the sun, moon, or object as measured from the horizontal (sea level or ground level). True altitude, or *corrected altitude,* is equal to the apparent altitude minus *refraction* minus the earth's curvature correction plus the *parallax* (that is, apparent altitude − refraction − earth's curvature + parallax = corrected altitude).

analemma—A chart that shows both the sun's *declination* (the angle of the sun relative to the celestial equator, or the path of the sun on the equinox at noon) and the equation of time. The equation of time is the daily difference between apparent "sun" time and clock time. There is a difference because the earth's orbit around the sun is an ellipse, which causes the speed of the earth around the sun to vary slightly depending on its position on this ellipse.

angel—A spiritual being or a guiding spirit. From the Greek word *angelos,* meaning messenger.

archetype—The original pattern or model from which all other things of the same type are made (*arche*, first + *typos*, mark of the blow). It is a prototype or source image of a symbolic form or principle that exists within the *collective unconscious*.

astronomy—The science of stars and other heavenly bodies, dealing with their positions, motions, size, and compositions.

azimuth—The measure of the horizontal angle from true north clockwise to the sun or moon's position.

bless—To make a person, object, or place holy and consecrated by a religious rite or by the spiritual projection of love, gratitude, light, or happiness.

cairn—Simple stone piles, historically used as tombs or coffins. Also, highly sophisticated megalithic observatories built with alternating layers of organic (turves) and inorganic material (small stones).

Candlemas—A calendar holiday that marks the first day of spring, the rebirth of nature, and the return of the Goddess from the Underworld.

chamber—An enclosed space formed by earth and stone.

collective unconscious—The part of the unconscious mind that serves as a common psychic foundation, present in everyone. It is a reservoir of commonly held associations of images and psychological states.

cosmology—The study and creation of theories concerning the nature of this holistic, ordered universe.

cubit—An ancient measure of length, specifically, the distance from the elbow to the tip of the middle finger.

cursus—A long, narrow passageway enclosed by two inner mounded banks and two outer ditches.

decad—The symbolic number of completion (ten). It contains all things in itself and marks a return to unity as well as the potential for rebirth.

declination—The angular distance of the sun or moon, north or south of the celestial equator.

degree—A unit of measurement equivalent to one ninetieth of a right angle.

deva—Nonphysical spiritual beings (from Sanskrit, *shining one*) of subtle energy and consciousness. Devas are nature's engineers, the creative intelligence and form-builders behind the entire universe.

dharma—The spiritual and religious teachings that guide us toward *enlightenment,* the purpose of human existence.

digit—An ancient measure of length, specifically, the width of the "pointer" finger.

distinction—Perfect continence. Once a distinction is made, the spaces, states, or contents on each side of the boundary can be indicated.

dolmen—Stone structures with a cap stone (*dol,* table + *men,* stone). Typically, a large flat stone supported by three or more standing stones.

dowsing—An intuitional technique for detecting earth energies and facilitating various spiritual practices (like *deva* communication) using a dowsing instrument such as a dowsing-rod.

dowsing rod—A Y-shaped forked stick or rod used as a tool to find *water lines* and *ley lines.*

dual—The symbolic number of plurality and *polarity* (two).

duality—The state or quality of being *dual*. The theory that the world is ultimately composed of, or explicable in terms of, two basic entities: *yin* and *yang*.

earth energies—The electromagnetic fields caused primarily by underground flowing water and ley lines that have the power to alter human consciousness. Analogous to the human body's acupuncture meridians.

earth figure—Piles of earth and turf arranged to form various shapes and figures.

earth foot—The original Roman and Greek measure for the foot was a little over one-eighth inch larger than the foot we work with today. One hundred Greek feet equaled one second of the earth's circumference (in other words, the earth's circumference divided by 1,296,000).

earth pyramid—Square or rectangular mounds of earth with flat slanted sides and a flat top area.

ecliptic—A great circle on the celestial sphere representing the sun's apparent path around the earth during the year. The angle (or obliquity) of the ecliptic is the angle between the plane of the earth's orbit and the celestial equator.

enlightenment—The ultimate purpose of human incarnation, enlightenment is the direct understanding of the true nature of reality. Enlightenment can also be described a transcendent state far beyond anything most humans believe possible or can conceive of.

ennead—The symbolic number that signals the vanguard of completion (nine).

entities—Nonphysical forms of consciousness. The two primary types of entities associated with earth energies are discarnate humans and nonhuman entities such as demons and evil spirits. Not to be confused with the spiritual hierarchy.

equinox—The fall and spring calendar holidays which occur when the sun crosses the celestial equator and day and night are equal.

feng shui—In Chinese, feng shui means "wind and water." A system of laws that govern spatial relationships and orientation in relation to the flow of energy. The basic aim of feng shui is to design a residence or a space of any kind so that it is in harmony with the earth spirit.

Findhorn—A community founded in 1962 by Eileen Caddy, Peter Caddy, and Dorothy Maclean in a caravan park near the seaside village of Findhorn in North Scotland (see www.findhorn.org). At first, Findhorn was a key force in publicizing the message of the *devas*. Today, they are "an international community and developing eco-village of about 350 people."

geomancy—Literally "earth divination." The techniques for creating places of power by consciously changing, altering, and building upon the earth's surface in order to evoke and encourage spiritual experiences.

geometry—The science of space and specifically, the branch of mathematics concerned with the properties and relations of points, lines, surfaces, and solids.

geopathic survey—A geopathic (*geo,* earth + *pathic,* disease) survey purges your home or space of the detrimental effects of negative earth energies and human and nonhuman entities.

Golden Section—The division of a line such that the ratio of the measure of the whole to the greater part is equal to the ratio of the greater part to the smaller part (see page 176), a proportion that is considered to be particularly pleasing to the eye.

henge—A ring of piled earth enclosing a circular sanctuary.

heptad—The symbolic number of perfect order (seven), it represents a complete period or cycle.

hexad—The symbolic number of the number of equilibrium, balance, and wholeness (six).

horizontal coordinate system—A mathematical system used to define the location of the sun, moon, or any other celestial object by the measure of two variables: *azimuth* and *altitude.*

human entity—A human spirit (ghost) who has died, left their body, but has not crossed over to the "other side" or been reborn, and is trapped in our world. Human entities can see and hear and but generally cannot be seen or heard by humans.

inshoot—The point where ley lines enter the earth. The center point of a ley-line *power center.*

invocation—The combination of the use of prayer, meditation, and will to appeal for help, intervention, or proper guidance.

karma—The sum of a person's actions in this and past lives that affect future lives. The law of karma states that for every action (physical, mental, or spiritual) you make, you receive a reaction. Virtuous actions bring future good events in your life, while nonvirtuous actions bring bad events.

labyrinth—A pattern on the ground made of stones, plants, walls, rope, or other materials that has a single path to a central point. The labyrinth is a symbol of inner wholeness.

Lammas—A calendar holiday that marks the early harvest and is celebrated by the "first fruits" ceremony on the full or waning moon.

Landscape Angel—The spiritual being responsible for a particular place or city.

ley line—A six-to eight-foot wide field of energizing energy that travels in straight lines, as seen from a "birds-eye" view.

limiting positions—More precisely, *limiting declinations.* The point on the horizon where the sun's risings or settings during the course of a year stop and reverse course. The moon has two limiting positions: the major and minor standstills.

long barrow—Extended mound or bank of earth that has one dimension significantly longer than the other.

L-rod—A dowsing tool that consists of a piece of metal rod bent into a right angle. L-rods are held in both hands with the long ends positioned to point straight ahead.

magus—A wizard or wise person who understands and practices the secrets of sacred space.

major standstill—A significant lunar event that occurs every 18.61 years. At the time of a major standstill, the moon sets very high on the northern horizon and very low on the southern horizon.

mantra—A special spiritual sound (*man*, mind + *tra*, liberation), often a Sanskrit word or phrase with a sacred meaning.

map dowsing—An intuitional practice used to dowse a place "long distance" via a map.

Martinmas (Hallowmas)—A calendar holiday that marks the beginning of winter. A fire festival is held to ward off hardship in the coming months of cold and darkness. Also known as Hallowmas, Halloween, and Samhain.

May Day—A calendar holiday that marks the first day of summer and is the time for the planting of the crops. Also referred to as Beltane.

maze—A pattern on the ground made of stones, plants, walls, rope, or other materials that has multiple paths to a central point.

medicine wheel—Stone figures in circular, mandala, and sun-like shapes primarily found in the American Northwest and Southwest Canada.

meditation—A deep and continued contemplation on a sacred word, image, deity, concept, or truth.

meridian—In astronomy, the invisible line drawn from the North to South Poles. In acupuncture, a pathway in the body along which vital energy flows.

metrology—The scientific study of measurement.

minor standstill—A significant lunar event that occurs every 18.61 years. At the time of a minor standstill, the moon has its smallest range of limiting declinations, specifically (+/-)18.3 degrees versus (+/-)28.58 degrees at the *major standstill.*

monad—The symbolic number of wholeness (one), the first discreet quantity which is self-generating (1 x 1 = 1) and includes all numbers.

monument—A large-scale sculpture of enduring value or significance, artistically and scientifically woven into the fabric of the earth.

mound—A raised mass of earth, which naturally assumes a small hill-shape.

mudra—A symbolic hand gesture used in certain spiritual practices.

negative water line—A polluted underground water stream that is detrimental to health.

nonhuman entity—A nonphysical being characterized by evil and darkness, the "dark" side of the *spiritual hierarchy*.

ocdoad—The symbolic number of perfected spirit on earth (eight).

outshoot—The place where *ley lines* leave the earth.

paired opposites—The technique of putting opposite images side by side to create a balanced wholeness in order to facilitate transcendental experiences.

paired similars—The technique of putting similar images side by side to call attention to the importance of an image or design element.

parallax—The difference between the apparent position and true position of the a celestial object. Because the earth is a large body relative to it distance from the moon, a correction must be made to account for the difference between observing the moon on the earth's surface versus from the earth's center (the point of observation assumed in astronomical formulas).

Pascal's Triangle—A triangular array of numbers. The triangle begins with 1 at the apex. The numbers at the ends of the rows are 1 and each of the other numbers in the row is the sum of the nearest two numbers in the row above.

passage tomb—A mound with an underground passageway leading into it.

pendulum—A dowsing tool that consists of a weighted object hanging from a string or bead chain.

pentad—The symbolic number of harvesting, completion, and marriage, as well as a representation of the most perfect manifestation or embodiment of any quality or thing (five).

polarity—The property of having poles, i.e., positive and negative ends or sides.

power center—A place where a *ley line* enters (or leaves) the earth and there is also an underground water spring. The presence of the ley and water energy creates a special electromagnetic field that not only alters consciousness, but retains strong emotions experienced at the site.

prayer—A solemn request for help, question, conversation, or expression of thanks directed to a spiritual being.

pyramid—A monumental stone structure with a square base and sloping sides that meet at a point at top.

recumbent stone—A stone set on its side.

refraction—The bending of light rays by the atmosphere. Refraction makes sunrise earlier and sunset later than usual.

sacred space—A spiritual artwork in a consecrated place.

self-surrender—To accept *enlightenment* or Supreme Consciousness as the goal of life and to consciously and mindfully move toward that goal.

solstice—The solstices are two of the most important calendar holidays of the year. At Summer Solstice, the longest day of the year, the northern hemisphere of the earth is pointed directly at the sun. The Winter Solstice marks the shortest day of sunlight in the year (in the northern hemisphere).

spiritual hierarchy—A vast evolution of spiritual beings that act in harmony and for the benefit of our own "earthly" evolution.

squared circle—The most important geometric form for the designer of sacred space. The name for the squared circle comes from not only the circumscribing of the circle by the square, but also from the ability to geometrically construct a unique square and circle such that the square's perimeter is equal to the circle's circumference.

stade—An ancient measure of length derived from the length of a stadium or approximately six hundred feet.

standing stone—The simplest and most elementary megalithic monument consisting of a single stone embedded vertically in the ground.

stone avenue—A parallel row of stones, usually found as a way of approach or departure from a central monument.

stone circle—The most elegant of the megalithic monuments, the stone circle or cromlech (*krom,* curve + *lech*, a stone) consists of standing or recumbent stones arranged in a circle, ellipse, or egg-shape.

stone figure—Stones arranged to represent the outline or shape of a figure, symbol, or likeness.

stone line—Two or more stones are consciously aligned to a special location or celestial event.

Supreme Consciousness—God, the highest consciousness in whom all things lie.

symbol—An object that represents something abstract. A joining together of concepts or ideas in order to reveal inner realities and truths.

symbolism—The use of *symbols* to represent ideas or qualities.

sympathetic vibration—A coincidence of rhythms between symbolic art (sacred space) and the person viewing it, enabling an exchange of information or feeling.

synchronicity—An acausal connecting principle or, in more basic terms, a meaningful coincidence not related in terms of direct cause and effect.

syzygy—The technique of placing opposite forms next to each other in order to create a new synthesized whole.

telluric—Energy arising from the earth.

tetrad—The symbolic number of earth, all natural phenomena, and terrestrial order (four).

theodolite—A surveying instrument with a rotating telescope for measuring horizontal and vertical angles.

thought form—A cognitive event, emotion, visualization of form, a feeling, or a state of consciousness.

transcendental—The state of consciousness wherein one goes beyond a limited stated of mind by completely understanding a situation, concept, or truth.

triad—The symbolic number of stability and innate structural integrity (three).

trilithon—a pair of stones set close together supporting a third stone laid across the top, e.g. at Stonehenge.

turf maze—A maze or labyrinth formed by removing the top part of the ground to create a channel. Either the raised turf or the channel (trench) can become the path.

transit—A surveying instrument.

Void—A symbol for emptiness, Void is a state beyond the comprehension of the intellect and represents that which is unknown to us.

water line—An underground vein of flowing water makes people feel passive.

yang—A Chinese word meaning literally "banners waving in the sun" or "shone upon." An archetype for active, male, light, firm, positive. The fusion of the fundamental components of the universe, yang and yin, is the source of all matter, energy, and consciousness.

yin—An archetype for passive, female, darkness, yielding, negative (see also yang).

Bibliography

This bibliography is organized by topic, including the categories:

- Megalithic Monuments
- Contemporary Sacred Space, Earth Art, Feng Shui, and Landscaping
- Meditation and Other Spiritual Practices
- Devas, Angels, and the Sacred Landscape
- Dowsing
- Death, Entities, and Ghosts
- Sacred Geometry and Number
- Ceremony, Symbolism, Myth
- Astronomical Alignments
- Sacred Fiction
- Secrets of Sacred Space Selected Web Sites

Megalithic Monuments

Barnatt, John, *Stone Circles of the Peak—A Search for Natural Harmony*, Turnstone Books, London, 1978. Excellent book on the use of number, geometry, and symbolic alignments in stone circles of central England.

Bayley, Harold, *Archaic England: An Essay in Deciphering Prehistory from Megalithic Monuments, Earthworks, Customs, Coins, Place-names, and Faerie Superstitions*, J. B. Lippincott Co., Philadelphia, 1920.

Bergström, Theo, *Stonehenge*, Bergström + Boyle Books, London, 1974. Picture book.

Bord, Janet, *Mazes and Labyrinths of the World*, E. P. Dutton, New York, 1975. Filled with many illustrations of mazes and labyrinths.

Bord, Janet and Colin, *A Guide to Ancient Sites in Britain*, Latimer New Dimensions Ltd., London, 1978. Great guidebook with nice photos, descriptions, and maps.

———, *Mysterious Britain*, Doubleday & Company, Garden City, New York, 1973. Good overview picture book on sacred space in England.

———, *The Secret Country—An Interpretation of the Folklore of Ancient Sites in the British Isles*, Paul Elek, London, 1976. The Bords really know their way around ancient England!

Brandon, Jim, *Weird America: A Guide to Places of Mystery in the United States*, E. P. Dutton, New York, 1978. A state-by-state guide to mysterious places, including many sacred places.

Burl, Aubrey, *From Carnac to Callanish: The Prehistoric Stone Rows and Avenues of Britain, Ireland and Brittany*, Yale University Press, New Haven, 1993.

———, *A Guide to the Stone Circles of Britain*, Ireland and Brittany, Yale University Press, New Haven, 1995.

———, *Prehistoric Avebury*, Yale University Press, New Haven, 1979.

———, *The Stone Circles of the British Isles*, Yale University Press, New Haven, 1976. Excellent analysis of stone circles on a region-by-region basis.

———, *Rings of Stone: The Prehistoric Stone Circles of Britain and Ireland,* Tick-nor & Fields, New Haven, 1979. Photographs by Edward Piper. Archaeological overview of British stone circles, including descriptions and beautiful photographs of fifty selected sites.

Castleden, Rodney, *The Making of Stonehenge*, Routledge, London and New York, 1993. Excellent book, with great detail on monument building techniques.

Chippindale, Christopher, *Stonehenge Complete*, Thames and Hudson, Inc., New York, 1994.

Cook, Warren L., *Ancient Vermont*, Academy Books, Rutland, Vermont, 1978. Proceedings of the Castleton Conference on Ancient Vermont. Excellent cross-section of opinions of the nature and origins of Vermont's stone structures.

Dames, Michael, *The Avebury Cycle*, Thames and Hudson, London, 1977. Wonderful exposition on monument/symbol/ritual connections. Recommended.

———, *The Silbury Treasure: The Great Goddess Rediscovered*, Thames and Hudson, London, 1976. Careful and detailed portrait of Silbury Hill as symbolic expression of the pregnant Earth Goddess.

Daniel, Glyn, *Megaliths in History*, Thames & Hudson, London, 1972. How megalithic design has persisted up to the present. Small, nice book.

Dibner, Bern, *Moving the Obelisks*, MIT Press, Cambridge, Mass., 1970. Interesting account of methods used to move and raise obelisks.

Dyer, James, *Southern England: An Archaeological Guide to the Prehistoric and Roman Remains*, Faber & Faber Ltd., London, 1973.

Eddy, John A., "Mysteries of the Medicine Wheels," *National Geographic Magazine*, January, 1977.

Edgerton, Harold E. & Brian Hope-Taylor, "Stonehenge—New Light on an Old Riddle," *National Geographic Magazine*, June, 1960.

Eogan, George, *Knowth and the Passage-Tombs of Ireland*, Thames and Hudson, London, 1986.

Feldman, Mark, *The Mystery Hill Story*, Mystery Hill Press, North Salem, New Hampshire, 1977. Overview of important historical highlights of the Mystery Hill site.

Fell, Barry, *America B.C.: Ancient Settlers in the New World*, Demeter Press, New York, 1976. "Controversial" account of Celtic discovery and colonization of America.

Fergusson, James, *Rude Stone Monuments*, John Murray, London, 1872. Many wonderful illustrations, a number of which were used in this book.

Forde-Johnston, J., *Prehistoric Britain and Ireland*, W. W. Norton, New York, 1976. Introduction to prehistory with emphasis on structures.

Foster, J. W., *Prehistoric Races of the United States of America*, S. C. Griggs, Chicago, 1873. Archaeological overview focussing on mound builders.

Fowke, Gerald, *Antiquities of Central and Southeastern Missouri*, Government Printing Office, Washington, D.C., 1910.

———, *Archaeological History of Ohio*, Ohio State Archaeological and Historical Society, Columbus, Ohio, 1902.

Giot, Pierre-Roland, *The Carnac Alignments*, Éditions Ouest-France, Rennes, France, 1993.

———, *La Bretagne des Mégalithes*, Éditions Ouest-France, Rennes, France, 1995.

———, *Prehistory in Brittany: Menhirs and Dolmens*, Éditions D'Art, 1995.

Glob, P. V., *The Mound People: Danish Bronze-Age Man Preserved*, Cornell University Press, Ithaca, New York, 1970.

Goodwin, William B., *The Ruins of Great Ireland in New England*, Meador Publishing, Boston, 1946. Many photos and drawings of New England stone ruins.

Grinsell, Leslie V., *Barrow, Pyramid and Tomb: Ancient Burial Customs in Egypt, the Mediterranean and the British Isles*, Thames and Hudson, London, 1975.

Habachi, Labib, *The Obelisks of Egypt—Skyscrapers of the Past*, Charles Scribner's Sons, New York, 1977. Historical account of Egyptian obelisks.

Hadingham, Evan, *Circles and Standing Stones: An Illustrated Explanation of the Megalithic Mysteries of Early Britain*, Walker and Co., New York, 1975. Good overview book.

Hancock, Graham, *Fingerprints of the Gods: A Quest for the Beginning and the End,* Mandarin, London, 1996.

Herity, Michael and George Eogan, *Ireland in Prehistory*, Routledge & Kegan Paul, London, 1977.

Her Majesty's Stationery Office, *An Illustrated Guide to the Ancient Monuments of Southern England*, London, 1973.

Heyderdahl, Thor, *Aku-Aku*, Pocket Books, New York, 1973. Good reading about Easter Island.

———, *American Indians in the Pacific—The Theory Behind the Kon-Tiki Expedition*, George Allen & Unwin Ltd., London, 1952. Interesting chapter on "Stone Human Statues and Megalithic Cult-Sites."

Ivimy, John, *The Sphinx & the Megaliths*, Harper and Row, New York, 1975. Believes Egyptians came to England and built megalithic monuments to learn astronomy.

Judd, Neil Merton, "Pyramids of the New World," *National Geographic*, Washington, D.C., January, 1948. Good article with photos.

LaFay, Howard and Thomas J. Abercrombie, "Easter Island and Its Mysterious Monuments," *National Geographic*, Washington, D.C., January, 1962.

Lemesurier, Peter, *The Great Pyramid Decoded*, St. Martin's Press, New York, 1977. Meticulous symbolic decoding of the Great Pyramid.

Le Scouëzec, Gwenc'hlan, *Bretagne Mégalithique*, Seuil, Paris, 1987. Big photos of megalithic monuments in Brittany. In French.

Longworth, I. H., *Prehistoric Britain*, British Museum Press, 1991.

Macaulay, David, *Pyramid*, Houghton Mifflin, Boston, 1975. Picture book on the construction of the pyramids.

MacLean, J. P., *The Mound Builders*, Robert Clarke, Cincinnati, 1885. General overview of mound culture.

Matthews, W. H., *Mazes and Labyrinths*, Dover Publications, New York, 1970. Reprint of 1922 edition. Recognized as authoritative book. Good chapter on maze and labyrinth design considerations.

Mendelssohn, Kurt, *The Riddle of the Pyramids*, Praeger Publishers, New York, 1974. Factual book on pyramid design.

Michell, John, *Megalithomania: Artists, Antiquarians, Archaeologists and the Old Stone Monuments*, Cornell University Press, Ithaca, New York, 1982.

———, *The Old Stones of Land's End*, Garnstone Press, London, 1974. Excellent book. Photos and alignments of Land's End stones and crosses plus excellent essay on megalithic science.

———, *Sacred England: A Guide to the Legends, Lore and Landscape of England's Sacred Places*, Cosmic Image Publications, Glastonbury, Somerset, England, 1996.

———, *The View Over Atlantis*, Garnstone Press, London, 1975. Excellent introduction. Recommended.

Moorehead, Warren K., *The Cahokia Mounds*, University of Illinois, 1929. Good scholastic overview with comprehensive bibliography on the Cahokia Mounds.

Morgan, Richard G., *Fort Ancient*, The Ohio Historical Society, Columbus, Ohio, 1965. Guide to the Fort Ancient earthworks.

Morrison, Tony, *Pathways to the Gods—The Mystery of the Andes Lines*, Harper & Row, New York, 1978. Book on Andes lines as pathways to shrines.

Paturi, Felix R., *Prehistoric Heritage,* translated by Tania and Bernard Alexander, Charles Scribner's Sons, New York, 1979. Overview of prehistoric European graphic art.

Peet, Stephen D., *Prehistoric America—Myths and Symbols or Aboriginal Religions in America*, Office of the American Antiquarian, Chicago, 1905.

Petrie, Sir Flinders, *The Hill Figures of England*, Royal Anthropological Institute of Great Britain and Ireland, London, 1925.

Phillips, Ford and Griffin, *Archaeological Survey in the Lower Mississippi Alluvial Valley, 1940-47*, Peabody Museum, Harvard, Cambridge, 1951. Detailed survey information.

Picker, Fred, *Rapa Nui: Easter Island*, Paddington Press, New York, 1974. Very nice photos and text on Easter Island.

Pidgeon, William, *Traditions of De-Coo-Dah and Antiquarian Researches*, Thayer, Bridgman and Fanning, New York, 1853. Wonderful commentaries on ancient mounds by an Indian medicine man.

Powell, J. W., *Twelfth Annual Report of the Bureau of Ethnology to the Secretary of the Smithsonian Institution 1890-91*, Government Printing Office, Washington, 1894. Seven hundred and forty-two pages on U.S. mounds. Excellent.

Priest, Josiah, *American Antiquities*, Hoffman and White, Albany, N.Y., 1833.

Purce, Jill, *The Mystic Spiral: Journey of the Soul*, Avon, 1974.

Putigny, Bob, *Easter Island*, Two Continents Publishing Group, New York, 1976. Good book on Easter Island. Lots of color photos.

Ranney, Edward, *Stonework of the Maya*, University of New Mexico Press, Albuquerque, 1974. Gorgeous photos!

Rothovius, Andrew, "The Adams Family and the Grail Tradition: The Untold Chronicle of the Dragon Persecution," *East West Journal*, November, 1977. Interesting article on the influence of megalithic tradition on the first English settlements in the New World.

———, "The Dragon Tradition in the New World, Part 2," *East West Journal*, August, 1977.

———, "Mystery Hill: An American Stonehenge," *East West Journal*, October, 1976.

———, "The New Thing at Mystery Hill is 4000 Years Old," *Yankee*, September, 1975.

Service, Alastair and Jean Bradley, *Megaliths and Their Mysteries: A Guide to the Standing Stones of Europe*, MacMillan Publishing Co., Inc., New York, 1979. A combination history and guide book to European megaliths.

Severin, Tim, *The Brendan Voyage—A Leather Boat Tracks the Discovery of America by the Irish Sailor Saints*, McGraw-Hill Book Company, New York, 1978.

Severy, Merle, "The Celts—Europe's Founders," *National Geographic Magazine*, Washington, D.C., May, 1977. Nice article on the revival of Celtic culture.

Sharkey, John, *Celtic Mysteries: The Ancient Religion*, Avon Books, New York, 1975.

Shortt, H. de S., *Old Sarum*, Her Majesty's Stationery Office, London, 1973. Guidebook.

Southwest Parks and National Monuments Association, *The Trail to Tsankawi—An Unexcavated Indian Ruin*, Globe, Arizona, 1999. Guide to this trail in the Bandelier National Monument.

Squier, E.G., *Aboriginal Monuments of the State of New York*, Smithsonian Institution, Washington, D.C., 1849. Reveals presence of many mounds all over New York State.

————, *Ancient Monuments of the Mississippi Valley*, coauthored by E. H. Davis, from the Smithsonian Contributions to Knowledge series, Bartlett & Welford, New York, 1845. Excellent reference book. Recommended.

Stover, Leon E. and Bruce Kraig, *Stonehenge: The Indo-European Heritage*, Nelson-Hall, Chicago, 1978. Stonehenge as a tribal meeting place.

Titterington, P. F., "The Cahokia Mound Group and Its Village Site Materials," St. Louis, 1938, reprinted by Cahokia Mounds Museum, 1977.

Tompkins, Peter, *The Magic of the Obelisks*, Harper & Row, Publishers, Inc., New York, 1981.

————, *Mysteries of the Mexican Pyramids*, Harper and Row, New York, 1976. Good reading. History, origin and purpose of the Mexican pyramids.

————, *Secrets of the Great Pyramid*, Harper and Row, New York, 1971. Great book on the Great Pyramid. Must reading.

Trento, Salvatore Michael, *The Search for Lost America—The Mysteries of the Stone Ruins*, Contemporary Books, Chicago, 1978. Excellent introduction to stone monuments in Northeast U.S.

Vatcher, Faith de & Lance, *The Avebury Monuments*, Department of the Environment Official Handbook, Her Majesty's Stationery Office, London, 1976. Concise handbook.

Viles, Donald M. and Charlene, *Tepic Cozen*, Garibaldi, Oregon, 1977. Descriptions of mounds and stone constructions in western Washington.

Wake, C. Stanilard, *The Origin and Significance of the Great Pyramid*, Wizards Bookshelf, Minneapolis, 1975, reprint of 1882 edition. Esoteric view of the Great Pyramid.

Wood, John Edwin, *Sun, Moon and Standing Stones*, Oxford University Press, Oxford, 1978.

Contemporary Sacred Space, Earth Art, Feng Shui, and Landscaping

Beardsley, John, *Probing the Earth: Contemporary Land Projects*, Smithsonian Institution, 1977. Available from Superintendent of Documents, U.S. Government Printing Office, Washington, D.C. 20402. Stock # 047–003– 00051–2. Catalog of exhibition on contemporary land projects and Earth sculpture. Very interesting.

Bourdon, David, *Designing the Earth: The Human Impulse to Shape Nature*, Harry N. Abrams, Inc., New York, 1955.

Bright, Greg, *The Great Maze Book*, Pantheon Books, New York, 1973. Author's own original mazes as well as photos and story of his "homemade" trench maze covering two-thirds of an acre.

Campanelli, Dan & Pauline, *Circles, Groves & Sanctuaries: Sacred Spaces of Today's Pagans*, Llewellyn Publications, St. Paul, 1993.

Chan, Peter, *Magical Landscape: Transforming Any Small Space into a Place of Beauty*, A Garden Way Publishing Book, Storey Communications, Inc., Pownal, Vermont, 1988.

Conder, Josiah, *Landscape Gardening in Japan*, Dover Publications, New York, 1964. Practical introduction with many examples relevant to sacred space.

Edkins, Rev. J., "Feng-Shui," *The Chinese Recorder and Missionary Journal*, Vol. 4, Foochow, 1872.

Eitel, Ernest J., *Feng-Shui: or the Rudiments of Natural Science in China*, Land, Crawford & Co., Hong Kong, 1978. Much quoted book on Chinese geomancy.

Feuchtwang, Stephan D. R., *An Anthropological Analysis of Chinese Geomancy*, Vithagna, Vientiane, Laos, 1974. Very detailed and researched presentation.

Goldsworthy, Andy, *Andy Goldsworthy: A Collaboration With Nature*, Harry N. Abrams, Inc., New York, 1990. Beautiful artwork.

Linn, Denise, *Sacred Space: Clearing and Enhancing the Energy of Your Home*, Ballantine Books, New York, 1995. Very nice practical book.

Lippard, Lucy R., *Overlay: Contemporary Art and the Art of Prehistory*, Pantheon Books, New York, 1983. Wonderful book on contemporary land projects.

McLuhan, T. C., *Touch the Earth: A Self-Portrait of Indian Existence*, Promontory Press, New York, 1971. Compelling compilation of Indian statements on the land as a sacred creation.

Osmen, Sarah Ann, *Sacred Places*, St. Martin's Press, New York, 1990.

Rossbach, Sarah, *Feng Shui: The Chinese Art of Placement*, E. P. Dutton, Inc., New York, 1983.

————, *Interior Design with Feng Shui*, E. P. Dutton, New York, 1987. The best book on feng shui I've found. Practical, and it works. I had the privilege of hearing Sarah Rossbach's teacher, Professor Lin Yun, at Jim Swan's first Spirit of Place conference.

Tiberghien, Gilles A., *Land Art*, Princeton Architectural Press, New York, 1995

Walters, Derek, *Feng Shui—The Chinese Art of Designing a Harmonious Environment*, A Fireside Book, St. Louis 1988.

Meditation and Other Spiritual Practices

Assagioli, Robert, *The Science and Service of Blessing*, Sundial House, Nevill Court, Tunbridge Wells, Kent, England, 1968. A small but very useful and practical booklet on blessing. Highly recommended.

Boyd, Doug, *Rolling Thunder: A Personal Exploration into the Secret Healing Powers of an American Indian Medicine Man*, Dell Publishing Co., New York, 1974. Good reading.

Brennan, Barbara Ann, *Hands of Light: A Guide to Healing Through the Human Energy Field*, Bantam Books, New York, 1988.

Finley, Robert, *The Bible of the Loving Road, Lao Tzu's Tao Teh Ching*, Bliss Press, Carbondale, Illinois, 1972. Limited edition of the best translation of the Tao Teh Ching I've ever come across. I printed this by hand for my Masters thesis when I was going to Southern Illinois University. Robert, where are you?

Lhundrub, Ngorchen Konchog, *The Beautiful Ornament of the Three Visions*, Snow Lion Publications, Ithaca, New York, 1991.

Mishlove, Jeffrey, *The Roots of Consciousness: Psychic Liberation through History, Science and Experience*, Random House, New York, 1975.

Norbu, Namkhai, *The Crystal and the Way of Light: Sutra, Tantra and Dzogchen*, Routledge & Kegan Paul, New York, 1986.

Rawson, Philip, *The Art of Tantra*, New York Graphic Society, Greenwich, Connecticut, 1973. Stimulating presentation of the use of cosmic sexual symbolism for sacred ends.

Redfield, James, *The Celestine Prophecy*, Warner Books, New York, 1993.

———, *The Tenth Insight*, Warner Books, New York, 1996.

Rinpoche, Deshung, *The Three Levels of Spiritual Perception*, Wisdom Publications, Boston, 1995. The most detailed and moving book on spiritual practices I've ever read.

Rinpoche, Patrul, *The Words of My Perfect Teacher*, HarperCollins Publishers, San Francisco, 1994.

Vinzons, Kamalanayana Q., *Ananda Marga Philosophy*, Ananda Marga Pracaraka Samgha, Philippines, 1970.

Wilhelm, Richard & Baynes, Cary F., *The I Ching or Book of Changes*, Princeton University Press, Princeton, New Jersey, 1985.

Devas, Angels, and the Sacred Landscape

Altman, Nathaniel, *Sacred Trees*, Sierra Club Books, San Francisco, 1994. The history of our reverence for trees.

Bernbaum, Edwin, *Sacred Mountains of the World*, Sierra Club Books, San Francisco, 1992.

Boyd, Doug, *Rolling Thunder*, A Delta Book, New York, 1974. Excellent.

Bubriski, Kevin (photographs) and Keith Dowman (text), *Power Places of Kathmandu*, Inner Traditions International, Rochester, Vermont, 1995.

Challoner, H. K., *Regents of the Seven Spheres*, Theosophical Publishing House, London, 1966. A very special book of devic communications. Highly recommended.

Daniel, Alma, Wyllie, Timothy, and Andrew Ramer, *Ask Your Angels*, Ballantine Books, New York, 1992.

Gennaro, Gino, *The Phenomena of Avalon—The Story of this Planet as Recounted by the Fairies*, Cronos Publications, England, 1979.

Hawken, Paul, *The Magic of Findhorn*, Bantam Books, New York, 1976 paperback. Harper & Row, 1975. Journalistic account of the Findhorn community.

Hodson, Geoffrey, *Fairies at Work and at Play*, Theosophical Publishing House, London, 1976 Reprint. Descriptions of fairies, gnomes, devas, etc., as encountered by clairvoyant Geoffrey Hodson.

————, *The Kingdom of the Gods*, Theosophical Publishing House, Wheaton, Illinois, 1976. One of the finest original introductions to the angelic kingdom. With many beautiful color plates. Highly recommended.

Hutton, Ronald, *The Pagan Religions of the Ancient British Isles*, Blackwell, Oxford, 1995.

LaChapelle, Delores, *Earth Wisdom*, The Guild of Tutors Press, Los Angeles, 1978. Excellent book. Recommended.

————, *Sacred Land, Sacred Sex: Rapture of the Deep: Concerning Deep Ecology and Celebrating Life*, Kivaki Press, Durango, Colorado, 1992.

Lehrman, Frederic, *The Sacred Landscape*, CelestialArts, Berkeley, California, 1988. Beautiful words and photographs of sacred places.

Michell, John, *The Earth Spirit—Its Ways, Shrines, and Mysteries*, Avon, New York, 1975. Nice picture book and introduction to the concept of the Earth Spirit.

Roads, Michael J., *Journey Into Oneness: A Spiritual Odyssey*, H J Kramer, Inc., Tiburon, California, 1994.

Spangler, David, *The Laws of Manifestation*, Findhorn Foundation, Moray, Scotland, 1975.

————, *Festivals In The New Age*, Findhorn Foundation, Forres, Moray, Scotland, 1975.

Steiger, Brad, *Medicine Talk: A Guide to Walking in Balance and Surviving on the Earth Mother*, Doubleday, Garden City, New York, 1975. Traditional Indian spiritual power and its application. Interviews with Twylah Nitsch and others.

Swan, James A., *The Power of Place: Sacred Ground in Natural & Human Environments*, Quest Books, Wheaton, Illinois, 1991.

Tompkins, Peter and Bird, Christopher, *The Secret Life of Plants*, Avon Books paperback, New York, 1973. Excellent introduction to concept of consciousness existing in plants and all matter.

Valentin, Ann and Virginia Essene, *Descent of the Dove*, S.E.E. Publishing Co., Santa Clara, CA, 1988. A must-read book for those with an interest in communicating with devas. Many good ideas on our personal responsibility to work on overcoming negativity on Earth and to become earth caretakers.

Dowsing

Baum, Joseph, *The Beginner's Handbook of Dowsing—The Ancient Art of Divining Underground Water Sources*, Crown Publishers, New York, 1976. Simple book on dowsing.

Bird, Christopher, *The Divining Hand*, E. P. Dutton, New York, 1979. Lots of fascinating dowsing facts, history, and adventures.

Cameron, Verne L., *Aquavideo—Locating Underground Water*, El Cariso Publications, Elsinore, California, 1970.

Cox, Bill, *Aquavideo: Locating Underground Water Through the Sensory Eye of Verne L. Cameron*, El Cariso Publications, Elsinore, California, 1970. Good descriptions of primary water theory and Cameron's amazing dowsing successes.

Cox, R. Hippisley, *The Green Roads of England*, The Garnstone Press Ltd., London, England, 1973 reprint. Presents evidence for the existence of ancient trackways linking ancient sites in England.

Devereux, Paul and Ian Thomson, *The Ley Hunter's Companion—Aligned Ancient Sites: A New Study with Field Guide and Maps*, Thames and Hudson, London, 1979

Fidler, J. Havelock, *Ley Lines: Their Nature and Properties: A Dowser's Investigation*, Turnstone Press, Wellingborough, Northhamptonshire, 1983.

Goodman, Jeffrey, *Psychic Archaeology: Time Machine to the Past*, Berkeley Publishing, 1977.

Graves, Tom, *Dowsing: Techniques and Applications*, Turnstone Books, London, 1976. Available in paperback in the U.S. as *The Diviner's Handbook*. One of the best how-to dowsing books available. Highly recommended.

———, *Needles of Stone*, Turnstone Books, London, 1978. Excellent research on Earth energies. Also recommended.

Hitching, Francis, *Dowsing—The Psi Connection*, Anchor Books, Garden City, New York, 1978. Historical overview with emphasis on scientific understanding.

———, *Earth Magic*, Cassell, London, 1976. Good general introduction to earth mysteries.

Lethbridge, T. C., *Ghost and Divining-Rod*, Routledge & Kegan Paul, London, 1967.

———, *The Legend of the Sons of God: A Fantasy?*, Routledge & Kegan Paul, London, 1972.

———, *The Power of the Pendulum*, Routledge & Kegan Paul, London, 1976.

Lonegren, Sig, *Earth Mysteries Handbook: Wholistic Non-Intrusive Data Gathering Techniques*, The American Society of Dowsers (ASD), Danville, Vermont, 1985. Can be ordered from ASD. Excellent, readable, understandable treatise on astronomical alignments.

———, *Labyrinths: Ancient Myths & Modern Uses*, Gothic Image Publications, Glastonbury, Somerset, Great Britain, 1996. Sig is one of the world's experts on sacred space.

———, *Spiritual Dowsing, Cosmic Images*, Glastonbury, Somerset, Great Britain, 1991.

MacLean, Gordon, *A Field Guide to Dowsing: How to Practice the Ancient Art Today*, The American Society of Dowsers, Danville, Vermont, 1976.

Mermet, Abbe, *Principles and Practice of Radiesthesia*, Watkins, London, 1975. Interesting stories on successful dowsing missions.

Nielson, Greg & Joseph Polansky, *Pendulum Power*, Warner/Destiny Books, New York, 1977. Covers use of the pendulum as an intuitional tool.

Pettis, III, Charles R., "Dowsing and the Design of Sacred Space," *The American Dowser*, Danville, Vermont, February, 1980.

———, "Underground Energy Patterns at Mystery Hill," *NEARA Journal*, Milford, New Hampshire. Also published in *The Ley Hunter*.

Ross II, Thomas Edward, "The Parastudy Experiment," coauthored with Howell Lewis Shay, Jr., *Radionic Quarterly*, December, 1975. Advances the idea of mental and spiritual neutralization of negative streams.

———, "Power Centers," taped lecture at 1976 American Society of Dowsers meeting, available from Alphasonics, Box 271, Nashua, New Hampshire.

———, "A View from the United States," coauthored by John D. Payne, *Radionic Quarterly*, Cirentester, Glos., England, March, 1975. The first written exposition on how to neutralize negative underground streams with steel stakes.

Ross, T. Edward and Richard D. Wright, *The Divining Mind: A Guide to Dowsing and Self-Awareness*, Destiny Books, Rochester, Vermont, 1990.

Screeton, Paul, *Quicksilver Heritage—The Mystic Leys: Their Legacy of Ancient Wisdom*, Thorsons Publishers, Wellingbourough, Northamptonshire, England, 1974.

Thompson, Clive, *Site and Survey Dowsing—An Anthology from the Journal of the British Society of Dowsers*, Turnstone Press Ltd., Wellingborough, Northhamptonshire, 1980.

Toulson, Shirley, *East Anglia—Walking the Ley Lines and Ancient Tracks*, Wildwood House, London, 1979.

Underwood, Guy, *The Pattern of the Past*, Abeland-Schuman Ltd., New York, 1973. Excellent "ground-breaking" book relating underground water to monuments.

Watkins, Alfred, *The Ley Hunter's Manual—A Guide to Early Tracks*, Pentacle Books, Bristol, England, 1977.

————, *The Old Straight Track—Its Mounds, Beacons, Moats, Sites and Mark Stones*, Abacus/Sphere Books, London, 1976 reprint. First book on leys. Recommended.

Death, Entities, and Ghosts

Alexander, Marc, *The Man Who Exorcised the Bermuda Triangle*, A. S. Barnes and Company, New York, 1980.

Blatty, William Peter, *The Exorcist*, Bantam paperback, New York, 1972. Harper & Row, New York, 1971. A worst-case example of dealing with entities.

Browne, Mary T., *Mary T. Reflects on the Other Side: A Compelling Vision of the Afterlife*, Fawcett Columbine, New York, 1994.

Eadie, Betty J., *Embraced By The Light*, Gold Leaf Press, Placerville, California, 1992.

Holdstock, Robert, *Necromancer*, Avon, New York, 1978. Novel on a negative entity inhabiting a stone.

Kübler-Ross, Elisabeth, *On Life After Death*, Celestial Arts, Berkeley, California, 1991.

Martin, Joel and Patricia Romanowski, *We Are Not Forgotten: George Anderson's Messages of Love and Hope From the Other Side*, Berkley Books, New York, 1992.

Maurey, Eugene, *Exorcism: How to Clear at a Distance a Spirit Possessed Person*, Whitford Press, West Chester, Pennsylvania, 1988.

Moody, Jr., Raymond A., *Life After Life*, Bantam Books, New York, 1988.

Morse, M.D., Melvin with Paul Perry, *Closer to the Light—Learning from Children's Near-Death Experiences*, Villard Books, New York, 1990.

Nuland, Sherwin B., *How We Die: Reflections on Life's Final Chapter*, Albert A. Knopf, New York, 1994.

Palmer, Greg, *Death: The Trip of a Lifetime*, HarperSanFrancisco, 1993.

Rinpoche, Sogyal, *The Tibetan Book of the Living and Dying*, HarperSanFrancisco, 1994.

Thurman, Robert A. F., *Inside Tibetan Buddhism: Rituals and Symbols Revealed*, Collins Publishers, San Francisco, 1995.

————, *The Tibetan Book of the Dead: Liberation Through Understanding In the Between*, Bantam Books, New York, 1994.

Sacred Geometry and Number

Arguelles, Jose and Miriam, *Mandala*, Shambhala, Berkeley, 1972. Very good overview of the mandala.

Berriman, A. E., *Historical Metrology*, Greenwood Press, New York, 1969. Very interesting book on ancient metrologies.

Borst, L. B. and B. M., *Megalithic Software: Part I, England*, Twin Bridge Press, Williamsville, New York, 1975. Mathematical analysis of ancient megalithic sites, cathedrals and even road patterns.

Bosman, Leonard, *The Meaning and Philosophy of Numbers*, Rider and Co., London, 1974. Excellent book on numbers.

Bourgoin, J., *Arabic Geometrical Pattern and Design*, Dover Publications, New York, 1973. Many full-page examples of Islamic geometric art. Possible to use these as pattern sources for designs.

Brown, G. Spencer, *Laws of Form*, The Julian Press, New York, 1972. Non-numerical, metaphysical arithmetic of logic. Recommended.

Brunes, Tons, *The Secrets of Ancient Geometry and Its Use, Volumes 1 & 2*, Rhodos, Copenhagen, 1967. Outstanding work on the use of geometry to analyze and create beautiful forms. Highly recommended.

Critchlow, Keith, *Islamic Patterns: An Analytical and Cosmological Approach*, Schochen Books, New York, 1976. Excellent book on the use of geometric patterns to reveal cosmological truths.

————, *Time Stands Still: New Light on Megalithic Science*, George Fraser, London, England, 1979. Photographs by Rod Bull. Excellent book on many aspects of megalithic science and sacred space. Highly recommended.

Davidson, D. and H. Aldersmith, *The Great Pyramid—Its Divine Message*, Williams and Norgate, Ltd., London, 1941. Detailed analysis of the Great Pyramid with lots of interesting illustrations.

Einstein, Albert, *Relativity—The Special and General Theory*, Crown Publishers, Inc., New York, 1961. I believe that someday all of the ideas in this book will be explained as part of a theory of consciousness.

Fuller, R. Buckminster, *Synergetics: Explorations in the Geometry of Thinking*, MacMillan Publishing Co., New York, 1975.

Heinsch, J., *Principles of Prehistoric Sacred Geography*, Zodiac House, London, 1975.

Heline, Corinne, *Sacred Science of Numbers—A Series of Lecture Lessons Dealing with the Sacred Science of Numbers*, New Age Press, Los Angeles, 1977.

Keller-von Asten, H., *Encounters with the Infinite: Geometrical Experiences Through Active Contemplation*, Walter Keller Press, Dornach, 1971. How to construct beautiful geometric forms, all presented in a contemplative philosophical framework.

Kenner, Hugh, *Geodesic Math and How to Use It*, University of California Press, Berkeley, 1976. Comprehensive introduction to math as used in designing geodesic domes.

Mandala Foundation, *Untitled limited edition on geometry, symbolism and life*, Terra Bella, California.

Martineau, John, *A Book of Coincidence*, Wooden Books, Powys, Wales, 1995. A fascinating book on the geometric synchronicity of the planets' orbits.

Michell, John, *City of Revelation—On the Proportions and Symbolic Numbers of the Cosmic Temple*, Ballantine Books, New York 1972.

Pennick, Nigel, *The Ancient Science of Geomancy: Man in Harmony with the Earth*, Thames and Hudson, London, 1979. Excellent introduction to geomancy. Recommended.

————, *Sacred Geometry*, Turnstone Press Limited, Wellingborough, Northamptonshire, 1980. Good book for those interested in sacred geometry.

Pettis, Charles R. and Sina Pettis, *Cosmic Geometry: Tantric Transformations*, Bliss Press, Ithaca, NY, 1976. A limited edition book I hand-printed in Ithaca, New York.

Pocley, Richard and Ron Ward, *The Energetic-Synergetic Geometry of R. Buckminster Fuller and its Application to Geodesic structures*, Design Department, Southern Illinois University, Carbondale, 1962.

Pugh, Anthony, *An Introduction to Tensegrity*, University of California Press, Berkeley, 1976. Only comprehensive explanation of tensegrity of which I am aware.

————, *Polyhedra—A Visual Approach*, University of California Press, Berkeley, 1976.

Research Into Lost Knowledge Organization Trust, "Chartres Maze, A Model of the Universe?," *Occasional Paper No. 1*, 1975. Investigation into symbolism and geometry of the maze in the Chartres Cathedral.

Taylor, Thomas, *The Theoretical Arithmetic of the Pythagoreans*, Samuel Weiser, New York, 1972. Excellent book on numbers.

Vandenbroeck, Andre, *Philosophical Geometry*, Sadhana Press, South Otselic, New York, 1972. A nice treatise on sacred geometry.

Willams, R. E., *Handbook of Structure, Part I: Polyhedra and Spheres*, Douglas Advanced Research Laboratories, 1968. Excellent introduction to polyhedra and their properties.

————, *Natural Structure: Towards a Form Language*, Eudaemon Press, Moorpark, California, 1972. Excellent source book on use of geometry to create natural structures. Recommended.

Ceremony, Symbolism, Myth

Cirlot, J. E., *A Dictionary of Symbols*, Philosophical Library, New York, 1962.

Cooke, Grace and Ivan, *The Light in Britain*, The White Eagle Publishing Trust, New Lands, Liss, Hampshire, England, 1971. Includes clairvoyant impressions of ancient ceremonies of light held at a number of ancient British monuments.

Cornford, Francis M., *Plato's Cosmology—The Timaeus of Plato*, Routledge & Kegan Paul, New York, 1971.

————, *The Unwritten Philosophy and Other Essays*, University Press, Cambridge, England, 1967 paperback edition. Excellent written essays on Plato and Greek thought. Includes an especially good one on the harmony of the spheres.

Hall, Manly P., *The Secret Teachings of All Ages: An Encyclopedic Outline of Qabbalistic and Rosicrucian Symbolical Philosophy*, The Philosophical Research Society, Los Angeles, 1969.

Jung, C.G., *Four Archetypes: Mother, Rebirth, Spirit, Trickster*, Princeton University Press, 1973 edition. Excellent psychological presentation.

———, *Man and His Symbols*, Doubleday & Co., Garden City, New York, 1969. Excellent book on psychology and symbols. Teaches about psychology in an interesting and involving way. Lots of beautiful art. Highly recommended.

———, *Mandala Symbolism*, Bollinger Series, Princeton University Press, Princeton, 1973 edition.

———, *Synchronicity: An Acausal Connecting Principle*, Princeton University Press, 1973 edition. Source reading for concept of synchronicity.

Kenton, Warren, *Astrology: The Celestial Mirror*, Avon Books, New York, 1974.

Neumann, Erich, *The Great Mother: An Analysis of the Archetype*, Princeton University Press, Princeton, New Jersey, 1972. Best book I know of on the Mother archetype. Highly recommended.

Santillana, Giorgio de and Hertha von Dechend, *Hamlet's Mill: An essay on myth and the frame of time*, David R. Godine, Boston, 1977.

Telesco, Patricia, *Seasons of the Sun: Celebrations from the World's Spiritual Traditions*, Samuel Weiser, York Beach, Maine, 1996.

Wolfe, Amber, *In the Shadow of the Shaman: Connecting with Self, Nature, and Spirit*, Llewellyn Publications, St. Paul, 1998.

Astronomical Alignments

Adzema, Robert and Mablen Jones, *The Great Sundial Cutout Book*, Hawthorne Books, New York, 1978. Good practical sundial book.

Aveni, Anthony F., *Archaeoastronomy in Pre-Columbian America*, University of Texas Press, Austin, 1975. Collection of technical papers on archaeoastronomy.

———, *Native American Astronomy*, University of Texas Press, Austin, 1977. Collection of fifteen technical essays on pre-Columbian astronomy in the Americas.

———, *Skywatchers of Ancient Mexico*, University of Texas Press, Austin, 1980. Excellent chapter on astronomy, with archaeoastronomy computer programs for the TI-59 calculator.

Brennan, Martin, *The Boyne Valley Vision*, The Dolmen Press, Portlaoise, Ireland, 1980. A study of the cosmology, symbol vocabulary, sundials, calendar, and artistry of the megalithic monuments in the Boyne valley.

———, *The Stars and the Stones—Ancient Art and Astronomy in Ireland*, Thames and Hudson, London, 1983. Excellent source of information on astronomical alignments.

————, *The Stones of Time: Calendars, Sundials and Stone Chambers of Ancient Ireland*, Inner Traditions International, Rochester, Vermont, 1994. Reprint of *The Stars and The Stones* with new epilogue.

Brown, Peter Lancaster, *Megaliths, Myths and Men An Introduction to Astro-archaeology*, Taplinger Publishing Co., New York, 1976. Excellent history of astro-archaeology.

Calvin, William H., *How the Shaman Stole the Moon: In Search of Ancient Prophet-Scientists from Stonehenge to the Grand Canyon*, Bantam Books, New York, 1992.

Chambers, R., *The Book of Days*, two volumes, W. & R. Chambers, Edinburgh, 1863. Lots of fun information on each day of the year.

Cleminshaw, Clarence H., *The Beginner's Guide to the Skies: A Month-by-Month Handbook for Stargazers and Planet Watchers*, Thomas Y. Crowell Co., New York, 1977. Easy-to-understand presentation on the sun, moon and planets. Good diagrams.

Cornelius, Geoffrey and Paul Devereux, *The Secret Language of the Stars and Planets*, Chronicle Books, San Francisco, 1996.

Gray, William, G., *Seasonal Occult Rituals*, Helios Books, Toddington, Cheltenham, Glos., Great Britain, 1976.

Hatch, Jane M., *The American Book of Days*, The H. W. Wilson Company, New York, 1978.

Hawkins, Gerald, S., *Beyond Stonehenge*, Harper and Row, New York, 1973. Astro-archaeological narrative on Stonehenge, Nasca and other sites.

————, *Special Report 226—Astro-Archaeology*, Smithsonian Astrophysical Observatory, Cambridge, Massachusetts, 1966. Mathematical derivations of astronomical calculations.

————, *Stonehenge Decoded*, Dell Publishing, New York, 1967. Important groundbreaking book.

Heggie, Douglas C., *Megalithic Science: Ancient Mathematics and Astronomy in Northwest Europe*, Thames and Hudson, New York, 1981.

Hoyle, Fred, *From Stonehenge to Modern Cosmology*, W. H. Freeman & Co., San Francisco, 1972. Good article on Stonehenge, related to Hawkins' book.

————, *On Stonehenge*, W. H. Freeman & Co., San Francisco, 1977.

————, "Speculations on Stonehenge," *Antiquity*, XL, 1966.

Kearnes, Hugh, *The Mysterious Chequered Lights of Newgrange*, Elo Publications, Dublin, Ireland, 1993. A wonderful view of Newgrange as the world's first light show.

Krupp, E. C., *In Search of Ancient Astronomies*, Doubleday & Co., Garden City, New York, 1977. Good overview of ancient astronomies.

————, *Skywatchers, Shamans & Kings: Astronomy and the Archaeology of Power*, John Wiley & Sons, Inc., New York, 1997.

LaChapelle, Delores, *Earth Festivals: Seasonal Celebrations for Everyone Young and Old*, Fine Hill Arts, Publishers, Silverton, Colorado, 1974.

Michell, John, *Secrets of the Stones: The story of Astro-archaeology, Penguin Books,* Middlesex, England, 1977. A short history of astro-archaeology.

Moore, Patrick, *Watchers of the Stars—The Scientific Revolution*, G. P. Putnam's Sons, New York, 1974.

O'Brien, Christian, *The Megalithic Odyssey: A Search for the Master Builders of the Bodmin Moor Astronomical Complex of Stone Circles and Giant Cairns*, Turnstone Press Limited, Wellingborough, Northhamptonshire, Great Britain, 1983.

O'Brien, Tim, *Light Years Ago: A Study of the Cairns of Newgrange and Cairn T Loughcrew Co. Meath Ireland*, The Black Cat Press, Dublin, Ireland, 1992.

O'Kelly, Michael J., *Newgrange: Archaeology, Art and Legend*, Thames and Hudson, London, 1982.

"The Origins of Science: The Astronomy of the Ancients," *Technology Review*, December, 1977. Entire issue is devoted to ancient astronomy.

Thom, A., *Megalithic Lunar Observatories*, Oxford University Press, London, 1973. Important reference and source book for lunar alignments.

———, *Megalithic Remains in Britain and Brittany*, coauthored by A. S. Thom, Oxford University Press, Oxford, 1978.

———, *Megalithic Sites in Britain*, Oxford University Press, London, 1967. Key reference and source book for astronomical alignments, geometry and metrology. Highly recommended.

Thom, A. & A. S., *Megalithic Rings—Plans and Data for 229 Monuments in Britain*, BAR British Series 81, 1980.

Waugh, Albert E., *Sundials: Their Theory and Construction*, Dover Publications, New York, 1973.

Sacred Fiction

Caldecott, Moyra, *The Sacred Stones Trilogy: The Tall Stones, The Temple of the Sun and Shadow on the Stones*, Popular Library, New York, 1977. Great story of megalithic magic. A fictional account of the ideas and techniques expressed in this book. Highly recommended.

———, *The Lily and the Bull*, Hill and Wang, New York, 1979. A novel on the struggle between the forces of good and evil. Highly recommended.

LeGuin, Ursula K., *The Earthsea Trilogy: A Wizard of Earthsea, The Tombs of Atuan & The Farthest Shore*, Bantam Books, New York, 1975. Excellent fiction!

Miscellaneous

Partridge, Eric, *Origins: A Short Etymological Dictionary of Modern English*, MacMillan Co., New York, 1958.

Raknes, Ola, *Wilhelm Reich and Orgonomy*, Penguin Books, Baltimore, Maryland, 1971. General introduction to Reich.

Reich Foundation, The Wilhelm, *The Orgone Energy Accumulator: Its Scientific and Medical Use*, 1951. Most practical thing I personally have seen on orgone.

Rogers, Steven & John R. Aument, *Cosmic Engineering*, Thoth Ltd., Boston, 1976. Tells how to make an orgone accumulator.

Token, Bob, *Space-Time and Beyond: Toward an Explanation of the Unexplainable*, E. P. Dutton & Co., New York, 1975.

Secrets of Sacred Space Selected Web Sites

There are many, many web sites on the subjects covered in *Secrets of Sacred Space*. Your favorite search engine can help you find the specific or general information you want. Here are just a few web sites to help you get started.

Ancient Monuments & Contemporary Sacred Spaces.

http://www.geo.org—The Geo Group.

http://easyweb.easynet.co.uk/~aburnham/ring/—The Stone Circle Web Ring Home Page: More than a hundred sites on all aspects of stone circles.

http://easyweb.easynet.co.uk/~aburnham/stones.htm—Megalithic Mysteries: A Photographic Guide by Andy Burnham.

http://www.serve.com/archaeology/ring/index.html—Archaeology on the Net Web Ring.

http://www.sacredsites.com/—Places of Peace and Power: The Sacred Site Pilgrimage of Martin Gray. Great photos and links.

http://www.mcli.dist.maricopa.edu/smc/labyrinth/—A Web of Labyrinths.

http://www.henge.demon.co.uk/general/contents.html—Chris Tweed's Contents: Photos and directions to ancient monuments in the UK.

http://www.neara.org/—New England Antiquities Research Association.

http://ireland.iol.ie/~tobrien/new.htm—Light Years Ago by Tim O'Brien: A Study of Cairn T, Loughcrew, and Newgrange.

http://www.webfactory.co.za/ecoshrine/—Voice of the Earth Eco-shrine.

http://www.beakman.com/sass/whatis.html—Sassafras Environmental Arts Center.

http://www.mkzdk.org/—A sacred space on the Web.

Astronomical Alignments.

http://www.wam.umd.edu/~tlaloc/archastro/—The Center for Archaeoastronomy.

http://hea-www.harvard.edu/~ruiz/—Web Pages of Tania Ruiz.

http://www.wam.umd.edu/~tlaloc/archastro/ae.html—Archaeoastronomy & Ethnoastronomy News.

http://www-hpcc.astro.washington.edu/scied/astro/astroarchaeo.html—History of Astronomy: Subjects include Archaeoastronomy, Ancient Astronomy and Ethnoastronomy.

http://www.as.wvu.edu/~planet/lnk_arch.htm—Archeoastronomy Links.

Dowsing and Geomancy.

http://www.newhampshire.com/dowsers.org/—The American Society of Dowsers.

http://www.geomancy.org/home.html—Mid-Atlantic Geomancy: A great site by Sig Lonegren, a veteran geomancer.

Acknowledgments

With a book that has been in process for over twenty years, there are too many who have helped for me to list everyone individually. But special thanks are due to John and Kate Payne, Rick Allen, Shrii Shrii Anandamurti, Carolyn Anderson, Mabel Demotte Beggs, Faye Bickle, Noreen Brownlie, Tom Bullock, Andy Burnham, Peter and Eileen Caddy, Mark Choi and Alex Gilman, Betty Cornish, Louise DeLaurentis, the Foundation of Light Cosmic Monument Study Group, members of The Geo Group and all those wonderful people who have taken my Sacred Space workshops and helped edit the manuscript over the years, Tom Hanna, Corson Hirschfeld, Dr. Robert Jangaard, Debbie Jones, Martin P. Levin, Kjersti Monson, Tom Lewis, Ann Kerns and everyone else at Llewellyn who helped with this book, Sig Lonegren, Dorothy Maclean, David McCreary, Steve Miller, National Geographic Society, New England Antiquities Research Association, Cheryl Nickel, Sue North, Tim O'Brien, Oxford University Press, John Paskiewicz, Bre and Morgan Pettis, Charlie and Louise Pettis, Claudia Pettis, Lydia Pettis, James Pierce, Richard Rangel, Ellis Robinson, Terry Ross, Byron Rot, David Rousseau, Tania Ruiz, His Holiness Jigdal Dagchen Sakya, H. E. Dagmo Kusho (Dagmola), Ryan Sansaver, Bill and Cathy Sawyer, the Seattle Arts Commission, Mike & Mickey Sweeney, Professor Alexander Thom, Acharya Yatiishvarananda Avadhuta, and Sidney, a special being in dog form, who was by my side for the entire construction of the Mutiny Bay Stone Circle.

Etymological References

Etymologies of key words appear throughout this book. My primary reference for etymological data was *Origins: A Short Etymological Dictionary of Modern English* (New York: The Macmillan Company, 1959) by Eric Partridge. I also used *Webster's New World Dictionary of the American Language* (Cleveland and New York: The World Publishing Company, 1966).

Figures

1.1 ©1990 Tom Bullock; **1.2, 1.5, 1.8** ©1979 Stephen Miller; **1.4, 1.6, 1.14, 1.25, 1.26** ©1975 Chuck Pettis; **1.10, 1.13** ©1977 Chuck Pettis; **1.22** ©1979 Chuck Pettis; **1.12** ©1997 Chuck Pettis; **1.3, 1.17** ©1998 Chuck Pettis; **1.7, 1.11, 1.15** reprinted from *Rude Stone Monuments in All Countries: Their Age and Uses* by James Fergusson (London: John Murray, 1872); **1.9** reprinted from *Archaic England: An Essay in Deciphering Prehistory from Megalithic Monuments, Earthworks, Customs, Coins, Place-Names, and Faerie Superstitions* by Harold Bayley (Philadelphia: J. B. Lippincott Co., 1920); **1.16** reprinted from *The Great Pyramid: Its Divine Message, Ninth Edition* by D. Davidson and H. Aldersmith (London: Williams and Norgate, 1941); **1.19, 1.20, 1.24, 1.27** reprinted from *Smithsonian Contributions to Knowledge: Ancient Monuments of the Mississippi Valley* by E. G. Squier and A. M. Davis, M.D. (New York: Bartlett & Welford, 1848); **1.21** ©1980: Artist–Deborah Jones, Photographer–Carol Betsch; **1.23** reprinted from *Traditions of the De-Coo-Dah and Antiquarian Researches* by William Pidgeon (New York: Thayer, Bridgman, & Fanning, 1853); **1.28** ©1974 James Pierce; **1.29** reprinted from *Prehistoric America: Myths and Symbols of Aboriginal Religions in America* by Stephen D. Peet, Ph.D. (Chicago: Office of the American Antiquarian, 1905); **1.30** reprinted from *Twelfth Annual Report of the Bureau of Ethnology to the Secretary of the Smithsonian Institution, 1890-91* by J. W. Powell (Washington, DC: Government Printing Office, 1894); **2.1** ©1998 Chuck Pettis; **3.3** © 1989 Chuck Pettis; **3.4** ©1977 Chuck Pettis; **3.8 3.9, 3.10, 3.11, 3.12, 3.13** original illustration by Carrie Westfall ©1999 Llewellyn Publications. **6.1** ©1997 Lydia Pettis; **6.2, 6.3** ©1978 Chuck Pettis; **7.1** ©1988 The Geo Group (the original Seattle photo provided to The Geo Group courtesy of Cosmic Images, Bellevue, WA); **8.1** ©1997 Chuck Pettis; **8.2** ©1995 Janice Chieko Kato; **10.1, 10.2, 10.3, 10.4, 10.6, 10.8, 10.10** ©1999 Chuck Pettis; **10.10** © 1977 Chuck Pettis; **10.5** illustration by Chuck Pettis after John Martineau's *A Book of Coincidence* (Wales: Wooden Books, 1995), 31; **10.7, 10.11** reprinted with permission from *Megalithic Lunar Observatories* (Oxford: Oxford University Press, 1973) by A. Thom; **10.9** reprinted with permission from *Megalithic Sites in Britain* (Oxford: Oxford University Press, 1967) by A. Thom.

11.1 © 1977 Chuck Pettis; **11.3** ©1997 Chuck Pettis; **11.2** ©1979 Stephen Miller; **12.2, 12.3** ©1979 Stephen Miller; **12.4** reprinted with permission from *Megalithic Sites in Britain* (Oxford: Oxford University Press, 1967) by A. Thom; **12.5, 12.6, 12.7, 12.11, 12.12, 12.13, 12.14** ©1999 Chuck Pettis; **12.34** ©1997 Chuck Pettis; **12.8, 12.33** reprinted from *Rude Stone Monuments* (London: John Murray, 1872) by James Fergusson; **12.9, 12.10** illustration by Chuck Pettis after Tons Brunes' *The Secrets of Ancient Geometry* (Copenhagen: Rhodos, 1967); **12.15, 12.16, 12.17, 12.18, 12.19, 12.20, 12.21, 12.22, 12.23, 12.24, 12.25, 12.26, 12.27, 12.28, 12.29, 12.30, 12.31, 12.32** by Mark Choi and Alex Gilman. All illustrations in chapter thirteen ©1999 Chuck Pettis with the exception of **13.1** ©1996 Chuck Pettis, and **13.6**, reprinted from *Smithsonian Contributions to Knowledge: Ancient Monuments of the Mississippi Valley* by E. G. Squier and A. M. Davis, M.D. (New York: Bartlett & Welford, 1848).

Color Insert

A, K, O, P, Q © 1998 Chuck Pettis; **B, C, D, E, F, I, J, N** © 1996 Chuck Pettis; **G** © 1975 Chuck Pettis; **R** © 1999 Photographer Stuart Mangold; **H, M** © 1995 Chuck Pettis; **L** Photo: Tim O'Brien.

Index